Damien Brown is an Australian specialist rural doctor. His bestselling first book, *Band-Aid for a Broken Leg*, recounts his experiences working for Médecins Sans Frontières on the medical frontline in Angola, Mozambique and South Sudan. He has now spent over a decade in remote Aboriginal communities in the Northern Territory, in larger urban and regional Australian hospitals, and for the Royal Flying Doctor Service in far north Queensland. Damien currently divides his time between Cairns and Melbourne.

⊕

'Bush doctoring is real medicine. Damien's journey is fascinating.'
Norman Swan, ABC Radio National, *The Health Report*

'*Bush Doctor* is a superb read, in equal parts entertaining and gut wrenching. Damien captures the wonder and humour of working as a medic in remote Australia without sugar-coating the hard realities. I loved this book.'
Sonia Henry, author of *Put Your Feet in the Dirt, Girl*

'With a light touch and occasional dark humour, Damien Brown navigates the physical and emotional challenges, the ethical conundrums and the irreconcilable contradictions of front-line medicine in remote Australia. Honest and self-questioning, idealistic and pragmatic, *Bush Doctor* is both a thoroughly engaging read and a refusal to look away from the entrenched and escalating health crisis among Indigenous people in the bush.'
Kim Mahood, author of *Wandering with Intent*

'Damien Brown's humanity shines through his writing.'
David Hunt, author of *Girt*

'While reading *Bush Doctor* I realised there are some jobs AI will never take!'
Rob Sitch, comedian and actor, ABC TV *Utopia*

'Written with honesty and humility, *Bush Doctor* is eye-opening and insightful.'
Benjamin Black, award-winning author of *Belly Woman*

'I am grateful to Brown for sharing such raw and grounded reflections about places and experiences I may never witness. His quiet observations speak volumes about the intersect of the ordinary and the sacred in this gem.'
Sally Gould, author of *Frog: The secret diary of a paramedic*

'Writing about what's difficult—illness, loss, culture, and difference—is an act of medicine in itself. This book doesn't shy away from the complexities of working at the edge, be it geographically, emotionally, and ethically. It reminds us that medicine is not just about saving lives, but about understanding them.'
Matt Morgan, author of *Critical*, *One Medicine* and *A Second Act*

Bush Doctor

A MEMOIR FROM
THE BEAUTIFUL, RUGGED HEART
OF OUTBACK AUSTRALIA

DAMIEN BROWN

Some names and identifying details have been changed to protect the privacy of individuals.

First published in 2026

Allen & Unwin
Cammeraygal Country
83 Alexander Street
Crows Nest NSW 2065
Australia
Phone: (61 2) 8425 0100
Email: info@allenandunwin.com
Web: www.allenandunwin.com

Allen & Unwin acknowledges the Traditional Owners of the Country on which we live and work. We pay our respects to all Aboriginal and Torres Strait Islander Elders, past and present.

A catalogue record for this book is available from the National Library of Australia

ISBN 978 1 76147 363 0

Cover design: Deborah Parry Graphics
Cover photographs: Andrey Moisseyev / Alamy (plane); iStock (road)
Typeset in 12/18 pt Minion Pro by Midland Typesetters, Australia

10 9 8 7 6 5 4 3 2 1

The paper in this book is FSC® certified. FSC® promotes environmentally responsible, socially beneficial and economically viable management of the world's forests.

For everyone who lives and works in these incredible places, and with respect for the Traditional Owners.

‘How do you cope with the poverty?’

‘I don’t have to. The poor do.’

—Overheard

Contents

Author's Note

A few years ago, I wrote a book about the time I'd spent working in Africa, in part because 300 pages was the shortest reply I could give to 'What was it like?' There were too many fascinating people; too many heartbreaking moments countered by uplifting or jovial ones, often at the same time; too many contradictions and nuances. That book ended here, with my first trip to work in Central Australia. In the years since, I've worked in many outback towns and communities and I've wanted to continue the story. But how to even begin? Most of it isn't mine to tell. I'm forever the outsider with my biases. And for all the amazing people I've met there—strong, proud, open and warm, despite difficult circumstances—the response elsewhere is cautious: 'Another book? Great! Oh, set mostly in remote Australia? Yeah, nah, I wouldn't do that if I were you.'

Our backyard is tricky. It's far easier to talk about other places. But whether I write about my experiences or not, this is where I work, and this is what I do every day. And I love it, for the most part. There's a price to pay, though.

As with much of life, there are few tidy beginnings or endings. There aren't many simple, neat stories that'll make for a nice narrative arc or illustrate a straightforward point. Things here are rich, and complex, and beautiful, and troubled, so I may as well start here, on the road as I come back with fresh eyes after a long break overseas. I need to get this down, because for reasons that'll become clear, my time here may be limited.

First, though, some disclaimers. This book was written after the fact. Mistakes or misrepresentations are my fault alone, and I hope that they'll be received in the spirit this is intended: a respectful telling of a bigger story. All events are true, to the best of my recollection, but some names, descriptions and details have been altered to protect confidentiality. The name of the town where much of this takes place has been changed to refer to the region instead, and timelines adjusted for privacy and ease of reading. The year when much of this is set has also been obscured. Language has been rendered as it sounds to my ear—beautiful, rich and idiosyncratic—which I hope is how it's perceived, and words such as 'blackfella' and 'whitefella' are used as I hear them in communities: commonly used descriptors, not loaded terms.

I'm mindful of the following as I write, and I hope that this is conveyed throughout: luck, good health and privilege have played a large part in my life, but many patients I meet are from different backgrounds and in difficult situations. When things get tricky in the places I work, I can leave. The people I work with often can't. Please consider this a content warning, too. Things can sometimes get difficult.

Anyway. I'd best get there.

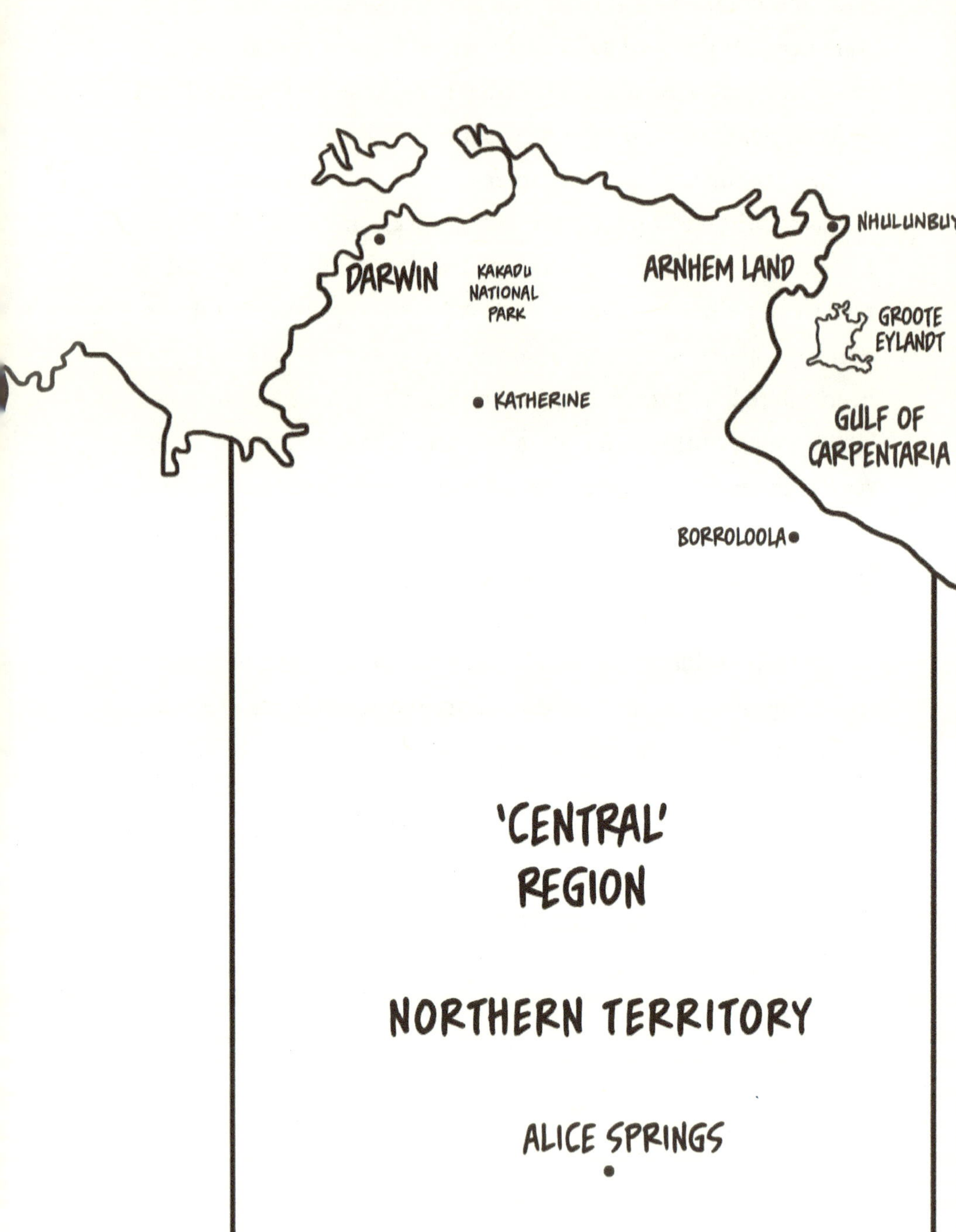
NHULUNBUY
DARWIN
KAKADU NATIONAL PARK
ARNHEM LAND
GROOTE EYLANDT
KATHERINE
GULF OF CARPENTARIA
BORROLOOLA
'CENTRAL' REGION
NORTHERN TERRITORY
ALICE SPRINGS

APUA NEW GUINEA
PORT MORESBY
TORRES STRAIT ISLANDS
HORN ISLAND
CAPE YORK PENINSULA
LOCKHART RIVER
AURUKUN
ORMPURAAW
KOWANYAMA
CAIRNS
TOWNSVILLE
QUEENSLAND
MOUNT ISA
AUSTRALIA
BRISBANE
SYDNEY
MELBOURNE

1

Anxieties

May, Central Australia

It's the middle of the dry season, in the middle of thirsty, brown-red country, and my rental car rattles up the highway. Roadside flood markers mock the landscape. There's been no rain for months. The weather here has two settings—wet or dry—but when the rain does come it'll saturate all this quickly. I've been caught before, watching the water suddenly rise to the doors of the little Toyota Yaris I'd borrowed—not an ideal outback vehicle—although it drained away just as fast. For now, the spinifex grasses and mulga scrub will need to huddle against the dry winds for months yet, under the desert sun, biding their time before a drink.

The roadhouse comes into view. I slow down and turn into the long driveway, stopping beside a fuel pump. It's been over three hours since I left Alice Springs and headed along this almost dead-straight highway, north through the centre of Australia, and I've got a couple more hours to go. My eyelids are getting heavy.

An old Ford Falcon pulls off the highway. It slows, sagging and rolling like an old boat, its back not far above the ground. A wake of orange dust ripples behind. The car stops on the other side of the fuel pump and two creaky front doors burst open, country music cutting out. A hand reaches out of the half-open window to grab at the outside handle of the back door, and there's some swearing; a giggle. Then the door pops. Bodies clamber out—five of them, all Aboriginal—and the car rises a few inches. A sixth person, a young boy, stays inside the car, standing on the back seat and watching me through the half-open window.

'Heya,' I say, as one of them fills the car. The others head into the little store.

'G'day,' says the man filling the pump, looking out towards the highway. The child's looking at me.

'Heya, fella.' I wave to him. 'How you going?'

He makes a little wave back. He's probably two or three years old, and I can't help noticing the nasogastric tube that's coming out of one of his nostrils, taped to his cheek and hanging loosely at the other end—an end that's usually attached to a bag, or a pump. I also can't help noticing the pyjamas he's wearing, 'Alice Springs Hospital' written on the front. Patients aren't usually discharged with either of these things, especially not while they're still attached. The child looks healthy and happy, though, despite the tube.

'Is he alright?' I ask the man.

'Yeah, he right,' he says.

'Good one.'

I wait a long moment. 'I'm just thinking about that tube and all,' I say. 'He looks like he gotta be in hospital?'

'Yeah,' replies the man. Then a long silence. This is often the case around these parts. People speak at their own pace, and trying to rush a conversation usually has the opposite effect. I give it time, look out at the horizon. Wedge-tailed eagles circle not far off, presumably over some roadkill—a kangaroo, or cattle from one of the surrounding stations, belly up and bloated in the heat. There are tens of thousands of feral camels out here, too, but I've fortunately never encountered one on the road. The cattle do enough damage to cars. Nothing jolts me more fully awake on these drives than seeing a bull through the side window as I pass it at 130 kilometres an hour, not having noticed it until then.

The fuel pumps rattle away.

'Yeah, righto,' I say to the man. 'Just wondering, you takin' the young fella back to Alice Springs later?'

Alice Springs, 300 kilometres south, has the biggest hospital in the region. There aren't many others in these parts. Central is the closest but it's far smaller, and Katherine is further away again. Darwin is another thousand kilometres up the road.

'Nah,' he says.

More silence.

'Which hospital you off to then?' I ask, hoping dearly that he's not going to say 'Central'.

'Central,' he says.

Ah. Central is the smallest and most remote one, and it's where I'm headed. We usually transfer the very sick kids in the other direction—to Alice, rather than from Alice.

'Yeah, right,' I say, finishing up and replacing the nozzle. 'Did Alice Springs send you there?'

'Nah.'

A long pause. He rubs his thick beard.

'But they say he's right to come, yeah? I'm just asking because I'm one of the doctors in Central.'

'Nah,' he says. 'But we takin' him. He right. He much better. More close to home, Central. We got family there.'

The others come out of the store, barefoot, hot chips and a couple of large bottles of Coke in hand. 'This fella workin' up Central way,' the older man says to the others. 'He a doctor there.'

'Ah yeah, I know you,' smiles one of the women. 'You look after my other boy before, remember?'

'I think so,' I say, although I don't exactly recall. 'He's good now?'

'Yeah, he right. He broke that arm. You mob put 'em needle in him and made him sleep. You pulled 'em right, made 'em straight.'

I'm flattered that she recalls. I've been coming here on and off for a few years, so I've treated many of these families. But networks are large, and there's also a persistent divide in town. Most Aboriginal people live in the 'camps' on the edges of town, and us health workers stay in our staff accommodation onsite, so there's little overlap aside from conversations at work or in the supermarket, or on the street.

'The little fella in the car, though,' I say to her, 'he's not too crook for Central? He's right to come out of Alice?' I notice that the man next to her is quite short of breath, too.

'Yeah,' she smiles. 'Tyreese be right in Central. You fixed his brother, you a good doctor.'

I smile and nod again. Her faith is touching, if a little misplaced. I trained as a 'specialist rural generalist', somewhat of an oxymoron of a title. It's the medical equivalent of a jack-of-all-trades-but-master-of-none, and the role doesn't exist in the cities. Up here I practise emergency medicine, anaesthetics, do the general ward rounds and some GP clinics. It's a great mix for these remote hospitals, but conversely, I don't have the depth of training in one area that a city specialist does. We also don't have the mountains of diagnostic equipment or referral options available in cities. A joke here is that Central has equal access to all of Australia's best beaches—all of them being at least a thousand kilometres away—but the same could be said regarding all major hospitals.

Mum climbs back into the car. The older man goes in to pay. The man who's short of breath shuffles past me, towards the car.

'How you going, Billy?' I ask. I recognise him from his many presentations to the hospital. He's a young guy, mid-thirties, wearing a cowboy hat and checked shirt tucked into jeans, a big belt buckle and old boots. Cowboy culture is big in these parts, a lot of people having lived and worked on cattle stations in decades past.

'Good, Doc,' he puffs.

'You looking a bit short-wind, yeah?'

'Yeah, little bit,' he says.

There's nothing 'little bit' about his shortness of breath. Billy's heart, despite his age, is big and floppy, and it barely pumps. He lives on a knife edge in terms of medications. He also likes to go bush as much as he can, to get away from the chaos of town and stay with his partner in the outback proper; but even a night or two of that will cost him if he leaves his medications in town, which he sometimes does. He doesn't like the obligation, I suspect.

Many don't. What Billy needs right now is a cardiologist, a kidney specialist and a high-dependency unit. What he'll get is me. In our little hospital. There's no way that someone can be equipped to deal with everything that comes through the doors in these places. Even a rostered night off doesn't guarantee respite from the job.

The last time I was here, a group of us went to watch a rodeo on a cattle station north of town and quickly found ourselves working.

'Just pull it hard!' implored one of the riders. He was holding his arm, his right shoulder obviously deformed. He lay in the paramedic's tent, and we'd been paged over the PA on the off chance we'd attended. The rodeos up here are unmissable—blackfellas and whitefellas all come, and all take it all very seriously. It's one of the few proper melting pots.

'Look, mate,' I replied, 'I'm happy to try, but I gotta be honest, I've had a few beers. All three of us have. And I can't guarantee without an X-ray that your shoulder's dislocated and not broken. If it's broken, there's a chance I could make it a bit worse.'

'Nah, she's right. Go nuts,' he said, laughing then wincing in pain. He was stoned on the green whistle, the inhaled penthrane painkiller the paramedics had given him. 'Someone just pull it!' he cried. His girlfriend was now supporting his arm as his mates filmed him, winding him up.

'Mate, you lasted like two seconds on that thing,' said one. 'Not even.'

'Nah, I filmed it. You rode him for like eight seconds I reckon. Watch this clip, docs.'

We did. It was impressive. They were 'ringers' from a station a few hundred kilometres away, immaculately dressed, as station crew almost always are at these events: R.M. Williams boots, Akubra hats, neat shirts, all covered in dust.

'Ahhh, someone just pull it, please!' he shouted.

'Guys, listen,' I said. 'I'm happy to do it, but we'll need some space. And no lawyers if this doesn't go well, okay?' I was only half-joking. Having a go was the right thing to do, but not exactly best practice without X-rays. 'It'll probably work just fine, but—'

'Doc, just bloody yank it!'

There was no yanking, but we manipulated it back into place over a gentle but sweary minute. The relief is usually instant, but we had a moment of doubt. 'Is it feeling better?' I asked, having felt a soft click. A more satisfying *clunk* is what I'd wanted. 'I'm going to lift your arm up slowly,' I said.

'Yeah, nah,' came the reply.

'That a yeah? Or a nah?' I moved his shoulder gently through its range of motion.

'Yeah. Ah, wait. Nah, it hurts up top there.'

'Yeah, but you can get it all the way up here, so it's almost certainly in,' I said.

'Yeah?'

'Yeah. We should still X-ray it tomorrow, though.'

'Nah.'

'Why nah?'

'I don't want to go all the way down to Central, Doc. I'd rather just see how it goes. Any chance you can strap it so I can ride again tonight? I reckon she'll be sweet as.' He was still stoned on painkiller and covered in dust, the rodeo in full swing behind us. Loud cheers and sudden *oohs* hinted at more patients to come.

'Not a good idea,' I advised. 'It really needs to heal.' But then in came the rodeo clown, fresh from a direct hit as he tried to distract a bull from a fallen rider. Much of his thigh was already a firm, purple-red, swollen bruise. Then in came a guy with a sore neck. Then . . .

Practising medicine up here is fascinating. The distances add to the challenges. Central Hospital serves a region the size of the UK, and the Aboriginal people in these remote areas have the highest rates of disease of any group in Australia. It was only 150 years ago that the first European made it here, and this highway bears his name: Stuart. In the mid-1980s, the last 'first contact' was made with a group of Aboriginal people, the so-called Pintupi Nine, who were living as they always had. Colonisation here is recent, and raw. The consequences unfold daily in these communities. It's why not all the medical work is pulling arms or stabilising medical conditions. A lot of complex social issues reveal themselves, and over the years I've come to develop a sort of mental buffer—a psychological crash helmet, maybe, or a learned desensitisation. You have to. Returning here demands it. Work must be left at work, and the lighter moments indulged in. Like this chat at the roadhouse fuel pump.

Billy and the others are squeezing back into their car.

'See you up there, Doc!' yells the mother.

The little boy waves.

'See you soon,' I say.

Their suspension sags and creaks. Doors slam, the country music fires up and the car sputters. A caravan zips past on the highway—one of the season's many grey nomads, the retired middle classes who travel Australia, some of who will arrive at our hospital with their own complex health needs, and at times little concept of what being out here implies. A letter from a private cardiologist in hand, requesting a full advanced work-up ASAP, or wanting a particular brand of a medication, and only that specific one.

'I come if I'm not right,' Billy says to me out the window.

'Please come either way,' I say. 'We can do a check-up, get your medicine right.'

'Yeah, I come if I'm not right,' he says, still short of breath. 'Maybe I be right.'

'Maybe. But maybe not. You look proper short-wind.'

'Only little bit,' he laughs.

'Nah, fair bit,' I laugh.

'Yeah, maybe fair bit. Alright, I come see you.'

And off they drive. Six members of the Warumungu Nation, bouncing off in a clapped-out Ford through an ancient landscape, descendants of the world's oldest continuously surviving culture. Carrying a dozen health issues, some Coke, juice and chips, and a nasogastric tube. Lives I can't imagine.

It's been months since I was last here. Old anxieties flood back.

2

Breathing

May, Central Australia

Working in the outback had never been my plan. I trained in a large city hospital where I was more than happy with the social life, the coffee shop in the foyer, the teaching and the many colleagues around to help. I was going to be an emergency specialist there, I'd decided. No one I knew had worked in remote towns, and it's not something I'd imagined for myself.

Many of these remote regions struggled for staff, I'd heard, relying on overseas-trained doctors obliged to be there for their visas, or Australian-trained doctors there for the short term. The international aid agencies had similar problems with staffing, at least with retaining people beyond the novelty of a first trip. Long before I went to Central, I'd hoped to work with Doctors Without Borders (Médecins Sans Frontières, or MSF), a seemingly obvious and exciting choice as an idealistic young doctor. But when I finally made it to the field on my first overseas posting, some local staff were confused as to why foreigners like me would want to come and work there. Even more so when I mentioned I was a volunteer.

'You mean, you're not paid?' one of the senior men asked, as we sat outside a brick and tin building. This was in Angola, in the south-west of Africa. Behind us, the wards were full of children with malaria and other infections.

'A little bit,' I said. 'An allowance, but nothing like in Australia.'

'Oh, so you had trouble getting work in Australia?' he asked. 'You had to come here instead?'

'No,' I laughed. 'I had trouble getting these six months *off* in Australia. I chose to come here.'

This region had just experienced three decades of civil war. Giving up an income wasn't a luxury that most Angolans could afford, and neither was taking time away from cultivating their land. The local school was a roofless building with bombed-out walls, and the town was mostly mud huts, surrounded by landmines.

'I don't mean to be disrespectful,' the health worker went on. His name was Roberto, and he'd been trained by South African surgeons during the war to perform essential surgery. He had no formal qualifications before that, but he operated delicately, doing emergency surgery and sterilising the instruments in a pressure-cooker on a wood fire afterwards. 'If you people aren't paid to be here,' he said, 'and you come from rich countries, from safe countries, does that mean you're not very good? I mean, why else would you come?'

I loved his question. He sounded as concerned about my competence as my motivations. Why indeed? In remote Australia we are well paid, but the same question comes up: *Why work here?* And why *keep* working here, when you can make as good a living, if not better, in more conventional places? I've been asked if I had trouble passing exams, as if that's the only reason I'd choose to come. And then there are the clichés about the personality types who gravitate to these places, like the Five Ms: the medics, missionaries, misfits, madmen and mercenaries, with some souls ticking a few boxes at the same time. 'Medic' is the only one for me, I tell myself, but that may be wishful thinking. Adventurism is part of it, too. Few people get to see these corners of the world or experience life in a remote community.

But maybe the more searching question is one I'd seen written in an aid worker's guesthouse in Africa: *What are you running from?*

In my case, I wasn't running *from* anything, but back *to* the continent of my birth.

I was born in Cape Town, South Africa, and grew up there until my family immigrated to Australia when I was fourteen. These were the last years of apartheid, the system of strict racial segregation, and a time of increasing uncertainty and violence, but I was oblivious to a lot of what was going on. We lived in a whites-only suburb and I went to a whites-only school, and our media was heavily curated by the government. I'd glimpsed the poverty—the homeless kids sleeping under sheets of newspaper in the city's centre, the impoverished townships and camps that the highways curved past as we drove fast, windows up and doors locked, to visit relatives—but it was always *over there*, on the other side of glass, away from my sanitised world. My memories of childhood are mostly far more positive. School rugby matches on Saturday mornings, with Table Mountain's steep, forested flanks towering behind us; hiking with my father in the nearby ranges, mindful of the baboons, which would climb through open hut windows or sneak into campsites to pilfer food; and family holidays at some of the country's many incredible beaches.

It wasn't until we came to Australia that I began to properly understand the problems in South Africa. Despite this, I'd always wanted to go back. Rose-tinted glasses may have been part of it, but I missed the accents, the food, the sound of the country's twelve official languages as you walk through town or flick TV channels, our extended family, and the cautious optimism of a country being reborn under Nelson Mandela. And I'd specifically wanted to go back as a doctor. I'd watched the local surgeon operate and was fascinated. My uncle had taken me to the run-down tuberculosis (TB) hospital where he volunteered as a pharmacist, and it looked like interesting, necessary work. Practising medicine seemed like a way to help. The poverty I'd witnessed often manifested as poor health: the chronic coughs of TB that many homeless people had, the HIV/AIDS crisis that was unfolding as we left, and the images of malnourished people elsewhere in the region. So maybe another of those Five Ms applied to me: missionary, albeit an agnostic one who believes in health care as a right.

As soon as MSF would take me, I volunteered. Six months in Angola followed. When I returned, I needed quick money before heading back to city-based training. A colleague suggested Central. They were always short, she'd heard, and they paid pretty well. I'd assumed it'd be a piece of cake after Africa.

Not at all.

By evening I'm in Central. It's been two hours since I saw Billy and Tyreese at the roadhouse. The sky's a purple dome, cloudless and salted with the first stars. The air is chilly. As I drive in, wedge-tailed eagles circle a dead kangaroo on the outskirts while crows contemplate it from the roadside. On the main street, pairs of shoes hang from powerlines by their laces. Kids wander around. Small groups of adults sit on benches and pavements, and metal shutters have been pulled down over shopfronts. It reminds me of the South African town my grandparents lived in, a small farming community—I'm an outright minority here as well. I'd felt this strongly the first time I came.

The little hospital is two blocks back from the highway. I park near the Emergency sign, then head inside to pick up the keys to the musty old cream-walled, green-floored flat I've been assigned for two weeks. I unpack and meet a colleague for dinner.

Billy comes in the next morning. He rings the doorbell at the ambulance entrance where his family have dropped him off.

'Mate, you look proper short-wind today,' I say, as I open the glass doors to the department for him. Two police vans are at the end of the car park, beneath the palm trees. A LandCruiser ambulance pulls into the driveway, arriving from a remote community.

'Yeah, I bin crook. All night,' he says, shuffling. He's wearing a thick flannel shirt and jeans, cowboy hat set neatly, and smells of wood smoke. I get him a wheelchair and push him to one of two resuscitation cubicles—called 'resus', the areas for the severely unwell. He gets onto the bed, and I adjust it so he can sit upright. 'Hardly been sleepin',' he says.

'I bet. Why didn't you come in earlier?'

A lot of patients here don't come in until their symptoms are advanced, or unless there are compelling difficulties at home.

'I took 'em tablets,' he says in half-sentences, puffing. 'Took 'em last night. I thought I be right.'

'You pee much?' I ask. Some of his tablets are diuretics that shift excess water from the body, to help his breathing.

He shakes his head.

'Is it worse if you lie down?'

'Yeah. Usin' lots of pillows.'

This is likely because of his heart failure. Even when he's stable and his condition is well controlled, Billy's heart pumps weakly. A backlog of blood builds up in his veins, causing fluid to seep into his lung's airspaces. I sit him forward and listen to his chest and can hear coarse, noisy crackles all over—the sound of fluid where it shouldn't be.

'You right to go on that mask for a while?' I ask.

He nods. He's used it before.

A South African intensive care doctor I worked with years ago, a man with a thick Afrikaner accent, used to ask people in these situations if they'd seen *Top Gun*. The question would initially confuse patients.

'But you've seen it, *ja?*' he'd ask, ceaselessly upbeat. 'Nice. Okay, well, remember Tom Cruise in that? With that big mask he'd wear inside the fighter jet? *Ja*, okay, we're going to set you up like Tom Cruise just now. We'll put a mask like that on, very tight. Big straps. It's going to be noisy. It's going to feel like you've opened that fighter jet canopy and put your head outside, but that's good. All that wind will push the fluid out from your lungs and back into your blood vessels. It'll help you breathe better. Okay? Good. *Ja*, let's go.'

I've channelled this explanation ever since.

We set up. Billy gives the thumbs up. Sue, an experienced nurse and the best soul in town for a coffee and debrief, readies the machine and tubing. I put a drip in and take blood, and another nurse fetches medications.

A heart transplant is what Billy needs. At 36 years old, he has severe heart disease—a degree of illness not usually seen until someone is in their sixties or older, and even then it'd be bad luck. Aging is sped-up out here. Disease processes are accelerated, shifted forward a few decades, often compounding each other. It's driven in large part by living conditions, poor food and crowded housing, the distance from adequate services, and various other 'social determinants of health' that are out of Billy's hands. He's had bad diabetes for years. He's also had numerous heart attacks, and needed stents inserted in Adelaide. Now his kidneys are failing. He's been declined a heart transplant by several specialists because of his many complicating illnesses. I've asked Billy whether he'd like consideration again, but he's said no. He likes to go bush with his family. He doesn't want to be tethered to more appointments and tests. 'I don't want that big cut, all them tablets,' he'd said.

The machine blows and beeps. He gives another thumbs up.

'You okay like that?' I ask.

He nods and says a muffled 'I'm right.'

I leave him for now.

So goes my first half-hour back. There are a few new faces here this morning, but there's no time for proper getting-to-know-yous: it's Monday, and a truism of emergency departments, or EDs, is that Mondays are incredibly busy. Aches and pains and fevers and splinters and insurance forms and things in eyes that had been endured or ignored all weekend suddenly need attention.

Most of the trainee doctors have changed over in the months I've been away, along with half the nurses. But otherwise it's as if I've never left. There's the same sign on the glass doors of our back entrance, saying: 'Stay cool! Please, no swearing, fighting, spitting or biting.' There's the same beautiful piece of Aboriginal art just inside the ambulance entrance, dots and footprints in warm, earthy colours, our three wheelchairs parked below it. The same large bug zapper above the ambulance entrance, sizzling and buzzing like a cheap motel sign. The same resuscitation mannequin we practise on, still lying on a trolley outside the patients' toilets, a white sheet pulled over it as if it were a corpse—something that's caused a few frights, and that needs to be moved. And there's the same cream-walled, neon-lit, far-too-small department with its five cubicles, two resus bays and two consult rooms, our work desks squeezed midway along the inner wall.

'Where do I find the CT scanner?' asks a new trainee doctor. Deb's her name, and she's just arrived from Sydney.

'In Alice Springs,' says Sue.

'Really? But you've got an operating theatre here, right?' she asks.

'Six of them,' says Sue. 'In Alice Springs.'

'What? How do you manage?' she asks.

'Pretty well,' says Faith, a Zimbabwean-born nurse. She's mixing Billy's medication. 'This hospital is very good. In my country, this could have been a referral hospital when I was training. It is not big, but look, there are two ventilators, and our pharmacy cupboards are full. We have every drug. And we have X-ray, and two ultrasounds. Two! And how many of your doctors are here now? Nine? Ten? For 30 beds? We used to have three doctors. Let me tell you, this is a very good hospital.'

I smile at Faith. She's been here for years, and she's kind and hardworking, never complains. A lot of staff here are migrants, many of them recent. A few South Sudanese men work at the nursing home down the road and, in this hospital, staff are from at least a dozen countries. There's rarely a queue of city-based Australians wanting to work out here.

Police arrive. They bring in a young man wearing handcuffs who needs assessment before going into custody. Paramedics bring in someone with chest pain. Not long after, the paramedics return with a baby kangaroo. 'Anyone want to bottle-feed him?' asks Liz, a paramedic who also volunteers as an animal rescuer. She un-swaddles the joey and lets him hop near our desk. The medical student jumps at the chance.

'They special nappies you get for him?' asks Sue, printing off an ECG trace for the new patient.

'Nah, regular Huggies,' says Liz. 'Extra small. From the supermarket.' Her phone rings again.

For a town of 3000 people in a region of 8000, this hospital is busy, even if small. Aside from the ED, there are two adult wards, a separate children's ward, and a few outpatient clinics. All of this is laid out around a central courtyard. Upstairs is administration and a pathology service. The Aboriginal Medical Service up the road provides primary care, but that's otherwise it for the area.

Last week's ward doctor is about to fly out, so I walk over to take the handover. Tyreese, the boy I met on the highway yesterday, is here—now in Central Hospital pyjamas, without a nasogastric tube. 'They took 'em out last night,' says his mum. 'We came straight away. He's right now, drinkin' more.'

He smiles as I squat to examine him. Lumps of moist Weet-Bix cling to his top like wallpaper glue. He does look much better. 'But why's he on the adults' ward?' I ask. 'No kids' beds left?'

'Nah,' says Mum. 'Doris here is his grandma. We just visiting her. Billy is his uncle.' Almost everyone in town is related or connected in some way.

'And what about you, Doris?' I ask. 'What are you here for?'

'Painin' in the leg,' she says, showing me an injury. 'Painin' big mob.'

The word 'pain' is used as a verb here: one doesn't 'have pain'. One 'pains' or 'is paining'. 'Mob' can be used for many things.

'Our mob' can refer to all Indigenous people, or a family, or other group. 'Big mob' or 'little mob' can mean a quantity, like 'a big mob of pain'. There are lovely idiosyncrasies of language here. The word 'deadly' is used to mean something that's great rather than lethal—as in 'That fella's deadly!' rather than 'That snake is deadly!'—which is not to be confused in a hospital. To 'yarn' is to talk, and yarning is an important thing here.

On the men's ward, a gentleman named Clancy Number Three is recovering from his emphysema. This is his full name: Clancy Number Three, written like that on all documents, 'Number Three' spelled out and capitalised, no other surname. I'd asked him if there was a Clancy Number One and Two, and he'd said yes, of course, and he'd known them well. They'd worked on a cattle station together decades ago.

'How are you this morning, Clancy?' I ask, and he stands up, straightens his hat and shakes my hand.

'I'm right,' he smiles. 'No more coughin'.'

His lung disease is likely from a lifetime of smoking. Tobacco was part of the rations and payments on cattle stations and reserves in the past, rather than money, and smoking rates in the region are high. There's irony in the love of cowboy culture among many here, to me at least; but the work often kept people on their land and was respected. I've heard many older men speak fondly of the long cattle droves to Queensland, the months of riding and camping, even though it was exploitative and unpaid.

'You're sounding great,' I tell him, listening to his chest. 'I reckon you'll be right to go home this afternoon. You happy with that?'

'Whatever you reckon, Doc,' he says.

I reckon whatever he reckons. He's earned his right to have a few days here if he'd like, having a break and running those hot showers dry. Billy, too. People like these two are a large part of the reason I keep coming back. For all the difficulties here, where else was I going to meet the likes of them—maybe even help a little?

After years of returning, I'm still caught off guard by the conditions. An experienced aid worker had cautioned me before I came here: 'It's harder than working overseas,' she'd said, 'because you don't expect it to be. And because it shouldn't be.'

Back to the ED after the ward rounds, and I walk in and stop. I look around. Take a deep breath. The department is full. The other senior, Emily, is mostly on her own. The three new doctors are struggling with software and computer passwords that don't work. Police bring in a young man who's injured and yelling, and the ambulance crew phones to say that they're at a car crash south of town.

'High-speed rollover,' says Liz on the phone. 'One's trapped, one's walking but injured. You got a pen?' She gives more details. 'Fire crew's setting up to extricate. Flying Doctors are aware. They're on another job but they're aiming to come to you afterwards. Our ETA's 45 minutes, if it goes well.'

I tell the team. Emily starts clearing a resus cubicle and we call another doctor from the GP clinic to help.

Billy is still on the mask in the other resus cubicle, improving slowly.

'You sure you're happy to stay in town?' I ask him. 'Even if you're proper crook in a few hours?' Alice Springs has an ICU; we don't. He's still young, and I really don't want to have the 'ceiling of care' talk with him now. Not rushed, not like this. He should improve soon, but if he doesn't, we don't have a lot more we can offer.

'Yeah,' he says, through the mask. 'Family here. I'm right.' He gives the thumbs up.

It's an awful feeling, to be short of breath like this. We often give medications for anxiety and pain to take the edge off, as people sit wide-eyed and sweaty, sometimes panicked, but Billy appears calm and breathes through it. We give him a little morphine to help anyway.

Two kids bounce into his cubicle as I adjust Billy's ventilator. They grab gloves, turn the taps on and jump on the floor scale, delighted by the beeps, but I direct them out. 'Where's your mum?' I ask.

'X-ray!' says one of the kids. 'What's your name?'

'Damien. Come sit with the joey, we'll get you some stuff to draw with.'

'What about a sweet?' she asks, but the vitamin tablets will have to wait. They jump straight back into Billy's cubicle anyway.

The medical student asks where she can get more milk for the joey, but we're going to need her help—this is an all-hands-on-deck scenario. The joey will have to babysit itself in the tearoom. Another man takes off his neck collar and walks out, says he doesn't want to wait anymore, calls us something under his breath, but the Aboriginal Liaison Officer tries to persuade him back.

'No chance,' she says, coming back a minute later, without him. Lynda's her name, and she's fantastic, another long-termer who knows everyone and everything in town. 'But did you see the woman in cubicle three?' she asks.

'The seizure patient?' I ask.

'No, the assault.'

'She must have also left.'

'And the kids in cubicle four?' she asks.

'Keeping Billy entertained. Could you keep an eye on them for a moment?'

She does. The waiting room buzzer goes. The police ask me to review their man in custody quickly, while Emily sets up for the car accident.

I look around. *Damaged bodies and proud souls*, I think, as I breathe in deeply. I'm glad to be back after months of working elsewhere, of having had a break from this, but I'm wary of what's ahead. The on call, the lack of sleep, the bad cases and the near-misses that'll add up again, because they can't not. The dilemmas and ethical issues. The culture clashes and stepping on toes at times. The challenge of helping with this in any meaningful way. And, more selfishly than I'd like to admit, how to stay okay in the process.

I have fourteen days straight of shifts. Before I know it, it's time for a short break in Melbourne.

3

Circulation

June, Far North Queensland

The sun also takes the week off when I arrive in Melbourne, lazing behind low clouds on cold, blustery days. The city is my short answer to 'where's home?' although I haven't worked here for years. It's where we landed when we migrated, and it's where I studied, and where I return between blocks of work.

This is an easy place to relax. The inner suburbs are full of parks and wine bars and cafes, and my days couldn't be further from what they're like when I'm working. I live in a progressive, student-filled part of town, tucked behind the so-called kale curtain. Steak done five ways doesn't dominate the menus down here, not even the classy steaks with frozen prawns on top. This is vegan and vegetarian territory. And food options aren't the only glaring differences. Here, I'm mindful of gendered pronouns when I'm meeting people for the first time; up north, a taxi driver asked me why I would work with 'the blacks'.

I've learned to switch expectations quickly, conversation topics even faster.

This fly-in, fly-out (FIFO) set-up is deliberate, though. It means a hospital like Central can keep a consistent group of staff returning long-term, if only part-time, rather than people burning out after a year or two. For me, it means that no matter how difficult a block is, I'm guaranteed a break. I'd lived up there for a year once, and I've spent months in other remote places, and it can get difficult. Cabin fever sets in—despite all the highlights. There are only the people you work with, the people you've treated and the people you're about to treat. Everyone's a colleague or patient. Over here is the person you diagnosed as having chlamydia, just hours ago, now serving drinks at the pub and avoiding eye contact, while at opposite sides of your table are two colleagues who've just split up, and who've both told you far more than you'd like to know about the other. They're going to need the roster rewritten so that they don't cross paths. Hosting a barbecue tomorrow night is the junior doctor you've all had to performance manage, but you do get on well with socially. And behind you, the family of a patient who's just died are sitting in the corner, quietly staring at their drinks—do you say hello? And if the hospital is suddenly short-staffed, too bad. You could say no to the overtime, but you'd be throwing colleagues under the bus.

So flying out is my release valve. An investment in doing this work for longer.

I own my small unit here in Melbourne, a half-unpacked base with the joy of my own bed, my books, a drum kit and a few art canvases, purchased in the waiting rooms of clinics and hospitals up north. What's missing is my girlfriend, Maya—conspicuously so.

The photos on my fridge remind me often. She's currently based in London for work, a once-in-a-career opportunity. The plan after that? We're working hard on it. For now, I'd settle with just living on the same continent.

Anyway, it's soon time to repack my bag—not that I'd ever fully unpacked. There's now just fresher laundry, and a change from my black hospital scrubs to the navy-blue uniforms of the Royal Flying Doctor Service, my other part-time role. Then it's a four-hour flight to Cairns, in Far North Queensland, and an acknowledgement that if carbon emissions are measured at the Pearly Gates, or on the scales of karma, or by whatever other metric lies in store, I could be in trouble. It's an aspect of this work I'm not proud of. But when I land in Cairns, the sky is big and warm, the sun's out and the Great Barrier Reef is iridescent along its green-blue fringes. It's a glorious start.

The weather is what worried me most when I took this job. It was cyclone season when I started. Trying to manage an unwell patient while flying, seated backwards, in a small aircraft at night, had worried me enough, but doing this while flying through a storm *really* worried me. I'd asked one of our pilots what would happen if we got caught in severe weather. Our aircraft are sleek, twin-engine Beechcraft King Airs that have been refitted with two stretchers and medical equipment, and they look sturdy.

'Yeah, nah,' he said. 'You don't wanna do that. The aim is to fly around the storms, never through them. That's why we take a bit of extra fuel in the wet season.'

This made me happy.

'I'd worry more about the birds,' he continued. 'There are tons of 'em. They'll sit right near the runways, in pools of water in the wet season. The brolgas are huge, bloody huge, but they'll usually stay still or just fly away. The magpie geese are a worry. They're stupid buggers. They'll fly straight up into ya. They'll look your way and still fly straight into ya. And the bustards are like bags of cement. Solid, hard little buggers. They'll do some serious damage.' Safety is everything for the pilots, though, and I've made enough landings in bad weather with them to be relaxed in the worst of it now. They're good.

I'd originally taken this job to round off my remote medicine training a few years ago, as it seemed to be the iconic 'bush doctor' experience. I've stayed on part-time or casual since, doing my best to plug gaps between my Central weeks. It's too interesting a job to leave. A lot of our flights aren't overly dramatic, though. We'll head off in reasonable weather to fetch patients who've been stabilised by staff on the ground, or who haven't yet deteriorated. Our role is often to be there 'in case'. We'll fetch people with heart attacks who are good for the moment, or kids with pneumonia who'll need oxygen and IV antibiotics, or those with bad injuries who'll need surgery in a bigger centre, among much else. 'Long periods of boredom, interspersed with moments of terror' is a description used about anaesthetic practice—a phrase borrowed from soldiers, apparently—and this job can feel similar. It's usually fine. But when cases are difficult, they can be *very* difficult.

A few days after arriving at Cairns, I take a phone call that begins mid-sentence. Never a good sign.

'. . . wait, I'VE GOT THEM. Hello? Oh my god, they're—'

The caller stops talking and I can hear shouting in the background.

'Hello? Sir, are you there?' I ask.

'You need to come, wait . . . GET THE HOSE, hello? Hello?' says the caller. There's more shouting and noise in the background.

'Hello? Give me your phone number and location.'

'There's been an explosion. There's two of them, you need to—'

The call drops out. We can't trace calls and they didn't leave a number. I start filling out a job sheet, but they don't call back. This isn't normally how jobs begin. We'd usually take calls from remote clinic nurses or a central coordinator, sometimes from people on remote properties, and have a detailed conversation. Problems can often be sorted with advice and medications, and if not, we fly up to 'retrieve' them.

I walk quickly to the nurse's and pilot's offices, down the corridor. Three of our aircraft are parked inside the hangar, metres away, where a handful of engineers are working on one. The sun's blazing through the hangar doors. The commercial airport is just across the runway. I find my two colleagues and tell them what I've heard.

'For real?' asks Baz, the pilot. 'And you didn't get a phone number?'

'And he definitely said two people?' asks Susan, the flight nurse.

'The phone number didn't come up,' I say. 'And I definitely heard *two* something.'

Susan starts taking out medications and equipment, although one of the other Flying Doctor bases may be closer to the scene. I call the coordination centre in case they've heard something, but they haven't. We pack two ventilators, two stretchers, two of most things, and Baz lets the refueller know, although we don't know how much fuel to load yet. A few minutes later, my phone handset rings. It's the original caller. There's been a fuel tank explosion on a cattle station and there are two patients, both awake but severely injured.

'What's the number and location?' I ask, putting us on speaker-phone and walking to the pilot's office. They're on a remote property, so Baz confirms the coordinates and queries the airstrip.

'Is there any lighting?' he asks.

'No, nothing.' But it's still only early afternoon now.

'What's the condition of the strip?'

'Dirt. It's unsealed.'

Baz fires off more questions. Has it been graded since the wet season? When did a plane last land there? Any powerlines or poles nearby? What's the exact length? We'll have a lot of equipment and weight. He does some calculations. 'We can do it,' he says, 'but we gotta be out before dark. It's a short strip; I can't take off safely with all that weight. Especially not in the dark.'

Susan takes out the last of the equipment and Baz meets the refuelling truck. I give first-aid instructions to the caller, then find my supervisor, Shelley, who's here coincidentally for a meeting. She's an experienced rural doctor and we'll need her help. She's happy to come with us.

Air-traffic control gives us priority, and we taxi ahead of commercial airliners, taking off over the sugarcane fields north of Cairns, heading to Cape York, the far northern peninsula of the Australian mainland. The property is about an hour's drive from an Aboriginal community clinic, so we call the nurses there to ask if any can help. Two of them will go now, they say. The three of us draw up medications and talk through a plan in the back of the aircraft, as Baz flies us north-west over coastal rainforest, then the Great Dividing Range, over dry eucalypt woodlands and towards the floodplains and marshes of the western side of the peninsula. To have one critically unwell patient in this confined space is a difficult job. Two is extremely challenging.

The aircraft descends. We fly low and bank hard over the airstrip as we near the property, to check the condition and to scare any wildlife. A colleague in the Northern Territory had once needed to circle a remote runway while they waited for a large water buffalo to move off, but the animal stayed put. The clinic car tried to nudge it off as the team looked down, but no luck. A few minutes later some other people arrived, and to the air crew's surprise they shot the buffalo, then dragged it off. The team landed safely, and an hour later were handed a few bags of warm 'buff' meat, a thankyou gift as they departed.

There are no animals today. The sun's bright and the strip's clear. We circle again and come in, bumping gently as the engines roar us to a quick halt. Two utes are waiting. Baz steps out and directs them to our rear door, and we unpack and reload our equipment. They drive us the short distance to a house.

A burned-out truck with melted tyres is smouldering, 20 metres from the front veranda. The grass around is torched black, hose-pipes snaking around it. The smell of burned grass and rubber is thick. It's dead quiet; unsettlingly so.

The man who'd called greets us at the veranda in a soft voice. The wait must have felt like an eternity. 'Thank you,' he says, and directs us in. Two other men are nearby with one of the patients. 'Greg's back there, in the shower,' says the man. 'He's bad.

This is Mick. We got him cooled off first. We covered the burns in clingfilm, like you said.'

Mick's on a sheet on the concrete floor of the large, open veranda. He's conscious and clearly in pain, so Shelley and Susan attend to him. I walk into the large, basic bathroom, just off the veranda, where the second man is lying on the floor. He's undressed and pale, shivering and wet from the shower. He's alert and sounds calm.

'Heya,' he says softly. 'Cheers for coming. I'm Greg.'

I kneel next to him and cover his waist with a towel. 'Nice to meet you, Greg. I'm Damien. Really sorry that we have to meet like this, though. How's your pain?'

'I don't have any.'

'Oh?' This surprises me. Full thickness burns are painless, as the skin's pain receptors have been destroyed, but partial thickness burns are extremely painful. He'd presumably have areas of both, as well as injuries from the explosion. 'No pain at all?' I ask.

'Nothing.'

I look at him from head to toe. He's pale. He smells strongly of fuel and smoke. With the torch on my phone, I can see black soot in his mouth and near his nostrils—a sign that his airways may be burned. There are no other obvious injuries I can see, but we'll need to get him out to look thoroughly.

'Welding a fuel tank,' says Greg, as I open a bag of equipment. 'Bloody hell, huh. We'd checked it, too. Looked empty. Was a beautiful morning.'

'I'm really sorry this happened, Greg. Let's get you out and comfy and down to Cairns. We'll take good care of you.'

He smiles slightly.

I've learned to project calmness in situations like this, even with overwhelming uncertainty—like now. Patients should believe that there's a plan, that this is normal for us, that they're in safe hands. Difficult discussions can come later. I do my best to sound lighthearted. Greg knows this is serious. My demeanour shouldn't amplify that.

He's worried now about the lack of pain.

'That must be bad, hey, if I can't feel anything?'

I tell him about endorphins and the shock response. We have great painkillers if he needs them, I say. I fetch clingwrap and blankets from our bags to help his body retain heat and moisture, then look for a vein for an IV. It takes me a while to find one.

'Are they bad?' he asks. 'The burns?'

'They'll need a lot of treatment,' I say. 'But you're doing great so far, Greg. We'll get you out and onto something nicer, then drift you off to sleep for the flight. I promise we'll keep you comfortable.'

Three nurses have arrived from the nearby community with more equipment. A handful of us crowd into the little bathroom to lift Greg gently onto a stretcher and carry him to the veranda. We systematically examine both men, running through the ABCs of resuscitation—assessing their airway, breathing, circulation, disability or conscious state, and exposing them to look for other injuries or signs. The aim is to find and quickly manage problems, in order of urgency, but in reality, a lot happens simultaneously. A secondary survey is next—a full examination from top to bottom, front to back. Many of our patients have already survived the critical first hour or two because of our travel times, a so-called 'trial of life'.

Greg's vital signs are stable—for now. In the coming hours his airway may swell and his circulation will become compromised. Shelley catches my eye as we examine him: there's no normal skin. None at all. It's all pale and waxy. Maybe we're confused about the appearance? He's conscious and chatting with us, and I've never seen someone with complete burns, so we must be wrong, surely? The other patient has burns to about 60 per cent of his body—an incredibly severe amount as well.

We huddle and discuss a plan. Baz reminds us we need to be gone before dark, and it's already late afternoon. Greg will need to be intubated—given an anaesthetic, a tube placed into his airway to protect it, and then connected to a ventilator. We'd normally also intubate someone in Mick's situation, but we think he'll be fine with a simple mask until we land. At least we hope so. To have both patients intubated creates its own risk.

We allocate roles and lay out the equipment. Monitors, a dozen pieces of airway equipment, oxygen canisters and tubing, battery packs, a suction pump and syringes. We perform a brief ultrasound to make sure Greg doesn't have a punctured lung.

Shelley, Susan and I kneel around Greg. Baz holds a sheet, shielding the monitors from sunlight. We give Greg some oxygen to breathe. He speaks to his mate, a few metres away, and his friend says he'll see him shortly in Cairns. Greg looks calm. He breathes slowly and deeply. We share a few words with him.

'Good to go?' Shelley asks.

We all nod.

Susan gives some painkillers, then the injection to drift him off to sleep. Then the muscle relaxant that'll stop his breathing, allowing us to intubate. We watch the clock. It'll take one minute to work. It's a long minute. He stops breathing. This is a critical few seconds now—his oxygen levels will drop quickly. We'd normally stand at the top of a bed to do this, but he's on the ground, so the position is awkward. I hunch over his head with the small video-scope and guide the plastic tube through his mouth, behind his tongue, to find his vocal cords and trachea. It's much harder than in an ED. I reposition myself on my elbows, and Baz moves the sheet for more shade. I pass the clear plastic tube over the scope and into his trachea—or at least I think I do. I'm not certain. I can't get positioned well. It may be in his oesophagus—catastrophic if not fixed quickly. The carbon dioxide sensor will confirm this, but the monitor resets itself as I connect the tubing. Awful timing. My heart thumps. We practise these drills, but these seconds are always stressful. We aren't breathing for him yet. Shelley leans over and performs a manoeuvre on the sensor to get it working, then peers over my shoulder at the tube and adjusts it a little, and she's happy. She's far more experienced in these jobs, and she's relaxed and unassuming.

The oxygen alarm sounds. Baz is onto it, stepping over to adjust the connections. Susan starts the drug infusions that'll keep Greg asleep. We do some blood tests on our analyser, then insert a urinary catheter and arterial pressure monitor. This all takes time, but he needs to be stable before the flight.

'We gotta hustle,' says Baz. 'It's gonna be dark shortly. This is not a good airstrip for the dark.'

But both patients are now having blood pressure issues. We adjust things, then secure the men carefully onto our stretchers, loading one on the back of each ute. We sit on the back beside them, holding pieces of equipment, and are driven slowly to the aircraft, past the burned-out truck that's still smouldering. The plane's rear loading door is narrow, and the stretchers are well over 100 kilograms with everything on them. There's constant alarms sounding and the risk of accidentally pulling out a tube. One at a time, we push each stretcher up the steep fibreglass 'slide' through the opening, around the tight corner, and onto the docking stations, where Susan secures them. It's sweaty work and there's equipment everywhere. Not a centimetre of wasted space.

Baz drives down the runway in one of the utes to check it, and a man on a quad bike checks the other side. The sky's darkening. Baz makes a plan for runway lighting: a ute behind us, shining its headlights ahead, and a ute at the far end, its tail-lights at the fence line. There'll be nothing down the sides. Toilet paper rolls doused in kerosene are an option, known as a 'dunny-roll take-off', but there's not enough time. This will have to do. Baz climbs back into the plane and shuts the door. I sit beside him in the cockpit for take-off because there's nowhere else for me to strap in with all the people and equipment. He quickly runs through his checks.

'We'll aim for the ute light,' he shouts, as the two engines whine through start-up. He radios the flight plan. The engines accelerate. I look back at Shelley and Susan, strapped in but leaning hard to adjust Greg's equipment as he's becoming more unstable, and Baz suddenly gestures ahead. He waves out the window to the group nearby and yells 'Cattle!' and points down the strip. I squint but I can barely see it—a bull has strolled onto the edge. The man with the quad bike quickly starts it again and races off, chasing the animal away, and loops back and gives us the thumbs up. Our plane immediately rolls ahead. It roars, bouncing and rattling at increasing speed down the dirt strip, and all I can see is the purple horizon and two red tail-lights ahead, the long shadows of the car behind us rapidly fading, and Baz clenching his jaw. I've never seen Baz clench his jaw. The lights are closer, then they're just in front of us, and then there's a fence right there but we're still on the ground. I'd lower my legs and pedal like the Flintstones if I could to help our little plane, but in no time the glowing red tail-lights are on us, under us, and we soar just above the fence line. I'd hug Baz if he wasn't adjusting landing flaps and banking, and then he turns and whoops: 'We bloody made it, Damo!' He's as excited as I've ever seen him, grinning, and I wonder if part of him is surprised.

The bigger problem is now in the back as we race to Cairns.

4

Don't Forget Glucose

June, Far North Queensland

Two ambulances are waiting when we land in Cairns. Under floodlights beside the hangar, we unload the men, manoeuvring them down a ramp and onto trolleys, along with the oxygen, monitors, tubing and pumps. Greg's blood pressure is highly unstable. Shelley, Susan and I accompany the paramedics on the fifteen-minute drive to the hospital, then reverse the process into the ED, where we're ushered to the resuscitation cubicles. A dozen nurses and doctors are waiting. We give a handover to the small crowd and switch over to the hospital's equipment, then load ours back into the ambulances and get a ride back to the hangar. That's it. A quick drink and some chips from the vending machine in our staff kitchen and an informal debrief. We're giddy with relief and adrenaline, and exhausted. The plane needs to be cleaned, and the paperwork finished still, so we settle in for another hour. I'll call for an update tomorrow, but our jobs are otherwise done. Nothing more. It's strangely final and anticlimactic.

What to do to wind down? A jog on the tourist-packed foreshore. A long shower. Takeaway dinner and a beer, and a half-hour of TV on the couch. Try to flick off that adrenaline and sleep. It takes a while, but the upside is that I catch my girlfriend on her lunchbreak in London.

Maya and I met in the UK while we were both studying public health for a year, taking a detour from our medical careers to look at the bigger picture of health care. She'd moved from Canada, as the university in London had a great reputation for global health and tropical medicine; I'd chosen it for the same reason. After a year living in that Central Hospital flat, London was pure indulgence: endless gigs and pubs and restaurants and places to fly to for the weekend, fantastic lecturers, and the upside of no on-call shifts and not running into a dozen patients at the supermarket. Maya and I hit it off immediately. On our first date, an older woman came over to our brunch table. 'I have to say,' she began, 'I've been sitting behind you two for a few hours, and you've spent more time chatting than I've ever talked with my husband. Ever, in 30-something years of marriage. And you still look so engaged. Marry her,' she nodded to me. That was a couple of years ago. I still shrug when mates ask how I ended up with her. 'No idea,' I laugh. She's smarter, kinder, has lived in some difficult places for work, and seems oblivious to her talents.

Tonight's a bit less romantic than London restaurants. I'm lying in the Flying Doctor unit in shorts, a ceiling fan paddling tropical air onto me and fruit bats squealing outside. She's in a bustling London park, office workers in smart coats in the background. We're literally worlds apart. Her morning has involved a series of meetings so far, part of her work on malaria control projects in East Africa. It's a completely different pace to my afternoon and work in general, and with a longer and broader view. I tell her about Baz's take-off and those ute lights rushing towards us, trying not to dwell on the medical details too much. She gets it, though.

'You're okay?' she asks.

Better for chatting with her, I say. And the team was great, which makes all the difference.

'And you went for a run?'

'Yup.'

'And you've watched some *Seinfeld*?'

'I have.'

'Then I have nothing else to offer you,' she laughs, tucking her black hair behind her ears, her phone propped on a park table. It's less than two months until we're together, we remind each other, and she says goodnight, and I melt, and the connection drops out, and I lament long-distance relationships. Honeymoon periods and sad goodbyes, then long countdowns to the next blissful weeks together, then more goodbyes. For a year we've been juggling London and remote Australia, and I'm not sure we could've arranged a more expensive flight path. We're determined to make this work, though. A week after this call, I get a care package from her, too. I *have* to make this work.

Handing patients over to another team is a constant part of the aeromedical job. There's the satisfaction of having played your part, and then others take over and you move on. But it's also a downside. You're never a part of their recovery. You arrive not knowing them, have a brief and intense interaction—on what's possibly the worst day of their lives—and usually never meet again. The other half of this Flying Doctor job is the opposite: the GP work in the remote communities. It allows for getting to know people in their own contexts, and over time it's become my favourite bit.

I arrive back at the hangar early the next week for a flight back up to Cape York, fresh coffee in my mug and the smell of aviation gas outside the hangar. There's a school bus feel to these mornings. We weigh bags, share quick handovers and enjoy the few hours of flying to catch up—mental and allied health workers, nurses, doctors and midwives among us. We staff five of the remote community clinics on the peninsula. All of them differ in terms of their geography and the clans and language groups present, but to an outsider like me there are some other notables.

Pormpuraaw is the most picturesque, to my eye, situated alongside a white-sand beach. It has the only drinking 'club' I've ever seen that requires you to be breathalysed to get *inside*. A positive reading means you'll be banned for a while, part of the Aboriginal council's strategy to reduce 'sly grog'—alcohol brought illegally into otherwise 'dry' communities. It's also the community I'd least want to overshoot the runway in, with a large, commercial crocodile farm at one end of its tiny airport.

On the east coast, Lockhart River is the largest community, a short distance back from another gorgeous beach. When I'd started there, an old sign hung at the front door stating: 'Proper sick and bleeding only, after 5 pm!' The area was a large base for American bombers in World War II and thousands of soldiers came for jungle training. It now attracts birdwatchers from all over the world, chasing species found only here and Papua New Guinea. The only non-coastal town we visit, Coen, was the site of a gold rush in the late 1800s. But it's the two others on the west coast that I usually get sent to—Aurukun and Kowanyama. They're the largest, at around a thousand people each, and they're also the most troubled, making the news occasionally for the wrong reasons.

We land a little after nine. Several people are waiting for the commercial flight out, chatting in the shade of a large tree. The bush is thick beyond the roadside, a river behind that. The clinic driver doesn't arrive and the phone reception is patchy, but after a while we reach a nurse. She drives down to fetch the three of us.

'Ah, yeah, I remember you,' says an older Aboriginal woman in the small waiting room. She's wearing a dress with bright yellow flowers against bold reds and deep blues.

'Lovely colours,' I say.

'It's my hunting dress,' she giggles.

'Really? It looks far too nice to go hunting in.'

'Brings me good luck, this one,' she says. 'I also got a dancin' one. And a jealousin' one.'

I ask what a 'jealousin' dress is, and she says that it makes her look so beautiful that other men stare, and her husband gets jealous. I laugh.

An elderly man at the reception desk looks over at me. 'I forgot your name,' he says. 'You that baldie doctor. We got two baldie docs here now.'

I smile. It's nice to be remembered for something.

The locals deal with an endless parade of FIFO workers. These clinics are permanently staffed by nurses, many of whom live here for years. They do the on-call work and see most patients. They also staff the ambulance service. It's an incredible job, and a tough one, a long way from friends and family and medical backup, and with patients with every imaginable injury and condition turning up. Most nurses form strong connections with the community and know the families well, but all have stories of difficulties and safety issues.

There's another familiar face as I step inside: an Aboriginal artist named Gloria. She comes in often to chat. I knew she was a good artist—she collects her own ochres nearby and bakes and prepares them, and she's a well-known weaver—but I'd had no idea of her international reputation until recently.

'Yeah, so, I got this letter,' she tells us in the corridor. 'They want me to go talk about my paintings there, but I don't wanna go.'

'You don't have to go,' one of the nurses says. 'It's your art, Gloria. Your time. You do what you want to do.'

'Go where?' I ask.

'Paris,' she says.

'Wait. Paris, as in France?'

'Yeah. But I bin' before. I don't like it.'

'You don't like Paris?'

'Too cold.'

I laugh. 'But someone will pay for your trip, right?'

'Yeah, some art mob. They always pay. I'm famous,' she says.

'And you don't want to go just for a week or two?'

'Nah. Too cold. And too busy there.'

I offer to go with her. I tell her I'll happily buy my own tickets and make sure she gets to see what she wants. Gloria's in her early sixties, a grey-haired grandmother and always a delight to be around. The trip would surely be fun. In contrast, this community, her home, has a reputation for violence at times, and staff have had to be evacuated following riots in the past. As lush and beautiful as the landscape is, this can be a harsh place. Visiting Paris rather than staying here is an overwhelming 'yes' for me.

'Nah,' Gloria laughs. 'Too cold. And no barra. We got barra season here soon, but that river there, the fishing's no good.'

Barramundi are an obsession in northern Australia. They're a great fish to eat. No barra in the river Seine is not a complaint I've heard before. I picture Gloria rugged up, a colourful beanie, standing in the shadow of Notre Dame with rod in hand, regretting the trip.

'Anyway, I been overseas before,' she says. 'People not so friendly there.'

Paris is off. Gloria suggests we should all go for a walk this evening.

I drop my bags at the dusty doctor's house across the road. A large cow and several dogs are lying in the shade of the tree outside. For three days, I'll be the only doctor, and then I'll fly out. There should be another doctor in town at the Aboriginal

Medical Service, but they've been short for months, so these days will be busy—a mix of straightforward consults and unexpectedly complex ones. This morning, skin and ears are the themes. In no particular order I see:

Impetigo, or 'school sores'—a bacterial skin infection that's common in children, and a potential cause of heart and kidney problems.

Scabies—an itchy skin infection, which is common due to crowded living conditions.

A sore ear due to a middle-ear infection.

A sore ear due to an outer-ear infection, or 'tropical ear'.

A sore ear due to a bug being in it—an easy fix with tweezers, a scope and a stoic patient.

Discharging ears due to a middle-ear infection that's perforated the eardrums. The young boy, who is, incidentally, dressed as Spiderman, holds his curly hair out of the way as I peer into each ear, his yellow, sun-bleached tips falling into the way. The holes are a possible cause of his delayed language skills, or are at least making them worse, and I refer him to an audiologist and surgeon.

A sore buttock, but this is our doing. A young boy is given a penicillin shot, the thick, white, painful injection he'll need every month, for years more, to prevent the recurrence of his rheumatic heart disease. It's another consequence of repeated infections due to crowded living conditions. He's terrified of the needle but the laughing gas eases this, his mum says, so we set it up. Whatever helps. A couple of minutes of giggling is a small reward for going through this a hundred times more over the years, which he'll need to, and his laughter is delightfully contagious anyway.

A sore breast is the next problem, and I tell the patient that there'll be a female doctor next week if she'd prefer. Cultural sensitivities here sometimes demand a same-sex doctor. But before I finish talking, she takes off her T-shirt. 'What?' she asks, holding the breast. 'But you a doctor, yeah? Nah, I'm not waitin'. You mob all know women's business, yeah?'

'We do,' I say, getting gloves, 'but I thought I'd offer it.' I tell her I'll get a female staff member to chaperone us.

'Nah, come on,' she says. 'I got the kids out there. I gotta get goin'. You a doctor, just check 'em.'

I do. There is a lump. I examine more thoroughly and refer her to Cairns for imaging and a biopsy; the travel coordinator will book the flight and accommodation.

These clinics are a whirlwind. A lot of the work is as much a chat as a medical consult sometimes, and the talking is important. People open up and share more each visit, but often we stumble unexpectedly into severe underlying medical conditions that derail everything else.

A man comes in complaining of a sore hand, but as I scroll through his recent results, I see that he's got end-stage kidney disease, likely from diabetes.

'Yeah, my kidneys been slow for a long time,' he says. 'You doctors always sayin' that.'

'Honestly, Reggie, this time they're proper crook,' I say. I explain that he'll probably need dialysis in the coming weeks or months, and that this will require planning. Dialysis is a dirty word for many, though. It tethers people to a machine for hours at a time, three days a week, forever, and he'll have to relocate to the city to start, possibly permanently.

'I dunno,' he says. 'I feel right. But what about my hand?'

I'll sort out his hand, I say, and suggest a family meeting tomorrow with the Aboriginal health worker and senior nurse. I want to make sure he understands, so that he can make a very informed decision. There's no interpreter here. More than 30 languages used to be spoken on the Cape, but most people speak good English these days. But I want to be certain he's clear.

'I'm gonna think about it,' says Reggie. 'I'm gonna pray tonight.'

'Please come back, though. Honestly, Reggie, they're proper crook. Not even slow. They're kinda sleeping.'

He nods. 'You send 'em driver tomorrow?' he asks.

'I will if he comes to work. He may not come.' But I leave a sticky-note reminder on my desk.

I'm always wary of missing these hidden medical issues. There's no prospect of doctor shopping here, often no possibility of a second opinion. Next week it'll be me again, then another colleague in two weeks, but patients may not return for months. I'm also mindful of waiting times. Spend too long with one patient and the others may leave without being seen, but too little and you're bound to miss something.

Diabetes and kidney issues are the themes this afternoon. There's another potential miss when a man limps in due to gout—from eating turtle, he suspects—and as I wait for the slow internet to access his notes, I check his vital signs and glucose.

'Whoa, John,' I say, 'your sugars are 22. Proper high.' This level is about four times higher than it should be. 'Did you have your tablets today?'

He didn't, he says. He ran out last week. So I have the first of many conversations about diabetes this week. I start with what he understands. I draw a few diagrams, explain that diabetes is too much sugar in the blood and use the analogy that it becomes like honey when it's left in the fridge—the sugar gets thick and crystallises, and can block small vessels in the eyes, kidneys and nerves, and bigger blood vessels in your legs, heart and brain. 'Don't forget glucose' is a prompt often used in resuscitation, because low blood sugar levels can cause seizures or drowsiness. I keep this in mind here, too, but for the opposite reason: patients' blood sugar levels are often far too high.

There are two paths from here, I explain to John. If we only partially treat him, complications will inevitably develop. But if we get his medications right and help him make some lifestyle changes, we can slow or even stop it. It's blunt, but it needs to be. He's in his early thirties and has three small kids, and I've seen enough severe cases—like Billy in Central—to know how this could unfold.

Diabetes is a scourge here. Among people living in remote communities, the rate is three times higher than for other Australians. Complications are also disproportionately greater. Almost all the diabetes here is type 2, and it usually presents in adulthood, caused by the body's resistance to the insulin it produces. There's a genetic predisposition, but it's also strongly related to diet and lifestyle factors, so conversations are sensitive. People can feel blamed, which ignores the bigger picture: that diabetes has become four times more prevalent over the last 40 years, worldwide. Lower socio-economic groups are disproportionately affected. Something significant is obviously happening, because a fourfold collapse in willpower and motivation—throughout all of humanity, at the same time—is unlikely.

Poverty drives poorer food choices. Here, there's only one store. Soft drinks and fast foods are an obvious go-to, and fresh vegies and fruit are expensive and often poor quality. Most kitchens are basic and homes overcrowded, making cooking unappealing and difficult, and the weather conditions don't encourage exercise. Even at the best of times, healthy habits are hard to form. I do my best to frame the discussion optimistically with John. He's a park ranger, smart and engaged, but he's caught at the confluence of economic and environmental factors bigger than any of us.

I refer him to the diabetic educator and others. No sugary drinks, I advise. Some portion control, and a half-hour a day of walking. I'll see him again tomorrow and we'll get some blood tests sent off.

'You're doing good,' I reassure him. 'This is only a problem if you don't know about it, and don't look after it. You're gonna do well.'

He's keen. He shakes my hand and hobbles to the waiting room, and I fetch his medications.

'The heroism of incremental care' is what Atul Gawande, an American doctor, called this: the small, sustained steps that can shift health outcomes hugely. I make no claims of heroism at this desk, but rather on the part of the millions of consults like this, daily, that can gently alter the trajectory of patients' lives. It lacks the drama of flying to an explosion, but it'll have far more impact overall. I'd even argue that many emergency cases are due to a failure of primary care. The severe infections, the heart attacks, the sudden kidney failure—a lot of this could be avoided or delayed with good preventive care. Dozens more retrieval aircraft could circle here all day, but it's surely better to prevent the need, or at least delay it. It's definitely kinder—and far cheaper.

Gloria's phone is out of range in the evening. These moments outside the clinic are the only chance I get to see the area, so I go for a quick walk alone. I head along the riverbank, past crops of cabbage palms, via the dirt road out of town through sparse eucalypt woodland. Thousands of corellas—small white cockatoos that settle here at this time of year and strip the trees bare—screech and squawk, but it's the dogs that I'm mindful of. During the day they lie harmlessly in the shade, panting and smiling, but when the sun sets, they're irritable and brave and full of energy, keen to stretch their legs with a chase and a nip of a passerby's ankle if they can.

A few years ago, I'd come across an older man beside a small lagoon out here, skinning a couple of kangaroos hung from a tree by their hind legs. 'Teaching the youngfellas hunting,' he'd told me.

Incredible, I'd thought, as he pointed out how to cut it. 'How'd you get them?' I'd asked. 'Spear?'

'Nah,' he'd laughed. 'Rifle. Twenty-two.'

These moments made this job unbeatable for me. In contrast, a dirt track nearby leads to the site of the first recorded contact between Europeans and Aboriginal Australians, Cape Keerweer. That was in the early 1600s. Dutch sailors clashed with the Wik People, and there were deaths on both sides. Colonisation didn't formally happen for another couple of hundred years, and up here it was even later, but by the late 1800s the first missions were set up in this region. Aboriginal people were forced onto them, or persuaded, or came seeking protection from the cattle stations and expanding settlements, and a 'Chief Protector of Aboriginals' was given legal power over all aspects of their lives. Many were sent to Palm Island for minor transgressions, and some children were taken from families, among so much else. Old ways of life were quickly undermined.

As with Central, I'm often struck by how recent this all was; the last of these missions was closed barely 60 years ago, and these communities are on their former sites. Pormpuraaw was the Anglican-run Edward River mission, for example, and Aurukun was the Presbyterian-run Archer River mission. And here I sit in the clinic, not even one average lifetime later, dispensing medications, filling in forms, having a yarn. Many of our patients were raised in these same dormitories.

The lagoon is now almost dried up. I turn and loop back through the suburban part of town, past kids playing in yards and on the street, in front of houses in various conditions. Abandoned cars rust beneath frangipani and mango trees in a few yards, and nicely fitted-out four-wheel drives and old sedans are parked in others.

Back at home, I shower and check pathology results for a few hours. The corellas settle as I climb into bed, but then the music starts: the dull thud of bass from a nearby house. I push my foam earplugs in, but an hour later there's more from another house. A clash of rock classics and hip-hop begins. Then, country music from a third house. Beyoncé, Archie Roach and AC/DC are all duelling. I push the earplugs in as far as possible, but then there's yelling. Shrieking. Voices of a man and a woman. The sound of a bottle breaking. A third voice chimes in. The cops will be called if it gets worse, but I soon hear them yelling from opposite directions, so it's over. I'm not sure how the kids manage to sleep well, or how they'll stay awake in school tomorrow.

The days are busy. On my last afternoon, I'm asked to quickly see a patient. 'Just some results,' says Helen, the receptionist. 'Super quick,' she says. But Murphy's Law guarantees that there's never a quick consult just before the plane lands to pick me and the other FIFO workers up.

The patient is having a cigarette out the front when I call her. She takes a deep drag as she comes in, flicking the butt. It sails past the 'No smoking' sign. She exhales the smoke as she walks down the clinic hallway. I'm not a fan of this. The whole clinic will stink of smoke for a while.

'Heya, I gotta be quick,' I say, waiting for the internet connection again. 'Just your results?'

'Yeah. I had check-up a few weeks before.'

'No troubles otherwise?'

'Nah.'

I scroll through them. She's mid-forties and her sugars are bad, kidneys slowing, liver function poor. I make a plan to see her for an hour on my next visit, and in the meantime chat briefly about goals. Less sugar, fewer cigarettes, medications every morning. 'You've gotta cut down on the smokes,' I say. 'It's dynamite with the diabetes.' We talk about some things that could help.

'But Doc, I like it,' she says. 'I need a smoke sometimes.'

I love the honesty, but I push back. 'You definitely don't need it,' I say. We chat more. She needs to make some changes. This is a fork-in-the-road moment for her, I say, but she suddenly tears up.

'I do, Doc. I need 'em. They help me.'

'What, the smokes?'

'Yeah, they help me.'

'They definitely don't. Help with what?'

She starts crying—big, heaving sobs that catch me off guard. I pass the tissues and look at my watch. I'm going to be late for the flight but I can't walk out right now.

'My son,' she says. 'Sometimes, he been hitting me. He got fasdee, you know? He a grog baby.'

It's an awful story. I sit quietly as she sobs and tells me. 'Fasdee' is a well-known term up here, an abbreviation of foetal alcohol spectrum disorder, or FASD. It's caused by heavy drinking when pregnant. Her son's a young adult now, and recently out of jail. He's separated from his partner and living with his mum, even though she doesn't want him there. Her husband has died. She doesn't work. She's closely related to someone who died by suicide last month. She doesn't want to report her son because she blames herself for his FASD and behaviour.

The pilot calls my mobile while I listen to her story.

'Sorry,' I say to her. 'I gotta take this. I'll be quick.'

'Where you at?' he says. 'We're baking on the runway here!' He's got two other communities to do pick-ups in still, he reminds me.

'Sorry. I'm coming.'

I step out quickly to talk with the nurse and mental health worker. They'll spend time with her now and follow up on domestic violence reporting. I have to run. I'll see her on my next visit. 'Don't worry about the smoking,' I say to her, sitting briefly, trying not to appear hasty as I pack my laptop and papers. 'I'm really sorry. I shouldn't have been so pushy.'

'You right, Doc.'

'No, I'm really sorry.'

This caught me off guard. *Never mind the blood sugar levels*, I think.

I have no idea up here.

We head to the runway. Bags and pathology specimens are loaded, and we're soon airborne, chatting, finishing notes and dozing not long afterwards, mouths open and heads lolling side to side. The sun's setting as we descend into Cairns, coming in low over yachts and waterfront restaurants. I'll probably head for sushi tonight, maybe a pub with a friend. And all of this just two hours from where we left. It's a world away.

This is the thing for me about working up here: you think you understand, then you realise you don't. You think you're making progress, but maybe you're not. The tablets for diabetes and high blood pressure are easily adjusted, advice easily dispensed and retrieval flights easily sent to dramatic scenes. But the background issues aren't simple. And they're rarely addressed. In the little consult room, in the few allotted minutes, politics and history and trauma and physiology converge. You nod, you listen, you type, you quickly explore barriers, then you apply band-aids and fly out. Brief visits, brief solutions. And during the flight, sometimes you cycle through the stages of grief. Denial is first, supposedly, although that luxury has long passed. After take-off, anger sets in. Anger at the lack of progress, the broken systems, the barriers beyond any clinic. Then, bargaining. *I'll work less*, I think, to delay burnout, take another holiday, although I'll possibly need to leave remote health altogether. But how can you leave this once you've seen it? Depression beckons next, but I skip past this—no point, it's not me who has to live up here. And as we descend, acceptance is on the horizon. But how can you accept any of *this*? If you do, it may be well past time to leave. Your standards have slipped. If you don't, you'll keep cycling through these stages.

The problems are even more striking after the months I've had working overseas. Time away hasn't helped—fresh eyes are sensitive.

Anyway. Sushi tonight.

5

Exposure

The Year Before, Central African Republic

There's a saying in medicine that 'more is missed by not looking than by not knowing'. I've been caught out by this. On a night shift a few years ago, we'd discovered a narrow stab wound on a drowsy, intoxicated patient. It was hidden beneath her darkly coloured bra strap. We'd previously missed the injury—self-inflicted, she'd later told us—and it could've been fatal if not properly managed. Another time, we'd found a tiny black scab on the buttock of a critically unwell patient, just millimetres in size. This was the only clue to typhus, from the bite of a small mite, also potentially deadly if untreated. So you practise being systematic. It's essential. This way, when you're rushed, or tired, or overwhelmed, it's automatic.

Exposing a critical patient adequately is an important part of this—the 'E' of the primary survey. You hastily cut off clothes, if necessary, although I do my best to avoid this in remote Australia. Wardrobes aren't extensive, and those backless, bumless hospital gowns aren't nice to go home in. As we did with Greg after the explosion, you look front to back, top to bottom. 'Fingers or torches in every orifice' was the teaching, but I'd like to think it's more dignified. You cover the patient in blankets and look in ears, nose, mouth, and do a 'per rectum' exam if indicated, although scans have made this last step largely redundant. And you remind yourself that this is a vulnerable, frightened person, not just a list of injuries—as it can feel like on a bad shift, when patients arrive one after another, a conveyor belt of quick assessments.

The need to phrase things carefully was an early lesson for me. A bikie club member was brought in after a bad accident. The trauma team 'log rolled' him onto his side, and my job was to assess his back, then put a finger into his rectum to check for internal bleeding and normal nerve function. The concern was that he had a spinal or pelvic injury. I donned two pairs of gloves and a generous amount of lubricant, and explained.

'You're gonna fucken what?' he yelled.

I explained again. He consented.

'Does this feel normal?' I asked, as I gently slid a finger in.

'I dunno, mate,' he yelled, clearly annoyed. 'What's *normal*? I've never had a bloke dare do that. And in a crowded bloody room, too. Is any of this normal?'

This got a laugh from the team—at me, not at him. 'Bloody hell,' he said, 'you're lucky I'm stuck on this bed.' But later he was more relaxed on painkillers. 'You coulda turned down the lights at least, bloke,' he said, 'and bought me a drink. You're lucky. I've nailed people for less.'

His discomfort was a good sign, though. His nerves were intact. When I'd performed the same examination on a young tourist in Central, after a high-speed car rollover, he'd asked, 'Feel what?' This was a severe problem. He was transferred urgently to the spinal unit in Adelaide and was discharged months later with quadriplegia, sadly.

Over time, I've come to wonder about *our* exposure as health workers. There are huge upsides to the job, of course, such as seeing other people's ways of living and helping out; but there are trade-offs. Being exposed to infections is one. I've had a few needle-stick injuries with patients' blood, including from a young soldier in a country with a high prevalence of HIV/AIDS. 'I probably wouldn't start preventive therapy,' said one infectious diseases expert, via email. 'Not with those tablets. They've got serious side effects. If you can't get regular blood tests, I'd leave it.'

I couldn't get regular blood tests where I was, so I did leave it, but another colleague had a different opinion the next day. 'You didn't start the tablets yet?' she asked. 'He sounds incredibly high risk. Are you sure you want to chance it?'

Nope, I wasn't sure. A few sleepless nights followed.

In South Africa, two of my former colleagues contracted *extremely* drug-resistant TB, a supercharged version of the already bad multi-drug-resistant TB. They'd needed painful injections for two years, every day, as well as handfuls of tablets, and months off due to the side effects.

The vicarious trauma is what I think about more, though. It'd have to add up: the compounding baggage of seeing the sad, the bad, the hopeless and the sometimes horrific. I'd dismissed this in my early years because I wasn't the one suffering these illnesses or deprivations. The patients and families were. I always got to go home. It seemed self-indulgent to talk about the impact of what I'd seen, when I'd only ever been a witness. But I don't think that anymore. There is a cost. And the exposure is cumulative. Empathy is essential, but it needs boundaries. Lines must be drawn. Exactly where, though, is an ongoing process for me.

Greg died from his burns the day after we brought him down. The other patient was transferred to a burns centre and is so far doing okay, although it'll be a long, stormy road ahead. It sits uncomfortably, knowing that we were the last people who Greg spoke with, but I'm heartened that he was comfortable and that the process was gentle. A colleague questioned whether we should've *not* put him on the ventilator, knowing treatment was likely futile, and been more upfront with him about his prognosis. Maybe. But we likely prevented him from dying due to airway blockage, an awful death, and we hopefully bought time for his family to get to him. Telling him about his grim prognosis out there wouldn't have been kind, as he had no time to process it and no loved ones to process it with. I think we did the right thing. I hope we did.

The exposure to violence is a growing downside for me. It's an increasing problem in EDs everywhere. But for all my time in Central, and despite its reputation, I've been assaulted only once there—by a skinny whitefella. I've been yelled at plenty of times and had to step away quickly from escalating situations, but this was a first. Leaving late after a night-time call-back, I could see a man beating a woman in the street, barely 50 metres from the hospital. I ran towards them but kept some distance, shouting that I'd called the police—a bluff, as I hadn't had time—but in a second, he lunged, grabbed my collar and swung. I turned and ran hard, tearing my shirt as I broke free. He chased, but I made it to the ED first and the doors fortunately opened immediately. He ran off, and when the police arrived minutes later and spoke with the woman, then checked the CCTV footage, they agreed that I was lucky. 'Ah yeah, we know him well,' said one officer. 'Heavy meth user. Good work getting away from him. Yeah, he'd have thumped you good and proper,' he said, patting my shoulder.

So for me, it's the skinny, angry guys that I'm wary of—not to trivialise the fighting that occurs in the community. It's a huge problem, but it's almost never directed my way. It's far more likely to occur between those who know each other. That said, I'm not a woman who has to walk home at night, or a nurse who needs to attend a late-night call-out to a remote house, and I'm sure I'd feel differently if so.

All of these exposures feel heightened for me in the field with MSF—the challenges, and the highs and lows. I'd spent time working with them again the year before I'd met Billy and Tyreese at that roadhouse. The contexts are very obviously different—one is in the middle of a wealthy Western country; the other is in a struggling country, in a conflict-affected region. But for all the differences, there are also some stark similarities. More than many of us Australians may like to admit.

'We fly there?' asked the check-in clerk, when I arrived for the first of my flights to the Central African Republic. It'd been years since I'd last worked with MSF. My previous posting had been in South Sudan, and I'd left suddenly due to safety issues and a run of patient deaths. I'd always hoped to work with the organisation again, but now that it was happening, it all felt as daunting and uncertain as the first time.

'I *think* you fly there,' I told the clerk. 'My itinerary says so.' This was at Amsterdam airport, after I'd spent a few weeks at MSF's Dutch headquarters doing project work.

'And the city,' the man asked. 'It's Bangui?'

I nodded.

'Can you spell it?'

I could, but I'd known little else about the country until weeks before, other than that there was a conflict there.

He typed for a while. 'Sorry. Can you spell it again?'

I did. He still looked unsure. He found something in the system, he said, put two tags on my bag, removed one, printed another, looked at his screen again, and I suddenly wasn't sure I'd ever see my belongings again.

I flew from Amsterdam to Morocco, then Cameroon, spending the night sitting in a brightly lit halal airport cafe. In the morning I boarded a half-empty Air France airbus, along with a few aid workers, French soldiers and diplomat types.

'Do you think it's very unsafe there?' the passenger beside me asked. He'd been fiddling nervously with the buttons of his blue suit, and introduced himself as a businessman. His question was absurd, though. The country was a few years into a civil war and I'd had multiple security briefings before leaving. 'Don't take this place lightly,' I'd been told, but I needed no second warnings. I knew how quickly things could deteriorate, and I'd reassured myself that this visit was only for a few weeks.

'Where are you staying?' the businessman asked. 'Maybe I can stay with you?'

'Your work didn't organise accommodation?'

No, he said. He didn't yet have work. He was coming for a few days to ask about diamonds. The economy was bad at home in Lebanon, and he'd met people who'd made good, quick money buying diamonds here. He'd never been to Africa before, he said. But the prospect of him staying with us was a non-starter. Aside from the clash with MSF's principles, their security is predicated largely on neutrality—only by not taking any sides and by providing care to all, rather than using guns, are they less likely to be targets. Arriving at the MSF guesthouse with a prospective diamond smuggler would've made for a memorable icebreaker, but was definitely off the cards.

There was no need to explain this further to him, because we soon descended over the city, where tens of thousands of people had taken refuge inside the airport grounds. A sprawling tent city surrounded the runway, and UN peacekeepers were visible with guns and armoured vehicles. And this, for me, was the surrealness of the field: weeks earlier, I'd been working in Australia; the day before, I'd wandered canal-side with Maya in Amsterdam; and now it was this: a slingshot to another universe. I wanted to be busy as soon as possible, because looking down at all that made me nervous and uncomfortable.

Two days later I *was* busy, standing in a hospital ward in the north of the country.

The smell is what had struck me the very first time I'd walked into a ward like this, in Angola in winter: the smell of too many people crowded into a room, their families sleeping on beds, next to beds, under beds, at the foot of beds, their small bags of clothing and food beside them. But in the Central African Republic it was the hot season, and the crushing humidity meant that doors and windows were at least left open. Air was fanned gently over feverish little bodies by worried parents' hands or pieces of clothing. This was another striking thing here: the colours. Against the drab brown bricks and the dusty ground, bright, beautiful dresses seemed the rule.

'Malaria,' said Matthieu, the French doctor. 'Almost all patients in here have malaria. All this side, all that side. We have two in each bed now.'

This was the *soins intensif*, or intensive care ward. All these MSF hospitals seemed similar to me—a collection of old and new brick wards, tents, cooking shelters, water points, latrines, outpatient consult rooms, and camping areas for patients' families. 'Intensive care' here meant you'd be *watched* more intensively, but little else—there were no ventilators or fancy monitors. Bags of IV fluids hung from wooden poles, and there were a couple of oxygen concentrators—noisy little compressors that could help a patient's breathing, provided that the generators were running.

There were twenty patients in the room, but it was quiet. There wasn't a lot of crying because these little bodies were tired, too busy fighting infections. There were another 40 children on the paediatric ward who weren't as severe, and dozens more would fill the malnutrition ward in coming months.

'A lot have meningitis, too,' said Matthieu. 'I did lumbar punctures on the severe children, and so many had meningitis. Look, we have three more to do this morning.'

A young boy started fitting on a bed nearby, and a health worker fetched an anticonvulsant drug. 'Okay, now four more to do,' Matthieu said. '*Putain*. So many sick children.'

The scene was bleak, but also one of hope: most kids would leave cured and healthy. The death rate in these hospitals was usually relatively low, less than 5 per cent, but there was, of course, bias in this: a patient had to make it to the hospital first, surviving the early illness and the long journey on muddy, washed-out roads, past various militias. Another 'trial of life', as with remote Australia.

These hospitals were places of huge contrast to me: part sad-looking ICU, part happy playground for recovered kids or their siblings; part family hotel, part palliative centre. There was a buzzing 30-bed maternity centre, but also a more sombre adult's ward, the site of occasionally heartbreaking 'I'm sorry, we can't treat this at all' conversations, where people picked up their belongings, thanked the staff anyway and walked home.

In a small room beside the ICU was a weeks-old boy with tetanus: back arched, enduring spasms, Mum quietly sitting beside him. He had a 50–50 chance of surviving, and it could've been prevented if his mother had had a tetanus booster and a clean place to deliver him. And in the yard just outside his door, two young girls were working hard, spurred on by the cheers of onlookers, to dislodge mangoes from the top of a tree with a long pole. 'Higher! No, to the left! Up a bit more!' It was almost festive.

On the paediatric ward, a little boy stopped me to shake my hand. 'What are all the dressings for?' I asked his mother. He had crepe bandages covering his scalp and three of his limbs.

'Burns,' she said, and then she sang and clapped and he did a little dance, jiggling and making the ward laugh, becoming more enthusiastic as the laughter built.

'And you, sir?' I asked a young man in a bed nearby. 'Why are you here?'

'I fell from a tree. I was trying to get the fruit from the top.'

'If you know how to get a wheelchair out here,' said Matthieu, 'I'd love to hear. He's now paraplegic.' But the paraplegic young man wanted to practise his English with me, not speak of wheelchairs.

All of this was within an hour of stepping onto the wards. You could throw almost any adjective at places like these, and it'd stick. I veered between hope, hopelessness, sadness and joy in any single moment. Only a handful of conditions accounted for most admissions, and most were fortunately easy and cheap to treat: malaria, diarrhoea causing dehydration, and chest infections. Some patients had TB and HIV, which are trickier, but MSF hospitals have good drugs and protocols. A surgeon and an obstetrician were also there, adding another level of care. Matthieu was exhausted, though. 'There are two of us covering the general wards, so every second night we're up for most of it,' he said.

It'd been years since I'd stood on a ward like this, but I remembered well the relentlessness. I also remembered asking myself what I was hoping to accomplish.

My role this time wasn't to treat patients, but to help improve quality of care—to help make care in these hospitals safer and more effective. I felt uneasy telling staff that initially, because everyone was already overworked. 'Tell head office we're down three doctors and a dozen nurses,' would've been a reasonable reply from them. 'And then put yourself on the roster tonight!'

But the need for the project was clear. These hospitals had a high staff turnover, and many staff had only basic training—interrupted schooling, in many cases, then postgraduate training for several months, rather than the years I'd been lucky enough to receive. And they were working in difficult conditions, and with limited resources, so medical errors were very probably occurring. Almost 10 per cent of patients suffered from an adverse event due to medical care in low- and middle-income countries, according to a large study in the *British Medical Journal*—and those were in stable environments, not conflict-affected ones. But where to even begin? The common conditions seemed the obvious place: making sure staff could safely triage, diagnose and treat them, and that there were clear pathways and responsibilities. A few specialists were going to support their areas, too.

The paediatric ward was where I started. After a few days of chatting, trying not to step on toes, I interviewed patients and staff. People were far too kind, though.

'Any problems during your stay?' I asked the mother of the dancing boy with burns. They'd been there for weeks.

'Nothing,' said Jean, the interpreter. French is the official language and mine was basic, although most patients spoke a local language, so I needed a translator anyway. 'She is very happy. She has no complaints.'

She was clearly being polite, because the wards were crowded, the yard a muddy construction site. Coughing from other wards echoed up the passageway.

'Great. But does she have any feedback at all? Anything that would make it better here?'

They chatted briefly. 'Nothing.'

'Does she feel safe?'

'In the hospital, yes. But outside the hospital, no.'

'Is the food okay?'

'It is very good. She is very grateful for it.'

'Is there enough privacy for the women, especially in the showers and toilets?'

'Yes.'

'And do health workers wear gloves when changing his dressings? And wash their hands?'

Everything was perfect, she said. She had no complaints. Neither did the paraplegic man who'd fallen from the fruit tree. He was young, still hopeful that he'd walk again, and he was very happy with the care. As was the mother of the infant boy with tetanus. The only request from any patients—in fact from *every* patient—was for MSF to please not leave. 'Before, we had to pay for treatment,' said one mother. 'And the hospital was not nice like this. It was not clean. Sometimes they had no medicine. We worry that when the fighting gets worse in town, you will leave. Please don't.'

This town had a population of 100,000 people, more or less, and this was the only hospital. The fighting had been going for years, splitting the country along religious lines, and a quarter of the population had fled their homes. And caught in the middle of all this, as usual, were women, children and men who'd surely rather get on with their lives.

The expats had plenty of suggestions for improving things. They were from a dozen African, North American and European countries, and gathered every evening around the large outdoor table, swatting mosquitos, often eating by candlelight.

'I just want the light to stay on when I'm operating,' said Pat, the Canadian surgeon. 'And we need a physiotherapist. We're getting a lot of limb injuries, a lot of gunshots.'

'I just want more sleep,' smiled Carrie, an American doctor on her first posting.

The Indonesian obstetrician was still operating on an emergency case, but she'd asked for a battery-powered blood fridge and newer operating table. The final list of requests was far longer. More staff, twice as many beds, and more training for the local health workers.

As for the Central African staff, they were also worried that MSF would leave. The midwives were hand-sewing curtains for their brand-new brick-walled unit as we chatted. They wanted more training, more equipment and a reliable supply of blood—a problem in many places, where people are reluctant to donate unless for family.

They were also concerned that at my age I wasn't yet married.

'Eh! No children?'

'Not yet. But one day. It's not too late, is it?'

'How old are you?'

I told them.

'*Eeesh*! Not even a girlfriend in Australia?'

I told them about Maya, but that our respective jobs were making it tricky to live together.

'*Non*, we will find you a wife here,' they said.

'That's very kind of you.'

'We must. Then you doctors will return, if you have a family here.'

'I'll marry him,' offered a voice from the end cubicle. She'd been groaning softly every few minutes. 'And then I will go to Australia with him.'

I thanked her. This was my first marriage proposal in years. South Sudan was the last, when a severely unwell woman with HIV had offered to marry me as a thankyou for commencing treatment. Here, I suggested that this woman's husband may take issue.

'We have four children already,' she laughed. 'He will be happy for the peace. They can come to Australia, too.'

By the next morning they had five children.

I've always found it hard to reconcile the people I meet with the chaos of their contexts. In Angola, a group of staff had prayed after a meeting for those mentioned in an MSF newsletter, a list of the world's trouble spots, and I remember thinking: *Don't you know this is a disaster, here, where you live?* Maybe so. Maybe not. But life went on, either way. Who were they going to compare themselves to? The country I was now in, the Central African Republic, was among the worst for making it through pregnancy alive, or childhood. I heard accounts of violence that I quickly tried to forget. And still, everyone showed up to work daily, and jovially.

Being an expat in these places has always been a bit uncomfortable to me: a parallel but separate existence. We move through, rub shoulders with the consequences of all those conditions, but never have to endure them—very hopefully. 'Don't shoot!

We're not part of the fight!' said the signs on walls, and we had 'grab bags' ready with essentials. If things got tricky, we'd be evacuated. On a normal day, a minute after leaving the wards, I could get a beer and send messages to Maya, then head to the river's edge or somewhere nice.

Each evening, I wandered down a track to the beautiful bend of a wide, quiet stretch of water, no hint of security issues, away from the UN peacekeepers' compound. I sat with others in the setting sun and watched hippos wallowing nearby, looking like bald, sunburned cows, only their ears and pink-brown snouts above the waterline. The kids pelted them with stones when they wandered too close to where people were bathing. I'd followed the sound of drumming one evening and found a group of women beneath a shelter made of branches, hammering on metal pots with sticks to lure winged termites from their nests. The vibrations apparently mimicked rain, tricking the insects, and the women had pots full of them. 'They're delicious when fried,' they assured me, offering me some.

To me, that African bush, the river and sunsets, all looked idyllic, despite the context.

A week later it wasn't so idyllic. I flew to another hospital, near the Ugandan border, and there was clearly a problem. Two staff were on satellite calls as I arrived in the compound, pacing, anxious-looking.

'They're missing,' said Claire, the coordinator. 'Our outreach team left this morning and haven't checked in.' Teams were expected to make regular radio contact when travelling, but there had now been hours of silence.

I put down my bags. 'A bad accident?'

She shrugged.

'What, kidnapped?'

'Possibly.' She was near a large wooden desk with the communications equipment—a long-range radio set, a satellite phone, and mobiles and laptops.

It could've been a car accident, but someone would have radioed. The likelihood was abduction. Multiple calls were made to the Europe and Bangui offices. The local police had sent a car out. There was a foreign military presence, too—anti-aircraft guns lined the dirt runway—but contacting them had to be done via higher levels.

I felt cold.

What if they were severely injured—*or worse?*

And what if this went on for weeks, or was only the start of an escalation?

There was no point me being there. 'Quality' seemed irrelevant. I felt bad even factoring myself into this, but abductions elsewhere had lasted for months sometimes, or even longer. I consider myself increasingly risk averse, with zero desire to die for this or any work, but there's a huge grey area in unstable places: they can feel safe until the moment they're not. I'd always operated under the belief that as health workers we're less likely to be targeted—we were treating all sides, the soldiers and their families, too, so why target us? This is an increasingly naive view, though. Safety is a relative concept, I've come to think, guaranteed only in retrospect when you're back out of the field.

They made more calls. We all paced. I didn't bother unpacking. I'd have updated Maya but it seemed selfish. Nothing she could do but panic.

Hours passed and we heard nothing.

More phone calls. The police came. Then the military, with lots of questions and maps.

Evening fell, and there were still no sightings or contact—but suddenly two cars pulled up and there they were! *All of them!* They got out of their damaged LandCruisers, and there were many hugs and tears. They'd been robbed and held at gunpoint, they said, but no one was injured. There were threats to kill the driver and take one of the women—frightening details, as they recounted them—but the attackers inexplicably backed down. The bottle of whisky and blocks of chocolate I'd brought were well received, and probably my most useful contribution to the visit.

At some point we slept, and by morning it was almost as if it had never happened. Staff wanted to keep working. Management in Bangui wanted them to fly out to debrief, but they declined. There were 1200 outpatients on HIV treatment and a busy little hospital, and they didn't want to leave the patients. Again, it all felt surreal; if you'd described this to me in a European bar a few weeks earlier, I'd have declined the trip. But some little clifftop of uncertainty had been stepped off, or so it felt when coming to the field. Things were largely out of my hands. You just went with it.

The next morning, I showered with a bucket in the warm early light beneath a large fig tree. I strolled the short distance to the hospital, past thick green bush, alongside singing schoolkids in their blue uniforms—many of them were Congolese refugees. The little hospital was full, painted like an old Caribbean guesthouse in oranges and blues and whites, green vines licking at the tops of the walls. The country was as beautiful as it was uncertain. I wanted to stay and see patients and be a part of the team, but I was also wary. Just be the affable foreigner, keep my head down, be humble and hopefully useful—this was all I could do.

The staff did fly out for debriefings the following week, and I went back to Amsterdam to write reports.

6

Fever of Unknown Origin

Still the Year Before, Chad

It was a reverse culture shock on arriving back in Amsterdam. The city was bursting with tourists, and colourful flowers hung in pots from antique bridge railings. At night I cycled alongside canals to the little unit I'd rented, and Maya came over, and we spent long hours together in cafes that spilled out onto cobblestone streets.

'We could live here,' she said, as we got lost along winding lanes. 'In one of these little lopsided homes. Maybe I should try to get a transfer?' We fantasised about it: both of us getting jobs with NGOs here, cycling everywhere with rugged-up kids, eating waffles and plates of cheese, no longer ships in the night with differing schedules. She was about to fly to Kenya for a month, just as I'd arrived back, and I still had work obligations in Australia after this. I'd been offered this job only temporarily and was relying on savings to cover anything more than rent, so this wasn't a start-a-family-and-build-a-life role. But it was stimulating, and I wanted to do this again down the track.

On weekday mornings, I gathered with MSF staff for updates from emergencies around the world. Afterwards, I worked on draft guidelines for the hospitals. This was a long way from the daily highs and lows of clinical care, though; my boss, himself a former clinician, had warned that this work wasn't one step removed from patients, it was ten steps. 'Clinicians struggle with this move,' he'd said. 'It's a big shift from the immediacy of hospitals.' But I'd long been interested in this side of health care.

An often-used analogy is that as a clinical doctor working at the bedside, you're pulling people from a river, one at a time, trying to treat them only after they've fallen in and half-drowned. In public health, you're dealing with the 'upstream' determinants of health, working at a population level to stop people falling into the river in the first place. This work appealed to me more as I saw the same medical conditions, year after year, often late in their course, when preventive measures could've averted them. I think of Billy with his end-stage heart failure, or that infant curled up with tetanus—all preventable, or at least delayable. Trying to pull on the bigger levers such as policy, education and research made sense, but I wasn't ready to give up clinical practice forever. Not yet. Maya had. She'd decided to move into public health for good, but her tolerance for office work was higher than mine. 'Death by meeting' was another warning my boss gave me, and after a few months of policy discussions and drafting documents as a group—sometimes debating section titles or font styles for days, each email cc'd further and wider in an ever-expanding inbox explosion—I was thrilled to head back to a hospital.

This time I was sent to Chad, a large country straddling the southern half of the Sahara Desert. It was another slingshot: drinks in Amsterdam on the Saturday, then dinner in a well-guarded hotel in the Chadian capital, N'Djamena, on the Sunday. Two days later, I was on a UN World Food Programme plane to the east of the country, sitting beside two African nuns, landing in time for lunch.

'It's really great,' I said, thanking the MSF cook who'd placed a battered pot of stew on the outdoor table. She was a Chadian woman, dressed in a glorious green headscarf and red dress. 'The beef,' I said, 'it's delicious.'

'*Pas boeuf*,' she corrected me, '*c'est chameux*.' It wasn't beef, it was camel.

There were plenty of camels along the main road, too—alive and well, tethered to each other, lumbering slowly under sacks of food—as our MSF LandCruiser rattled past. At the hospital gate, the two guards greeted me in different languages.

'*Ça va*?' asked one, dressed in a shirt and jeans.

'*Salaam alaikum*?' asked the other, wearing a long, white djellaba robe and sandals.

A young boy nearby opted for English. 'Yes, hello America!' he shouted from his donkey.

'No, no!' I corrected him. 'Hello Australia!' This was worth clarifying given the region's shifting conflicts.

Stepping through the high metal gate into the main yard, I wondered again what more could be said of these busy, remote hospitals once you'd seen a few. To paraphrase an often-used quote, every good hospital is the same, but every under-resourced, struggling hospital struggles in its own unique way. Three things there stood out to me: the very different standards of care, a looming malnutrition crisis, and the lack of women's rights.

The doctor overseeing the program was in his small brick office, scrolling through spreadsheets, when I met him. A roll of toilet paper stood at the centre of his desk.

'That a problem here?' I asked, nodding at the roll.

'My friend,' he laughed, 'you will see. Oh, you will see!'

And oh, I did see. It was a reliable low point of these postings, the moment a universe of new organisms introduced themselves to your inner world. I watched two goats lick from the patients' drinking taps as I was shown around the hospital a little later, and I braced for another round of weight loss.

'Don't put that in your report,' Sébastien laughed, shooing the goats away. He was the Rwandan doctor supervising the medical team. Nearby, patients and their families sat around the large, sandy compound, resting under the wards' shaded verandas.

'This is a tricky set-up,' Sébastien said. 'The government runs this hospital. We support it. But it can get complicated.' MSF provided women's and children's health care, and TB and HIV care, and the government did the rest. 'We supplement the government staff's wages to make it the same as our staff,' he said. 'And we provide all their medications. But still, there are two very different levels of care.'

The government representative told me not to report on his side, but I did look around—briefly, for the sake of interest—and it was sobering. Mattresses lay on the floor, and some patients had only cloth between them and the hard, unclean ground. I saw few staff and very little equipment. But the reality was that it was probably no worse than other hospitals in the country.

So why was MSF here, in this town? It was a way to keep a presence in the region, Sébastien told me. Darfur, in western Sudan, is just to the east, and the Central African Republic is to the south. Hundreds of thousands of refugees had come over the border in past years. There were also periodic disease outbreaks and food shortages. This 'shared model' between NGOs and governments was used increasingly to help build capacity, and to support these struggling services, although there were obvious challenges. But we were, of course, guests in these countries. Programs can't be run unilaterally. Access to vulnerable populations requires negotiation. 'Without Borders' references MSF's values and spirit, not the practicality of entering and working in a country as one pleases, least of all as foreigners. Helping to support and train local staff seemed the more useful thing we could do, ideally making ourselves redundant.

The maternity ward had all of these problems on display, and more. Issues of gender and culture were simmering when I walked in. No small things in these parts.

'I cannot accept this,' said Patricia, a tall Kenyan midwife, as she pulled back the pink curtain of a small plywood-walled cubicle. A young woman was in labour, lying quietly in her yellow dress and headscarf, drenched in sweat. Three others were labouring in neighbouring cubicles. Wall fans blew hot air at them.

'She is not progressing,' said Patricia. 'She has been like this for hours. And her haemoglobin is thirty, can you believe this? *Thirty.*'

This was a severe anaemia, well beyond what many people survive. She urgently needed a blood transfusion and a caesarean section, but her husband had refused and walked off. 'He will not discuss it,' Patricia said. 'Now I must try to find another man who can consent for her.'

And what did the woman want? She bit her lip during her contractions and made little sound. Patricia spoke with her via the local health worker, translating. She couldn't consent, she said. Only her husband could, or a senior male relative. What would happen would happen, she said quietly. It was God's will.

'Honestly. I cannot accept this,' Patricia fumed. She stepped outside to make some phone calls. 'Why do the men get to decide?'

I agreed. I'd found this to be the most challenging aspect of working in the region previously. I'd argued angrily with a husband in South Sudan who'd refused a simple procedure for his wife. It was a stupid, hot-headed thing to do on my part—but I was exasperated, and the woman was going to die without it. He stood there as calmly as if declining another drink in a bar—just shrugged and said, 'No.'

There was no easy solution I could ever see in these situations. To ignore this woman's autonomy went against Western medical ethics, and everything I'd been taught. Patients must make their own decisions. But to override the husband's wishes would be to insult him, and his culture, and possibly endanger staff—even the project. And this wasn't my culture or country, nor Patricia's.

Patricia stepped back inside. 'The government doctor is coming soon,' she said. 'He is tall, and a man, and he speaks Arabic, so maybe this will help. I don't know. You must come and watch if we go to theatre. You must see. It can be very difficult.'

The therapeutic feeding centre was a happier place than maternity that afternoon—even if the underlying reason for its existence wasn't. Big-eyed, skinny children would arrive, listless and irritable, and over subsequent weeks be gently nursed back to health. By the time they were ready to leave, they'd be running around and playing. It was like watching wilted flowers bloom. A relief and a joy—the epitome of a necessary intervention.

'This girl is almost ready to go home,' said Sébastien, who also ran this unit. The girl smiled broadly, a little milk moustache on her lip. Her mum sat beside her, in a royal-blue dress and beautifully patterned green headscarf, and again I suspected that unwritten rule: the more austere the environment, the brighter the clothing. All the mums dressed like this. They sat quietly beside their children, nothing to read or watch, just soft conversation and the cries and giggles of a few kids.

'We have 60 beds for malnutrition,' Sébastien said. 'For now, we are okay, but soon there will be two patients in each. Last year we had three children in some.' He was the only doctor for the unit, along with a few dedicated nurses. This was a huge job. The treatment of these children is surprisingly tricky. Weakened little hearts struggled with the food and fluids after going without, and their immune systems were fragile. Treatment had to progress delicately, and the scope for errors was huge. My plan was to spend most of my time on this unit, sorting out resources and helping to run teaching. There was a preventive component, too, with at-risk households being given sachets of high-energy food. Much of this had been done before, but the hope was to make it routine, and to simplify available material. A gentle, sustained nudge—I hoped.

'You are married?' Sébastien asked me, as we walked to the TB unit. I gave him the abridged version.

'You?' I asked.

He nodded. He had a wife and two children back home in Rwanda. He'd been training in paediatrics there before joining MSF, and now saw his family every three or six months. But this paid better, he said, and there was the possibility that he'd be transferred to Europe one day. For me, the job was a financial liability, but for him it was the opportunity of a lifetime. 'You must make sure you have a wife and children,' he said to me, as we crossed the yard.

I nodded.

'It is important for a man,' he added.

I nodded again, bracing for the suggestion.

'Maybe we can find you a wife here?' he said.

I nodded, and later relayed his offer to Maya. 'Maybe we should wear fake wedding rings in the field?' I messaged, half-jokingly.

'Oh, I've got a bunch of them,' she pinged back.

Patricia called us late afternoon. 'We need three bags of blood,' she said. 'All of us staff, please, we must all get tested for compatibility.' The Chadian doctor had managed to get an older relative to consent for the woman's transfusion. 'And Damien,' Patricia asked, 'can you operate?'

I couldn't. But the Chadian doctor could, even though he was an intern.

Patricia quickly corralled the theatre staff, half of them employed by MSF, half by the government, and blood matches were found. A unit was drained from each of three staff, and the first was given to the mum a moment later, still warm from the donor's body. The mum was helped to walk to theatre, across the courtyard, pale and breathing fast. She looked terrified as she stepped in. The room appeared Soviet-era—old white tiles, a cracked floor, a metal table with big levers. I was anxious on her behalf. The anaesthetist was a local nurse and used only ketamine, something we use for sedation back home, a safe option although the patient's eyes would probably open at times during surgery. This was disconcerting to see, but she'd be 'dissociated'—unaware, and with good pain relief.

The intern and his assistant scrubbed in. A nurse painted the belly with antiseptic. Sterile green sheets were draped over the patient, and Patricia got ready to look after the baby. I watched from the side. *This wasn't a case for an intern*, I thought, but he worked methodically, if slowly, and got the baby out within minutes—a boy. Patricia took him and supported his breathing and dried him vigorously. Incredibly, he was okay. Patricia spent a few more minutes with him, then swaddled him and handed him to another midwife. She stepped out, exhaling deeply, and I exhaled watching her exhale. Mum was now getting her third bag of blood, and they were starting to close her up, so I left.

The temptation in these places was to judge. Watching the surgery, I saw a few opportunities for potential errors, even a couple of near-misses. But the standards of 'back home' can't be applied. There are always many ways to do things. Battles need to be chosen. A Kenyan colleague in the Northern Territory had told me that he was surprised when he'd first come to Australia. 'You doctors get handheld for years here,' he'd said, 'and you call the boss for everything. You can't even do caesars! We do these straight after medical school.' But he'd been embarrassed by his gaps in other areas, he'd said, like the management of kidney disease, or how to use the more expensive drugs and tests he'd never had access to—this was all our bread and butter, not his. 'And you are so careful,' he'd said. 'You scan everything, you refer everything, you are always writing all these long notes in case you get sued. You are all very worried. Sometimes, no one seems to make a decision.'

Needs are so obviously different between contexts, and so are the ways of practising. Even between hospitals in Australia, things are done differently. There are always multiple ways to approach a problem. Many are safe and reasonable, and only some are worth correcting. Those are usually 'systems' problems anyway, such as a patient not getting reviewed soon enough because responsibilities aren't clear, or drug errors occurring repeatedly due to unclear labelling or protocols.

Ultimately, I didn't want to be the blow-in foreigner, with no understanding of the context, making unneeded suggestions. Patient safety is always worth addressing, though, but the balance can be fine. And again, the aim, as I saw it, was to support people. Although the intern had surgical skills, and I didn't . . .

The thing that could make or break a posting was often your fellow volunteers—the group you'd share every mealtime, meeting, evening and day off with. That you'd hear every possible story, joke, opinion, rant, regret, fantasy and past romantic escapade from, many times over, for six to twelve months. You'd probably witness a few complicating romances thrown in, too, and by the end of it all you'd leave with incredibly close friendships, despite possibly never meeting again.

This team was large, and included Rwandan and Congolese doctors, a Dutch nurse, a Tunisian program manager and a Kenyan midwife. I walked each evening with a few of them, down to the wadi, the bone-dry, sandy riverbed flanked by palm trees, which would flood in the wet season. Children fetched water from wells dug into the sand, and young girls did the laundry in other wells, laying the colourful clothes around the edges. At a shallow mud quarry along one bank, hundreds of mudbricks had been cut and lifted out by shirtless men, who stacked them into large, neat piles by hand. A wood-fired kiln nearby was being loaded by others. The scene could've been centuries old, save for the printed T-shirts and cheap Nokia phones.

A long-term posting here would be incredibly difficult—extremely isolated, and with an edge. I was stopped a couple of times by older men: 'Why are you in our country? Yes, but why in this town? Yes, but why are you walking around?' My views on these trips have come to be rapidly changeable, depending on the moment. I could see this all as an unspoiled, traditional, family-centric scene, or as an oppressive, patriarchal, impoverished one. Or both, and everything in between. Patricia had found this aspect very difficult. 'Most women I see have been cut,' she'd told me, referring to genital mutilation. 'It causes so many problems, especially for childbirth. I get very sad.'

This region is particularly difficult for women. Three-quarters are illiterate, and the risk of a mother dying from childbirth is *200 times* that of Australian mothers. Access to contraception is limited, and there's the issue of consent and other glaring cultural differences.

Walking around, the bigger questions again screamed out to me. Was any of this effective? Did anything improve in the longer term? Was my trip here actually useful in any way? Or was this partly 'voluntourism' by someone who could afford the time off? I never have a good answer. I have to believe that some of this contributes, even if minutely, even though not all aid or development programs have had positive effects. Many have undermined locals and existing systems, and there's plenty of robust discussion and literature on the topic. But overall, many things have improved. It does me good to recall this. It's too easy to buy into the clichéd narrative of these places as hopeless, as never improving. It's wrong, and it lets us all off the hook: what's the point if nothing works?

In the last twenty years, the number of childhood deaths worldwide has *halved*. Most people living with HIV are on treatment, including in Sub-Saharan Africa, and treatment is now so effective that it essentially prevents transmission. Maternal deaths have declined by around a third, and childhood malaria deaths by even more. Things do change. Even simple interventions such as a 'surgical checklist'—a list of basic things to be checked before an operation, such as allergies and the operation site—have halved surgical deaths in some regions.

Not that we should forget the huge inequities and challenges, or the ongoing conflicts. Many of these gains could also be undone quickly by bad policies and funding cuts. But I do think it's helpful to pause occasionally and consider the progress—and that it's therefore possible to do more. My view walking around was biased: South Sudan, Chad and the Central African Republic, the three last places I've gone with MSF, are the lowest in the world on measures of development. They're outliers. But the gains overall are real, due mostly to the efforts of millions of local people—not a few foreigners and agencies.

As for this project, supporting this hospital is *something*. It's a safety net while longer-term forces play out. That seems worth it.

On my last Sunday, Sébastien was called to see a new patient, and I went along. A young child had arrived with malnutrition and a high fever, and I knew her look well: big wide eyes on a thin little body. She was too tired to notice the IV going into her hand—never a good sign. Her mum stood quietly and towelled the girl's forehead. The Chadian nurses prepared medications and gave the therapeutic milk. Everyone was patient and gentle and methodical, but the little girl was puffing hard, a little sprinter deep into a race.

We checked for malaria, but the fever could've been from many other things. The malaria test came back negative within minutes. What else could we do? We could only make educated guesses. In that part of the world, infections are still the main cause of death, unlike heart disease and cancers back home. The list of possible causes was as long as the list of tests was short. We gave her broad-spectrum antibiotics. Sébastien looked for other clues, such as signs of HIV/AIDS, hepatitis or TB. We went back to first principles from old-school tropical medical textbooks, feeling for a huge spleen that could've been leishmaniasis—a parasitic illness—or for a slow pulse that could've suggested typhoid fever. We felt for a big lymph node in the neck that could've been due to sleeping sickness, or TB, or lymphoma, or . . .

It could've been a hundred things. A thousand, even. We had tests for only a handful. We did what we could. Step by step and gently—and in most cases it would have been enough. Most children would be sitting and smiling with a milk moustache a few weeks after arriving, and kicking a ball outside the unit after a couple of months.

But this little girl ran out of puff. She just tired, slowed down and stopped. Just like that. No warning. No poignant moment. No calls to the family in time. Just silence.

Sébastien listened to her chest. There was no point doing CPR. She was too malnourished. It'd just have prolonged the trauma. Sébastien closed her eyelids and shook his head gently at the mother, who started crying quietly. She took the colourful cloth that would've been the bedsheet and swaddled her daughter in it, and the nurses started cleaning, and some other women came in and consoled her, and not long afterwards she walked out of the hospital carrying her daughter.

'I'm sorry,' I said to Sébastien. 'You okay?'

'Yes,' he said softly. 'It's very common here. Very common.'

It was very sad. I remembered the first time I'd experienced this in Angola. The family thanked us for trying. The crying rippled through town and I couldn't sleep afterwards. I wondered if there were other things I should've done, but it happened again. I emailed specialists and memorised all the treatment protocols, and then I learned to sleep okay afterwards, because I had to, and because Sébastien was right: it is common.

We headed back to the staff compound. Near the entrance, four young girls in headscarves were squatting, playing a game with pebbles on the sand. Today was Patricia's birthday, and she'd baked a cake in an iron pot in the fire. The coals had overcooked the outside to a rock-hard crust, but Sébastien kept saying, 'Mama, this is better than any cake they sell at the airport in Nairobi! It's delicious!', which was sweet because I'm not sure he believed it. Maybe he did; maybe all the cake at Nairobi airport really was even drier.

We sang happy birthday outside. Thick smoke from the wood fires reddened the sky. Patricia wanted to extend her contract for another year, she said, because there was so much more work to do there, but there were far easier jobs she could've taken.

The contradictions never ended. The bittersweet reality on the wards, the precariousness of life around them—all this only sharpened the contrast.

I'd decided not to extend the role in Amsterdam. I had a few months left that I'd finish, and then someone with far more expertise in quality would be coming. Maya needed to spend more time in Canada for family reasons in the months ahead, and I'd been getting emails from Central. 'We'll be happy to pay you nothing if that makes it more appealing,' said my boss there, Chris. 'You're welcome to volunteer here if that makes it better. Just get your arse back. The needs aren't any less.'

Touché.

More flights to Europe. A few months more of office work. Beautiful catch-ups with Maya, and time with her in London. A difficult goodbye.

More flights back to Australia. A 'How ya goin', luv?' from the airport cafe worker when I landed, and time with family and friends.

It was good to be home.

7

Geography of Gratitude

July, Far North Queensland

My parents and I have a kind of 'don't ask, don't tell' policy about the trips I go on: I don't tell them the bad things, they don't ask. They're amazingly relaxed. They're far more interested in Maya, anyway, although they'd also have a fair idea about conditions in the field. Mum grew up near Johannesburg, a vibrant but troubled city where you slow down at traffic lights but try not to stop at night, to avoid being robbed. And for a retired businessman, Dad's had his run of adventures. He hitchhiked to Mozambique—which back then was about to descend into civil war—to surf when he was still in school, without telling his parents. And, like all white South African men of his day, he was conscripted to the military. Namibia was where he was sent, near the Angolan border, not far from the town that I was sent to 35 years later with MSF.

'Never been busier!' said Mum, filling me in on their recent months. The three of us strolled on a long, windswept beach in the small coastal town they'd retired to, and spent a few days catching up. 'I don't know how we managed to find time to work,' Mum said, 'when we could have been doing all these other things instead.' They were more active than me these days, spending most mornings 'supping'—stand-up paddle boarding, Dad explained, now more down with the beach terminology than me. He was playing in a band, too. It was great to see. They'd both had their run of health scares in recent years—breast cancer, a brain tumour and cardiac surgery among them, all fantastically managed by our public system—so this was well earned.

Friends were also happy to have me back in Melbourne. Some hadn't realised I was gone.

'What, Europe? Really?' asked a good mate. 'You were living there? Damn. Lucky you. I tell you, though, you have no idea what these bloody private schools cost these days. We had an interview for Luce last week. And we've just put Tegan on a waiting list. Full fees for three of them. Nightmare.'

This I didn't doubt.

It wasn't only FIFO work I was doing, apparently, but also a FIFO social life.

In Cairns, it's a little before 6 pm, the start of a nightshift. I take the handover from the day team. The large hangar doors are open to the north, looking out over thick, rainforest-covered hills, and the sun's setting behind them. As an office view, this is hard to beat.

'The refueller's available up there?' asks Rob, the pilot on tonight, checking the aircraft.

'Confirmed,' I say.

'And it's just the one patient?' he asks.

'Yeah, and their escort. A one-month-old baby and their mum. Four kilos and 75 kilos.'

'And the helicopter's definitely online for our last leg?' he asks.

I call the statewide coordination centre to confirm. 'The weather's good up there,' they say. 'The helicopter's online. They're expecting you.'

We're good to go. Wendy, the flight nurse, wheels a trolley full of medical equipment across the hangar, and I pass the packs up the stairs.

'And you've definitely told me the right destination?' Rob asks as he calls the refueller.

I laugh. This is a mistake I'd made once, never again. Shortly after take-off a few years ago, I'd had a small panic as I'd ruffled through the handful of job sheets on my lap. 'Uh, I did say Kowanyama, yeah?' I'd asked him.

'No. You said Aurukun.'

'Uh-oh.'

'Uh-oh what?'

'Can you steer this thing to Kowanyama instead?'

He could, fortunately. It wasted a little fuel, but plans were quickly altered and we changed heading. There's an extra layer of checking before departure these days.

I re-confirm tonight's destination. Rob starts the tug, a little vehicle that looks like a ride-on lawnmower, and pushes one of the three aircraft back, onto the tarmac. The refueller arrives and takes Rob's order, then climbs his ladder and connects a hose from his truck to our wing. Fuel isn't usually loaded before the destination and weights are confirmed, because too much creates a weight problem for take-off, and too little means risking a rendezvous with reef or rainforest. Meanwhile, I return calls to clinics where two other jobs are pending. This flight will be a long trip, though—five or six hours at least before we're back—and the other jobs are less critical, so they'll have to wait. We take a quick toilet break, grab some snacks, fill the coffee flask, and soon take off, banking into the last light of a tropical sky, climbing gently over sugarcane fields and river inlets, the ocean to our right and thick rainforest to our left.

Tonight we're heading north to the Torres Strait, beyond the tip of mainland Australia. This is a trip made best in daylight, because below us is a land of superlatives. To our right is the largest living structure on earth, the Great Barrier Reef, which hugs the coastline for more than 2000 kilometres. The oldest rainforest on earth is below us soon, too—the Daintree, older than the Amazon by millions of years. For long stretches along this coast, dense patches of forest end along white-sand beaches, the reef not far offshore, itself creating endless variations of patterns from above in the azure waters—love hearts and circles among them. On a clear day, the view is incredible. A few of the world's deadlier things are down there, too, like the salties, or saltwater crocodiles, cruising along beaches and rivers, territorial and stealthy and best avoided entirely; and the box jellyfish, capable of causing cardiac arrest within minutes. There's also the more common Irukandji jellyfish, seldom fatal, but still able to ruin a holiday with a syndrome of severe pain and 'sense of impending doom'. If no one is swimming at a perfect-looking beach, there's probably a reason.

Calls come through on the satellite phone occasionally. Most are from the nurse-run clinics in Cape York or regional hospitals, and we'll have to divert if their patient is more urgent. A clinic calls now about someone having a mental health crisis. 'She's been okay to take oral sedation,' says Des, an experienced nurse. The connection is patchy. 'We've spoken with psychiatry in Cairns. They want her down in Cairns. Family want her down there, too.'

'Psychotic features?' I ask.

'Yes. Voices. Threats of self-harm. But she's been lovely with us.'

'Flown out before?'

'Once. No issues.'

I take the details and apologise to Des. We won't be refuelled and ready until around 2 am, so it may have to be the daytime crew. The pilots are strictly regulated as to how many hours they can fly, and our current patient needs to come down urgently. Des may be up all night. 'This happened last week, too,' he says, 'and we're two nurses short at the moment.'

I empathise. It's a huge burden for the clinics. But our other bases in Townsville and Mount Isa are also busy, and his patient is at least safe. There's nothing else we can do, unfortunately. For now, Wendy and I discuss a plan for the patient we're about to pick up, catch up on staff gossip, take other calls, and watch as Rob lands us smoothly on Horn Island in the Torres Strait.

It's dead quiet and dark when we land and more humid, too. Port Moresby, in Papua New Guinea, is not far to our east, closer now than any Australian city. Two pilots and a helicopter are waiting for us in the nearby hangar.

'You bring the KFC?' Rob asks me as we transfer our gear. I laugh. I'd been told that you can swap a bucket of KFC for an esky of fresh lobster up here, if you call one of the airport crew ahead of time to arrange it. There are no eskies that I can see here, and I suspect an urban myth.

Wendy and I strap into the back of the helicopter. Rob will stay with our plane. The engine starts and whines, building slowly to a roar, and the cabin rattles. The pilots turn around to confirm we're good. We give the thumbs up. Slowly, we rise into a pitch-black sky, heading gently forward and out over the ocean. There's no horizon that I can see, and I watch the pilots adjusting things behind glowing, otherworldly cockpit screens, as if we're in a video game—an extremely expensive one.

This couldn't be further from a nutrition ward in Chad, geographically or resource-wise. The truism with aid work is that coming home is harder than going, and I still felt that, even months after leaving there. In the field, you're overwhelmed and busy and don't have time for pondering, but when you get home the disparities jar. The reverse culture shock is real. I'd felt it years ago, and I still feel it to a degree every time I return to Melbourne from remote Australia. The initial homecoming is great: you have a loved one who meets you at the airport, a comfortable bed and deep sleeps, restaurants, no security issues, no goats licking taps, and no colleagues needing toilet paper on their desks.

But then the chasm between home and what you've seen in the field begins to grate, often in the smallest ways. Patricia and Sébastien are still back there, about to have 100-plus critical kids in the unit, and I was choosing a colour for my old kitchen cupboard in a hardware store, then queuing for *the* best coffee—for this week, anyway, according to the blogs, although there were 50 other cafes that I could try nearby. It's disorientating. The temptation is to immediately sign up for another posting; the itch becomes intense. But you have to ride it out. And you have to remind yourself that comparing home to the field is simplistic, even self-righteous. 'Normal' life here isn't less meaningful, even if it's less dramatic most days, and it was never going to be as simple as forgoing a coffee to save a life. So the adjustment is yours to make. Not doing so is a sure road to resentment—or being a pain in the arse at dinner tables.

What do you do with everything you just saw, though? Maya and I watched the musical *The Book of Mormon* while I was staying with her, and she'd joked that theirs was the better advice for dealing with a difficult thought: 'Turn it off, like a light switch,' sang the actors. 'Just go click!' Another line I'd overheard was closer to how I felt: 'How do you live with the poverty?' someone had asked, and the reply was that they didn't have to—the poor did. I only transited through these worlds.

I worry that there's a narcissistic aspect to overthinking this too much. How many of the patients I've seen would get to indulge in navel-gazing, or have adjustment periods? But I'm mindful of self-care, in part because I've ignored it for years. A career is a marathon, not a sprint—there's no point flogging yourself for a while and then limping away, as a few souls have done up north. So I do a little maintenance these days. I jog up the highway in Central, a rock in each hand in case the dogs sneak up. I'd attended a 'yoga for stiff white men' class, sold by the title, and I continue with it. And I take time out of remote communities often, and read, or noodle around on my guitar or drums, or stay with my parents on the coast. And I take an active interest in conversations about school fees and football scores and renovations, because this is the world I actually live in. There's no point comparing it all the time.

The cabin rattles. We fly on through complete darkness. It's a moonless night; we could be going up, down, sideways or hovering still, and I wouldn't know. There's nothing that I can see to orientate myself. 'Never mind storms and hitting birds when you're in a helicopter,' Baz had teased when I'd started. 'Worry about that Jesus nut, the one above your head.' This nut was the only thing holding the rotors on, apparently. 'Just that one little thing. If she comes off, you'll meet the big fella pretty quickly.'

The flight's only a few minutes long. We soon see lights.

'Secure in the back?' a pilot asks through our headsets.

Thumbs up.

A landing pad comes into view. We move towards it, descend slowly and hover over it, just beside the hospital. The skids gently reach for the ground, skittish and jerky like a nervous bird, and we touch down. The roar of the engine becomes a whine, and they give us the okay. We climb out and stretcher our gear into the small hospital.

Wendy knows her way around this place, so I follow her. She's been doing this for almost twenty years. She's an ICU nurse and midwife, and as with most of these jobs, I just follow the nurses. They know what they're doing.

'They're here!' says the nurse looking after the child as we enter the nursery. 'Fantastic! Thank you for coming.' She introduces us to the patient's large family. I've never been thanked more as a doctor than in this job, even though others have often done the hard work by the time we land, and we just swoop in for the final bit. In contrast, when I'm in the ED, I'll sometimes spend hours sorting things for a patient, making calls and writing letters, only to get a muted 'Yeah, cheers' at the end—or occasionally a complaint about the waiting time, or sometimes an earful. No one wants to be in an ED. But arriving in the Flying Doctors uniform, people are incredibly grateful. Sometimes even *too* grateful. Expectations can be high.

We've arrived to pick up complicated, unstable cases in the past, and staff have stood back and said, 'Great, the cavalry is here!' and then left, and I've looked at the patient and thought: *Uh-oh. This guy wouldn't survive a haircut right now. He's critical. How are we going to get him into an aircraft, let alone to Cairns on a bumpy trip for hours? Someone call retrievals!* Then I'll notice my colleague's uniform and realise that *retrievals is us.* There is no Plan B, no time for impostor syndrome. So you do the systematic thing: the ABCs, phone for advice if need be, put lines in, chat with the family, clarify expectations. And very occasionally the decision will be to just stay here, to keep them comfortable, with family, to die on Country.

But not tonight. Our patient is stable, and tiny. She's one month old and has severe bronchiolitis, a viral chest infection, and she's getting high-flow air and oxygen via nasal prongs. It's similar to what Billy gets in Central, and it'll keep her little airways open and improve her breathing.

We switch her to our equipment. Wendy takes time securing everything. Mum farewells the grandparents and aunts and uncles and cousins, and the entire trip is reversed. Back onto the helicopter. Back into the dark. Back onto the airstrip. Back into our plane. And back down to Cairns, our precious cargo secured in a capsule. Wendy fits bright yellow earmuffs over bub's ears to protect them from the noise—'Mini-Muffs', says the writing on the side—and the infant girl is breathing quickly but otherwise stable. Mum watches out the window. This is her first time on a plane, she says. She's a young woman with limited English, a Torres Strait Islander—Melanesian people who're closely related to Papua New Guineans, and who live on a few of the nearly 200 islands between Cape York and Papua New Guinea.

For me, these borders highlight the randomness of your birthplace, and what that can mean for your opportunities—or the lack of them. And how arbitrary these lines can be. Papua New Guinean citizens sometimes come to Australian-run clinics on the Torres Strait Islands via boat. The journey is relatively short, a couple of kilometres, and if they can get there, they'll be given free emergency care. We've brought a few down to Cairns Hospital at times. If they can't get there, they'll need to manage in the struggling health system back in Papua New Guinea.

A young woman enduring an obstructed labour in a small Papua New Guinean village may have no trained attendants to help her, and possibly a long, painful journey to somewhere bigger. But if she's near the coast and her family have access to a decent boat, Australia's resources may soon be able to assist. I've seen these hard, binary divisions many times overseas.

Before joining MSF, I'd spent a couple of months at a clinic on the Thai–Burma border. A limited pool of money was available to help some patients access higher-level care at larger Thai hospitals, and many times I watched the Burmese staff having to weigh up who'd get the money and who wouldn't. A 25-year-old man with kidney failure, needing dialysis? Nope, sorry. The costs would be ongoing for years, and high. He'd be offered palliative care. But a young woman needing once-off abdominal surgery that'd likely cure her condition? Or a six-year-old needing heart surgery? Yes. These were fixable—*if* the money could be found that month.

Here, on my side of the border, I've never come across a medical decision being made over money. Not in any hospital or remote clinic. Most people don't live in systems anything like what we have. For all the flaws and inadequacies of our system—and there are many, a lot of them below us as we fly over remote communities now—I'm frequently reminded of how lucky we are.

Most of us, anyway.

8

Haemodialysis

August, Central Australia

This is my routine again: Central, a short break, Flying Doctors, repeat. There are roster gaps in these and other services, too, so the difficulty is saying no. It'd be easy to end up working every day of the year. I do my best to draw boundaries, but it's easy to let them slip.

I fly to Alice Springs and spend the night with friends, for a barbecue and wine in a suburban backyard. Under that vast, glass-clear sky, we can see the silhouette of the MacDonnell Ranges behind us. Dining in the desert. In the morning, I stock up with groceries and drive north. 'Hippies use backdoor' says the sign outside the roadhouse toilets where I stop to refuel. At the front of another roadhouse, two green alien mannequins are walking away from their little metal craft. 'UFO capital of Australia!' the sign declares. In Central, it's shoes dangling from powerlines and metal shutters over shop doors welcoming me to town again.

Turning off the main road, I pass the overgrown bushes outside the post office. A few years ago, I'd seen a person's legs poking out from under these as I walked to dinner with colleagues. 'You okay?' we'd asked, kneeling down, looking through the leaves. I'd expected the worst—a bad assault, maybe even a dead body. There was no movement. I climbed deeper into the scrub and saw a near-naked woman, still breathing but not responding.

'Oh my god. Call the ambulance,' I said to my colleague. 'Shit, better ask them to send the cops, too.' I gave the patient a shake to try to rouse her. No response. Her other clothes were scattered nearby and would probably be used as forensic evidence. I tried again to wake her, but the ambulance and police were there in a minute. They attached monitoring and got their scoop to carry her out, but she suddenly woke up.

'Leave me alone!' she yelled.

They questioned her. Surely she'd been assaulted? What about her clothes being scattered around?

'I'm sleeping!' she said. 'I was hot. I took 'em off. Why you buggin' me?'

We convinced her to come to the hospital anyway for a check-up and social worker review, and ultimately just to sober up. There were no signs of assault that we could see.

This is a difficult town. I'll sometimes gently prod intoxicated people sleeping on pavements. 'You right, fella?' I'll ask. A lot want to be left alone. A few need an ambulance, but they'll often have a sandwich and leave the ED quickly. Others wake up and walk off. The sober-up shelter closes in the daytime, so you can't call them.

I do wonder what the footage would look like in retrospect, though: a whitefella doctor prodding an intoxicated person, leaving them because they asked to be left, but they then end up succumbing to something vaguely related a day later—or three months later. Or something completely unrelated a few days later, even.

I have moments when I think working here is one of the best jobs in medicine. This is a spectacular region: wide-open skies, red soil, tough people. It's a privilege to be here. But I have moments when I fear that nothing is changing, and that this is going to bite me, personally and professionally—because basic psychology suggests as much, and because the laws of probability almost guarantee bad medical outcomes. There's a lot of grey area decision-making up here that heightens the risk. Like the many head injuries we see, for example, that we can't assess properly without a CT—we observe them closely instead, which is almost always fine, although the closest neurosurgeon is hours away anyway. There are often legal issues we become involved with, such as child protection and domestic violence concerns, some of which may require a court appearance and close scrutiny of what we wrote or did, even years later. And many patients leave hospital against our advice, at significant medical risk. 'The only way to never make mistakes is to never see patients,' one of my bosses once told me. We can't force someone to stay, or to come, or to do what we say. Autonomy is the rule. And so my aims here are revised: harm reduction, not fixing things. Becoming more comfortable with uncertainty, in an era in which certainty is demanded of doctors by the public, media and law. And trying to do all this sensitively, in a region in which culture and trauma and dysfunction wash constantly through the hospital.

But if you adjust your standards, at what point are they too low? Is this you being realistic and pragmatic? Or cynical and lazy?

These thoughts bounce around during my commutes here, between podcasts and playlists, while scanning for roadside wildlife, swaying road trains and overloaded old Fords. I've vowed to myself to resign at times. But then I'll have moments when I love this job again.

And then I'll have moments when I dislike it again, like when I'm being verbally abused—because someone's had to wait, or because they want a sandwich. The 'C-bomb' is a popular go-to, or 'baldie' something-or-other. Mostly I'll laugh. Occasionally I'll change an adjective and throw it straight back, and their relatives will laugh. Other times I think, *Righto, find someone else to yell at, I'll leave.* I can empathise, but I don't have to stand here and cop the abuse. No one in health care should.

And then I love the job again: a cute kid in an AC/DC onesie presents with a chest infection, and lovely parents. Easy fix. Best job in the world.

And then I dislike it again: a police report that I need to fill in; a depressing, detailed, graphic write-up about objects versus bodies. *Worst job*, I think.

And then Clancy Number Three comes back, cowboy hat set neatly, kind and gentle. And I love it.

And then Gloria the artist phones from up north. 'When are we gonna go fishing?' she asks, and I love it even more.

And then . . .

And then . . .

These opposing states often coexist.

Billy's sitting alone in a resus cubicle as I walk into the ED. 'Where you bin, doc?' he asks, pulling his Top Gun mask away from his face.

I lean over to silence the alarm. 'Working with the Flying Doctor mob,' I tell him. 'How have you been, Billy?'

He nods, still puffing. 'You bin right?' he asks.

'Not bad for a young fella,' I say, and he chuckles wheezily. He is the young fella here, though—a few years younger than me. 'How about you, though?'

He catches his breath. 'Not so good,' he says. 'Short-wind comin' quick now.' He's taking his medications regularly and at maximum doses, but he hasn't been able to go out bush for a while. 'Too crook.' He shakes his head.

Billy's been on the mask for a few hours, sitting quietly overnight in the cubicle with the lights dimmed. His cowboy hat's on the trolley beside him and his flannel still smells of wood smoke. Outside the hospital, a strong wind spatters dust across the car park. Night temperatures drop to the low teens at this time of year, but days are a perfect 30 degrees. Humidity is nearly non-existent, making eyes and skin constantly dry, but this is by far the nicest time of year to be here.

'Better get you on this for a bit longer, Billy,' I say. *Back into that cockpit again, mate. Really sorry.* He's tired of it. The mask has to be strapped on tightly and becomes sweaty and uncomfortable, but he needs more.

'Sista,' he calls to Sue, one of the senior nurses, as she walks past. Sue's my go-to person for a debrief. She's seen a hundred of us doctors come and go up here, and even more patients. 'My god,' she'd laughed when I arrived back. 'You think you can work in Europe, and just come back to work out *here*? You think that's gonna stick? I give you a month.' We've both talked about leaving here, often, and yet here we both are. It's hard to put the lid back on this work once you've opened it. The place gets under your skin.

Sue puts her head around. 'You okay, Billy?'

'When you right, cuppa tea?' he asks.

She nods. 'Just give me a few minutes.'

'Four sugars,' he says.

'Nah, one sugar,' I laugh. Tea with heaps of sugar is a thing here. Maybe it's a hangover from the ration days when tea, sugar, flour and tobacco were the staples and in short supply, but a sugar shortage is clearly not an issue these days. 'Four will make it like a soup,' I tease. 'Your blood sugars will go nuts.'

'No breakfast.' He shrugs.

'How about two?' I say, although higher blood sugars are the least of his problems at this stage. He smiles and gives the thumbs up.

'Two's good.' He pulls the mask back up and I help him with the straps. He says something else, but the ventilator compressor and *whoosh* of air is all I can hear now: the gentle tussle of a metal machine against a failing human heart. Pressure gradients and the physiology of fluid shifts play out in Billy's chest, gently and slowly. It's having diminishing returns for him. There's a phrase I've heard up here, that to grow old is to 'catch old age'. I hope Billy catches it.

I'll organise another meeting for him, if he'd like, with his family and the Aboriginal Liaison Officer. We need to be very clear about what he wants, and what he'd like his limits of care to be.

So here we go again: a completely different spectrum of illness compared with rural Africa, but no less confronting.

My first trip to Central was for two weeks, about ten years ago, and I wasn't sold. Actually, I couldn't leave quickly enough. I saw chaos and dysfunction, both inside and outside the hospital, and the fact that I hadn't expected it in this country was a part of what I struggled with. The hospital was relatively unsupported, with a quarter the number of doctors we have now—if enough could be recruited that month. There was no consistent level of training required. If you had sensible, hardworking colleagues around, fantastic. If not, tough, you did what you could. One locum spent his afternoons skateboarding in the car park, having been kicked off a training program. Another was trying to get away from the party scene and substances, so they'd picked the most remote town they could find a hospital in. Most locums were fantastic—competent and kind, and loved the work—but many never returned, because they had regular jobs to go back to, or because of the conditions. A group of experienced nurses kept things safe, prompting us newbies and sometimes calling Alice Springs ED themselves if they were worried. So it wasn't the working conditions that got me back.

I'm also not the typical outback type, whatever that is. But if it's anything like that guy who dislocated his shoulder at the rodeo, or Gloria the artist, with her own barramundi fishing boat, then I'm way off. When I was visiting Darwin one week, I ordered a steak at a pub, sitting beside mine workers I'd been fishing with on a mate's boat.

'A steak, hey?' one of the guys said as I put in my order. 'Wouldn't have picked that for ya.'

'Oh yeah? Why's that?' I'd asked.

'I dunno. I just figured you were one of those vegos, you know? One of them, what do you call 'em? Vegan blokes. Some hippy type from Melbourne or Sydney.'

'Hipster?'

'Yeah. That one. Soy milk in the lattes, cycling to yoga, all the answers to the problems up here. That sort.'

I cringed and laughed. It was time to invest in a faded blue vest, and to trade in the boardshorts and sandals for boots and a decent belt buckle. He was partly right. I am a city person, and I do bring a yoga mat up here, although I hide it in my luggage. But I had no answers to the problems back then—and none now.

I fell into this work slowly. First for the convenience of casual work and an adventure, then for the medicine, then the people. I returned often, usually between overseas posts and city-based jobs, and then switched from emergency medicine training to rural and remote medicine. I was completely out of my depth, but fascinated.

The wards are freezing. Unlike the Central African Republic, there's no fanning of relatives required here. Bright beanies are pulled low and creamy-white hospital blankets tucked high, and yet the air conditioners are running on full. I'd tried for a while to get the temperature turned up to 'bearable' for patients, but there was a strict chain of command for these things: managers to make an appointment with, emails to send, toes to avoid stepping on. Health care loves bureaucracy.

'Come on, doctor,' says Mavis, in the first room. 'I'm freezing, I wanna go outside. Can you see me first?'

I can, but we need to get everyone together. It used to be just me and a nurse on the rounds, but now it's me, two other doctors in training, a medical student and up to four interpreters, depending on the day.

'I gotta be at court by ten for work,' says Lisa, one of the interpreters. 'They got a busy day there. All the lawyers flying up.'

'I gotta drive to Alice,' says Angela, another interpreter. 'My husband's got an appointment. Then we got a land council meeting.'

'Come on,' says Mavis, putting her head out of the women's room. 'It's too cold in here.'

It's our cue. We start. Mavis is a woman with severe liver disease who develops confusion if she worsens even slightly. She was admitted again yesterday with an infection, but seems better today. Her blood results should be back in an hour or so, I tell her, and she says she'll wait on a bench in the sunny courtyard.

Doris, Tyreese's grandmother, is in the next bed. She's been here for weeks after surgery for a bone infection, and she's waiting for physiotherapy. 'You're like a teenager,' I tease her, 'always busy on that phone.'

'Playin' cards,' she giggles, and shows us the screen. The games used to be played with real cards spread out on the bedsheets, against others on the ward.

In the next bed is Jeannie, who tells us exactly what she needs: a needle to get fluid out of her belly. It's a periodic procedure to relieve pressure from ascites, a build-up of fluid caused by her long-term hepatitis and now cirrhosis.

So begin the ward rounds. It's the opposite of a successful public health intervention: late-stage diseases, preventable injuries, and downstream consequences of upstream issues.

The men's room is the same. There are four patients, and the list of recent problems among them includes a stroke, a below-knee amputation, a heart attack, diabetes, treated TB, an above-knee amputation, pancreatitis, a head injury from a car accident, alcohol withdrawal and bronchiectasis—permanent lung damage from repeated infections. And all of these men are under 50, two still in their thirties. We don't have a male interpreter today—to keep men's business and women's business separate is preferred for some things, and essential for others—but I'll come later to talk privately with two of them about drug and alcohol counselling.

A lot of what we do here, in my mind, is provide respite. Somewhere to sleep comfortably, an uncrowded space with regular meals, no obligations and no grog. The antibiotics and other medications do their bit, of course, but the time and space to heal is just as important sometimes, if not more. The body goes a long way to sorting itself out. People usually open up in the days after their ED presentations, too, and their families visit, social services are put in place and things shift. Very slightly—and maybe only temporarily. But it's a shift. *Incrementalism.* A small nudge.

It's easy to judge some of these social issues. I have in the past. It's a striking change from the acute diseases on the MSF wards, the infections that are often easy to cure. These chronic diseases and social problems are more difficult, but the common theme is that our environment and context hugely affect our health. In Chad and the Central African Republic, the lack of basic services and infrastructure contributes to the infections. There's less chronic disease there because diets are simpler, if often inadequate. Many diseases also go undiagnosed. Here, a cocktail of social determinants drives these conditions: the cheap, highly processed foods; the poor and crowded housing; the unemployment; the loss of traditions and social structures; the trauma; the substances; the mistrust of many services, and many other barriers.

In the kids' ward, there's at least some successful prevention today. A three-year-old has just got out of the bath, and his thick hair is slicked back and coiffed to one side. 'He looks like Elvis,' his mum laughs.

'We worked hard on that,' says Joyce, a Congolese nurse.

The boy giggles in excitement from all this attention. He's on antibiotics for a chest infection and now improving, less likely to become an adult with chronic lung disease like Ron, who I saw a few doors back. And the two-year-old girl in the next room is also going well, being treated for scabies and skin sores, reducing her risks of kidney disease and rheumatic fever, among much else. Small but important wins.

Exercising outside becomes more difficult as the weather heats up. Flies will become an increasing problem soon, too, and these aren't any skittish, city-slicker flies. They're fearless outback flies that go straight for your eyes and nose, and they're persistent, and either blind or undeterred by swatting.

For now, the evenings are still relatively cool. When I'm not on call, I'll head for a quick run after work, past the Memo Club, just half a block from the hospital, then up the highway. Friends had messaged me from the club during a brief stop on their drive across Australia recently.

'My god,' they'd said. 'Wow.'

'Meat raffle tonight?' I'd messaged back from overseas, thrilled that they were seeing the region.

There was, they said.

'Two red mobility scooters parked near the gaming room entrance?' I asked.

Yes, they said. Actually, there were three.

'Ambulance crew getting a quick dinner in uniform, eating near the photos of Charles and Diana's visit on the wall nearby? A ridiculously big caravan parked badly outside, half-blocking the entrance?'

Yes, they replied. Was I here? How did I know?

My excuse was the countless dinners and work debriefs in a town with a single dining option within safe, quick walking distance.

Across from the Memo Club is the dialysis unit. It runs late into the evening, six days a week, a constant trickle of people coming and going. The Renal Bus picks up their patients, two sessions daily, while the Memo Bus picks up its own patrons, some of whom may become the ED's patients later.

The dialysis unit here is busy. This town has sixteen dialysis machines—more than anywhere else *in the world* per capita, at least from what I can tell from an online search. Despite that, there's a long waiting list. But we at least have the machines;

people living in remote communities have to relocate to Alice or Darwin or bigger cities to first start dialysis, often permanently.

Kidney disease is an epidemic here. Aboriginal and Torres Strait Islander people need dialysis at ten times the rate of other Australians, more so in remote areas. Diabetes is a large contributing factor. A kidney transplant would be far better treatment, but there's a huge shortage of donors. The Flying Doctors have raced here twice in my time to fetch someone when a compatible donor has suddenly become available, a fantastic win, if rare. The kidney specialists are here monthly, reviewing their patients, but the need is still growing. We hospital doctors have little to do with the unit—their nurses run it, and they call their specialists directly—but if they do call us, it's usually an emergency. Which is what happens later this week.

Sue takes the phone call. They tell her that someone's unconscious and it's not just a faint—they're confident it's something worse. Emily and I run the half block to the dialysis unit. We're ushered inside where a man's slumped in a reclined chair. Half a dozen staff are connecting monitoring equipment and taking out the dialysis lines running into his arm. Emily gets the handover as I feel for a pulse.

'Sir, can you open your eyes?'

He just groans.

'What's his name?'

'Sam.'

'Sam, open your eyes!' I squeeze his shoulder.

A groan. I feel for his carotid pulse.

'He had a sudden collapse an hour into dialysis,' says one of the nurses. 'He was fine before.'

'Has he got an output?' asks Emily. The blood pressure machine is still measuring.

'Yes, but weak,' I say. 'Did he bleed? Any issues with dialysis?'

'Nothing. And his blood tests were okay before. Blood sugar's normal.'

'Sam? Open your eyes!'

He groans softly again.

'Have we got the defibrillator pads here? Airway equipment?'

One of the dialysis nurses pushes the large crash cart closer. I try to lay Sam's chair flat as I support his jaw to help his breathing, and the nurse puts the pads on his chest.

'Sam!' I call. His breathing slows and he doesn't answer.

Emily starts compressions. She presses deep and fast and I try to ventilate him with a bag and mask connected to an oxygen cylinder. The chair is now reclined but it's soft, an awful surface to do this on.

'The defib is ready,' says Michelle, the nurse manager. I don't know most of the staff in this unit, though, or their names.

'Okay, charge.'

'Charging!'

Emily continues compressions and we hear a rib crack, a normal but unpleasant sound during compressions. There's a loud *beeeeeep!* as the defib charges. I take the oxygen mask away.

'Hands off,' calls Michelle.

We all stand back and watch the monitor. He's in ventricular fibrillation, a chaotic rhythm where the heart twitches rather than contracts rhythmically. It can often be shocked back to normal—as long as it's done quickly and nothing else significant is wrong.

'Everyone clear?' Michelle calls.

There are nods and yeses. We step right back.

'Delivering shock!'

A loud alarm sounds. Sam jolts violently. Emily immediately starts chest compressions again. Fifteen other dialysis patients are watching all of this, and a few gasp. They're connected to their own machines and can't be taken off quickly, and they'd all know Sam well—some are likely relatives. Someone wheels some screens around the area but there's no real privacy.

'Let's repeat his potassium urgently,' says Emily. High potassium could be a cause in these cases. She's already sweating from the CPR so we clarify roles: two people to draw up adrenaline and other drugs, one to write down what's happening, one to call out at the two-minute mark. The orderly steps in to continue the chest compressions. We're now following a standard resuscitation protocol: two-minute cycles, pause and check, shock if indicated, give drugs.

'How are we going to get to the ED?' I ask.

'I've called the ambulance,' says another nurse. 'They said ten minutes.'

The chair squeaks and wobbles under the force, and I think of these poor people having to sit there and watch this. I continue to support his breathing, holding the mask firmly with one hand, the other squeezing the bag every few seconds. I stop briefly and insert a Guedel airway, a hard plastic mouthpiece to help his ventilation. 'We need to get him onto a firm surface,' I say.

'Coming up to two minutes.'

'Okay. Continue compressions. Oxygen away. Everyone else clear. Charge.'

'Charging.'

Loud beeps.

'Charged! Hands off!'

We watch the monitor. He's still in ventricular fibrillation.

'It's shockable. Everyone clear?'

I glance around during the pause. Sun's streaming through the windows, across the renovated unit's freshly painted walls with artwork and medical posters, and the long row of dialysis chairs down this side with everyone watching.

'Delivering shock!' calls Michelle.

The machine beeps and Sam jolts violently again. Compressions immediately continue. Patients sometimes regain consciousness suddenly if their circulation returns to normal, yelling out or flailing at the person pushing on their chest. I've been accidentally kicked when this has happened, a huge fright but an ultimately happy one.

'A milligram of adrenaline, please,' calls Emily.

'Going in now,' says a nurse. 'Flush going in. Adrenaline given.'

In an ED this is easier with adequate space and equipment. Here, the stress is heightened, but everyone speaks calmly and clearly.

We hear another rib crack.

'Let's get him onto the floor,' I suggest. He's a well-built man and it'll be tricky in this small space. The aim is to interrupt CPR as little as possible, because even brief pauses worsen outcomes. A resus bed would be better, but we don't have one. We agree that if the ambulance isn't here in two minutes, we'll shift him to the floor. We debate running him on a narrow trolley down to the ED while doing CPR, but it's half a block on a rough footpath. 'Does he have an advanced care plan?' I ask.

'He's for everything,' confirms Michelle.

'Potassium's normal,' says another nurse. I ask someone to call the ED and tell them to set up.

'We're coming up to two minutes,' says the scribe.

We watch the monitor. The other patients sit in silence. Sam's still in ventricular fibrillation.

Another shock. His body jumps again, and we immediately lift him onto the floor, seven of us moving awkwardly, and we restart compressions. The next drug goes in, and the ambulance pulls up, and after the next shock we lift him onto their stretcher. *This poor man*, I think. He's still a thousand kilometres from the nearest cardiac centre in Adelaide—*if* we can get his heart going again.

Emily and I climb into the back of the ambulance and we continue CPR, then unload him into the ED. In resus, we intubate him and the sequence continues. One of the registrars puts in a bigger line and takes blood.

'Coming up to two minutes,' the scribe says.

'Okay. Continue compressions. Oxygen away. Everyone else clear. Charge.'

'Charging.'

We go through the cycle again and watch the monitor.

'Wait, is that sinus rhythm?' This is great if so—a normal rhythm.

We watch. 'Yes! Has he got a pulse?'

Emily feels. 'Yup. The carotid is decent.'

This is fantastic, but it's not the end. He'll very likely worsen again, and we haven't addressed the underlying cause, possibly a heart attack. We do an ECG and chest X-ray and other tests, and start medications that'll support his heart. Emily talks with the ICU and Flying Doctors in Alice, and they divert an aircraft. Incredibly, they're on the ground within an hour, and I think, *Great, the cavalry is here!* They spend time doing their thing, and Sam is stabilised and slowly loaded back into the ambulance, sedated and on a ventilator. They pull out and drive him to the airstrip, all very carefully.

We exhale. He's still in a critical state. But out here, in this town, this is a victory. We've bought time.

Weeks later, long after the afternoon's events have been forgotten, Sam walks into the ED. 'Someone wants to say hi,' says Emily, who's on shift again.

9

Impaired Judgement

August, Central Australia

Here's a good problem to have in a hospital: Chris, one of the other senior doctors, has offered to do a coffee run for the ED doctors this morning, but one of the nurses said that he earns more than enough to get everyone else coffees as well. She's joking but not joking, and there are fifteen takers. He's struggling with the list.

'Skinny latte, extra hot,' says the new Kiwi nurse.

'Small cap,' says Emily.

'Almond milk flat white,' says a new medical student.

'You know this is from BP, right?' Chris reminds them. The BP service station is currently the only coffee outlet in town. But they're undeterred.

'Decaf with soy,' says the social worker.

'Regular latte, full cream,' says Faith.

'I'm not asking for this stuff from a petrol station,' Chris says. 'It's embarrassing.' The list goes on, though.

I come along as a carrier. Chris fetches his car from a hospital-owned house two doors up, behind a high metal fence. He moved to Central a few months ago, with his wife and young son, after a few years of FIFO work between here and Melbourne, and he's also the medical director for the year. We've got a fair bit in common; he grew up in the UK and trained there before migrating to Australia, and he'd also spent some time working in Southern Africa.

We drive up the main road. This is a continuation of the Stuart Highway between Adelaide and Darwin, and most of the region's shops and services are clustered along it—a clothing and furniture store, the police station and courthouse, the Indigenous-run Northern Land Council, the Aboriginal legal services centre, a chemist. A few pubs and restaurants are scattered among them. Away from this main area, there's a sober-up shelter and a women's shelter, a fantastic Indigenous history museum and a language centre. The football oval's just behind us, and the AFL games here are a must-watch. Families drive in from remote communities, and the players are skilled and graceful and sometimes rough, their athleticism on awesome display. It's better not to be on call on a finals night, though. Parties and rivalries go on long past the final siren.

The BP guy takes our order. 'I know, I know,' says Chris, rolling his eyes. We wait beside the frozen kangaroo tails filling an ice-cream fridge near the entrance—long, hairy, cling-wrapped poles of fat and meat, cooked on the fire as is. I've seen a few patients with them on the wards, and I've also treated someone who'd been assaulted with one. 'Headache, beaten with roo tail,' said the triage note, not even an exclamation mark.

'Bad month in town?' I ask Chris, as we take our own coffees to the patch of lawn near the fuel pumps and wait for the rest.

'No, not really,' he says. 'Why?'

'Looks a bit like a war zone,' I say. 'I mean, it's not quite Central Africa, but everyone looks wounded, no?' Two groups of adults are sitting cross-legged near us. One of the women has bandages on her forearm—from bad dog bites, says Chris—and the woman beside her has taken her prosthetic leg off and laid it beside her. A man behind them has a bandaged forehead, another man's on crutches and a woman's wearing a forearm cast. A couple of the young kids with them have loud, moist coughs, and a few are cradling bottles of soft drink and packets of fried chicken. Ours is a biased scene, I realise. We're not seeing the people who're at work, or running the council, or driving the buses, or being park rangers, or looking after households.

'I'm gonna growl you!' says one of the elder women, as the man with crutches hops over to them. I know him from work. He's a talented artist but he struggles with binge drinking. 'Stop humbuggin' me!' the woman scolds him. To humbug is to hassle or beg from someone, and it's not uncommon to see signs in pubs or shops asking people not to. There's a strong obligation traditionally to share resources with family, I've been told; this was essential in the past but can cause problems now.

The man hops over to us. 'Heya, Docs,' he says.

'Heya Tommy,' I say. 'What happened to your leg?' There are sutures on his forehead as well.

'Alice mob,' he says. 'I been long-grassin' down there, but some fellas get cheeky with me. Had to go for X-rays and everything.'

To long-grass is to sleep somewhere rough, literally in the long grass at times, and a long-grasser is a person who may be homeless or might just be travelling. Hospital documents sometimes list an address as 'long-grass'. I've been asked down south not to use the term, but no one can suggest a replacement. 'Homeless' doesn't fit. Some, like Tommy, do have homes, but they'll long-grass when away.

Tommy hops off. The kids come over to ask our names and exchange high fives.

'It all looks pretty normal to me.' Chris shrugs. 'I mean, normal for here.'

'Maybe,' I say. 'Was it always this bad?'

'It was,' he says, but I'm not sure anymore. I hear Elders on the ward saying it's far worse. And Chris and I have probably lost any objectivity. I still catch myself judging this place harshly at times, especially when I hear yelling or breaking glass at night or have to step past an early afternoon brawl outside the supermarket, but I remind myself of how recent the displacement here was. An Aboriginal reserve was established a little over a hundred years ago, just up the road, and the Warumungu were corralled onto the poor land. They were then shifted further to a site without enough water, then years later moved a few hundred kilometres south of here, all to make space for the telegraph line, then the cattle properties, then the goldmines—and all the people that those attracted, and the alcohol and violence and diseases they brought. Only in the 1960s, sometime after the missions closed, were the Aboriginal people here 'settled' back, although this time into camps on the town outskirts, loosely separated by language and kinship groups, and with no amenities. These days, the camps have around a thousand residents. Most accommodation is council-owned brick houses, but there's a huge shortage, so what does exist is crowded, inadequate and often hot. When I occasionally drop off a patient or carer, or if I make a home visit, I'm often shocked. Some houses are okay, but many have crowded bedrooms, pest infestations, mattresses outside and not enough bathrooms or toilets. Air conditioners are frequently old or broken. There are tin sheds on the edge of town, all that some people can find—literal ovens in this heat, with no plumbing. They remind me of the informal squatter settlements in South Africa. A common address in medical notes here is: 'c/o post office, Dump Camp'—actually Marla Marla Camp, but known for the nearby garbage tip—or Mulga Camp, or Warlpiri Camp, or others. Sometimes the address is just: 'Tin Shed, Mulga Camp.'

Again, the contrast is stark. In Chad, the poverty is absolute. Here, the poverty is undeniable, yet people have TVs and smartphones and cars parked outside homes. Cigarettes are 50 dollars a pack, but smoking rates are high. A bottle of spirits sells for 200 dollars on the black market—a way of getting around the alcohol takeaway sales restrictions—but a purchase isn't rare. I'd also spend money on easing the days if I lived here, though. My colleague was right: working here is harder than in Africa, because you don't expect it to be like this. And because it shouldn't be.

'You've just been lazing in Europe and Melbourne too long,' says Chris, as I walk gingerly to the car with the box of coffee cups. 'You've become all soft and gentrified.'

Chris has a line I've heard him say when someone new arrives here, inexperienced but confident about the problems and solutions, lecturing us all at work. 'Yup,' he'll say when they're out of earshot, 'there goes another one who cares too much to actually stay here.' They'll be back home in no time, he'll suggest, working in a nice private practice, an Aboriginal artwork from town on their wall, lecturing forever about their weeks here.

I laughed when I first heard him say this. It's cynical, but there's maybe a little truth to it. Those who're the most absolutist, the most opinionated about solutions, fall the hardest. They burn out. But I don't think you have to *not* care to stay up here. Most doctors here are passionate and engaged. But if your passion runs constantly towards outrage, you'll flame out—and you're useless to the roster if so.

For me, finding a healthy middle ground is an ongoing process—some space between caring enough to show up daily, engaged and empathetic, versus becoming so disheartened or frustrated that you walk away. That space can feel narrow at times.

Emily and I alternate being on call, giving Chris a break. Next week, Emily will leave, and Chris and I will share the on-call duties. There's a registrar in the hospital overnight, a mid-level or senior trainee, and we're only called if more support is needed.

On the first night, I come in to help get a drip into a young child. 'Baby Shark' will be in my head for days now, after Mum plays it over and over again as a distraction.

On the second night, there's a car accident on the highway. Emily is up most of the night, and I wake up only to the sound of the Flying Doctors landing. She's exhausted when she comes back in the next afternoon.

On the third night, I sleep well. On the next one, I get a call to say there's a woman in early labour. 'No need to come in,' says the night doctor. 'She's still very early. This is just a heads-up.' But it's 1 am, and I can't do anything with a heads-up except think, and childbirths here aren't great because we don't have a working operating theatre if problems arise, so I sleep fitfully. At 5 am I get the call. She's delivering. I run over, but the midwife is there and Mum and bub are healthy, so all is good.

Days are busy, too, so the fatigue catches up with me. On Saturday night, I'm in bed early, deep asleep on the musty old mattress, when my mobile rings. I wake enough to press it to my ear.

'Yeah?' I ask.

There's mumbling.

'I can't hear you.'

Mumbling.

I take my earplugs out. 'Yeah?'

'The paramedics called,' says Mo, the night doctor. 'They're en route to a house. Something about breathing difficulties or an airway problem. The house is apparently only two minutes from here—'

'I'm coming now.'

I go from horizontal to dressed in a few seconds, hopping to pull on shorts, a T-shirt and shoes. I run across the yard of the staff compound, pillow lines on my face, mind hazy like a fever dream under the security floodlights. I'd normally take a few minutes to dress and collect my thoughts before coming, splash cold water on my face, but he said the magic word: *airway*. There's no time.

I dash into a resus cubicle. Staff are moving a patient out to clear space. 'Any updates?' I ask.

'They haven't called back,' says Mo.

They must be busy on the scene.

I open the airway trolley and quickly lay out the essentials: masks, tubes, suction equipment and even a scalpel, because years ago a similar call was for three patients who'd had their throats cut. *Three patients*—in the space of fifteen minutes, in an ED that has only two resus cubicles. One of the patients was sitting up, panicked-looking and holding their neck as blood and air gurgled between their fingers. They urgently needed to be intubated to protect their breathing, but this had to be done below the wound, which paradoxically meant cutting their neck further. Another had a similar injury but not as bad, and the third had bleeding that we could control. It's a knee-trembling procedure, to have to cut a person's neck—a once-in-a-career thing, so statistically I'm safe until retirement. But this is Central.

The ambulance pulls into the driveway. I double-check the equipment and run through the emergency plan with Mo and two nurses. The ambulance reverses and we meet them at the hospital doors, and a paramedic gets out the side.

'Sorry,' she says. Kate's her name.

'My god. Dead?'

She shakes her head.

'Prank call?' Grog runners sometimes call fake emergencies to an address far from a main road to divert police, I'm told, but I've only heard of that happening in remote communities.

'Nope. Real call,' says Kate. 'Just a big, big miscommunication. Isn't that right, Mavis?'

The paramedic opens the back doors of the ambulance, and her partner, Jo, gently pushes out the trolley. The patient is sitting up and seems to be breathing okay. I recognise her.

'Hello,' she says. I know Mavis well—she was on the wards only recently with complications of liver failure. She's sniffing through a blocked nose and clutching a tissue. 'I never said I can't breathe,' she says. 'I told my family I'm not breathing right. *They* called you mob and said I can't breathe. I just gotta blow, then I'm right. Look.'

She blows her nose. She's right—she can breathe.

'The family called,' says Jo. 'Sorry. You must have got called before we got there.'

'That was me,' says Mo, the night doctor. 'I wasn't sure whether to wait or get you just in case.'

'Better just in case,' I say. And much better this than an actual airway issue, we agree.

Mavis looks apologetic. 'I reckon I just need Vicks rub,' she says.

I reckon so, too. Mavis is a sweet middle-aged woman, and she easily becomes confused if she misses any medication or develops an infection. We admit her until the morning.

Many nights on call are fine. I might get a phone call or two, but sometimes nothing. I'll cook on the little stove in my unit and FaceTime Maya, or a few of us will walk to the Memo Club for dinner. On any given night, a good portion of the hospital staff are also at the club, dining in a room decorated with war memorabilia, or ordering a drink next to one of the regular barflies in their faded singlets, parked at the counter for the long haul. If the head chef is here, I may get a free side dish or two, because he's adamant that I treated his young boy one day—although I honestly don't recall. It's very kind of him.

Another dinner option is Chris's house, or squeezing into one of our staff units, but this means that I'll have to buy beers or wine. Tonight I'm off duty, and we're heading to Chris's place, so I'll need to take something. I hate buying takeaway alcohol up here. I'll get questioned by a police officer stationed outside each of the half-dozen outlets. 'Where are you planning on consuming this?' I'll be asked, as they check my licence. 'Melbourne, hey? You're a long way from home.'

'Yeah, I am,' I'll say. 'I'm just drinking at the hospital flats.' But this sounds as bad to me as saying 'in the park, by myself' or 'alone in my car'.

'And you're not buying this for anyone else?' I'll be asked.

'Nope.'

'Righto.'

And then I'll wander in and grab a bottle of pinot, or some overpriced IPA beers, and I'll recognise at least one person who I've previously counselled about *their* alcohol consumption, and I'll wish I hadn't come inside, and that I hadn't parked the car, stickered with a 'Northern Territory Government' sign, out the front, although there are a few cars like it beside it. And I'll tell myself that because I'm into smaller quantities of the fancier stuff it's okay, and I'm not being completely hypocritical . . .

Alcohol here is an ugly, hot-button issue. Regulation is an ongoing minefield. There's a book about this town's battle for restrictions a few years ago, written by a well-known Aboriginal author. The restrictions were *wanted* by many Aboriginal Elders but opposed by whitefellas and the industry. These days it's my own tribe, city-based liberals, who largely oppose the restrictions. I also used to, but I really don't know anymore. Many Aboriginal people oppose the restrictions, too, of course, and policies are forever shifting, and it's all against the ugly backdrop of long-running control, coercion, dispossession, and the Federal Government's 2007 'Emergency Intervention', which sent in defence personnel and banned alcohol and pornography in remote communities. Now there are 'mobile police beats' located outside takeaway stores, a 'banned drinker register', daily purchasing limits, and increasing rates of—

The clerk interrupts my thoughts. 'Those are on special,' he tells me.

'These?'

'Yeah, the pinot. She's a pretty good drop.'

'Yeah, righto,' I say. 'I'll take another bottle, then.'

'Yeah, goodo. Why not, hey?' he says, and scans my driver's licence as required by law, and I put on my sunnies and hat before I walk out, partly to hide.

I *hate* buying grog up here.

Being on call can be a difficult aspect of remote medicine. The fatigue is real. It's often after hours when the more challenging cases present, and when the underbelly of the town reveals itself. It's when the severe assaults occur, and the rollovers of overfilled cars, and the police cases, and the sure-to-be coroner's cases, and the truly awful cases that you don't forget.

The more surreal moments happen after hours, too. A man knocked on the door here a while ago, asking for pain tablets. 'What's the trouble?' I asked, then noticed the large bloodstain on his T-shirt. 'Whoa, fella, what's going on there?'

He showed us the handle of a knife. The rest of it was still embedded in his chest.

'My god, mate, let's get you a stretcher,' I said, but he walked towards resus without any help and sat down. We did far better than pain tablets for him: he got a blood transfusion, antibiotics, a tube into his chest to drain the blood and air, and an urgent flight to Alice Springs.

In the late hours of another night, ward nurses called me to help manage an elderly man who'd become confused and agitated. I'd arrived to find him standing on his bed, frightened-looking, convinced that a dog was at the foot of it. This was likely delirium. None of us could reassure him or get him to take any medication, though, and he was becoming distressed and at risk of falling, so I jumped on the bed with him, hoping to coax him down and to take medication. 'We'll keep that dog far away,' I promised.

'It's not a dog,' he'd said, wide-eyed. 'It's a dingo! It's gonna get your foot there!'

He was terrified. I couldn't reassure him; he kept kicking at the dingo, so I also kicked at it, shouted at it, danced with him and colluded with his hallucination as we convinced him to take something to reduce his distress, which he finally did. Broken hip avoided.

Then there are the overtly bizarre cases; the ones where you read the triage screen, giggle with colleagues then step out and manage it with a professional demeanour. Such as the drunk traveller who'd peed on an electrified cattle fence, and wanted his penis X-rayed to make sure all was fine. Or the European tourists who came in with a daddy longlegs spider in a jar, a harmless, tiny little thing, petrified that it had bitten them in their van, having heard the standard 'everything out here can kill you' stories. Or the guy who asked for a male doctor, concerned that he'd 'Cooked me balls, Doc', because the kids had opened the microwave door on a low counter just as he'd walked past. Would I mind please checking them?

Another man shot the tattoo of his football club's logo after their grand final loss, furious with them, inexplicably ignoring that the tattoo was on his ankle. He shattered his joint and I'm sure he's never walked properly since. It's still the only gunshot wound I've seen in Australia.

Another night, a retired grey nomad limped in, having spiced up an evening with his wife, he explained, by forcing his genitalia through a thick metal washer from his toolkit. This was an improvised 'ring' to keep things firm, he said, but he now couldn't remove it. Neither could we. *All* of his genitalia had been jammed through, and it was an increasingly swollen mass. Our ring cutters failed, so for the better part of an hour a few of us worked at it with a small, handheld grinder. One colleague dripped water on the grinder to stop things overheating, another held swollen things out of the way as I worked the blade, like council workers trying to saw through a slab of pavement.

'Not getting too hot there, mate?' I shouted occasionally, mindful of what was at stake for him.

'Nah, all good. She's a bit tender, though.'

'Yeah, I bet. So anyway, you came via Uluru, yeah? Okay weather so far?'

Not all of these things happened in Central, for sure, and every ED staffer has a hundred similar stories. And if you can't laugh at these more than you get upset about the disasters, something will give.

In the cities, you get to spread the on-call load among many specialists, taking one night a week, or even one night a month. Here, you can't. I arrived in a new town once and had to cover anaesthetics for two weeks, day and night, as well as the normal ED shifts, because the other providers had to suddenly leave. I'd initially refused, but this meant that expectant women couldn't deliver there and would have to stay in a larger town, in case they needed theatre, and all elective surgery would be cancelled. Patients from remote communities who'd travelled here for operations would get sent home. So, of course, you say yes, but then you worry. You sleep poorly. And you become anxious that you'll make errors you shouldn't. During an emergency surgical case one night, I was giving the anaesthetic and sat to write notes and thought, *Which case is this on the table again? The self-inflicted stab wound to the belly? Or the ruptured appendix?* Both were young women. I looked over the curtain. 'Stab or appendix?' I asked the surgeon. He looked just as tired. We'd both been at work for almost twenty-four hours. And then: 'Wait, did we give this dose of fentanyl yet?'

After a bad run, my phone can start to feel like a hand grenade beside my bed, primed to explode at any moment. I wake often. Is my phone on? Did I miss a call? I check the settings and try to fall asleep. Wait—that dog barking . . . is it attacking someone? And what's that rustling in the kitchen? Great, just a cockroach. *Dammit, now if I don't get to sleep, tomorrow's going to be even more of a mess . . .*

This is one reason why I fly out. We're well staffed here, for now, and being on call every second or third night is doable—just. I've also started lying to myself. *Whatever comes in will be easy to manage*, I tell myself, so that I can drift off. *Nothing could go wrong. There's no condition that we can't easily manage out here. No women will possibly go into early labour tonight. All the drivers are obeying the speed limit, seatbelts on, cars not overloaded with passengers, and no startled kangaroos will hop onto the highway. No severe pneumonias are evolving, no fights are brewing, and no firecrackers are being lit by someone who's about to point the barrel at their mate . . .*

Denial has its uses.

10

Knowing Little

September, Far North Queensland

Denial has its place in other domains, too. Having to do relationships long distance has led to previous break-ups—or at least contributed to them hugely. Or so I tell myself. A few months of psychoanalysis on a couch may reveal otherwise, but the theme has come up often enough. Maya has experienced the same, too. *When you're everywhere, you're nowhere* is a saying that resonates.

My aim had never been to move around this much, only to follow the interesting, meaningful work—and to enjoy it. As a junior doctor, I headed to Peru to study tropical medicine, to get a foot in the door with aid agencies. Afterwards, a colleague put me in touch with a clinic on the Thai–Burma border. It was run by Burmese refugees, he said, and he'd worked there, and they were happy to have me for a few months. My girlfriend at the time took leave to come along, and we loved it. And what wasn't to love? The medicine was eye-opening, and the health workers were grateful for any textbooks and resources and teaching we could give. At night, we ate Thai food at local markets, then cycled home past saffron-robed monks sweeping their monasteries or collecting alms, then past rice fields, to our little guesthouse. This was how I wanted to spend the coming years, I decided.

At the time, MSF was considering my application. The placement they offered me was for six months in Angola, and I couldn't have said yes more quickly. This was a country I'd heard about as a child, a place my father had been involved with, and it'd be my opportunity to get back to Southern Africa and work as a doctor. My girlfriend wasn't thrilled about me leaving for so long, but I selfishly saw no dilemma. I wanted both: the relationship and the volunteering. I'd be back in a few months, I promised, and we could carry on. And I'd probably do this again later, but we could have a normal relationship in between. Wisely, she left. Family was her priority. I envied her that. My family was all over the map. I had no strong emotional ties to Melbourne, or any city other than Cape Town, but I hadn't lived in Cape Town for twenty years and was rarely in Melbourne. So for me, anywhere where work was meaningful was good for a base; old friends would always be there, and new friends could be made. My ex-girlfriend went on to start a beautiful family with a great guy, and the loss was entirely mine.

South Sudan is where I ended up a year later, with MSF again, but the trip was messy. I'd initially signed up for Somalia, but that was aborted due to the murder of staff I'd not yet met. Mozambique was next, to help with a cholera outbreak, but that project was closed when things settled and the local staff were laid off—not a happy time for them. And then there was South Sudan, busy and fascinating and with huge needs, but I finished early due to safety concerns and the high numbers of deaths, among other reasons. I was still single at the time—probably just as well for any potential partner who'd have had to endure my debriefs during this emotional roller-coaster.

When I got home, I disappeared into a rabbit hole of writing. This is another easy way to stay single: move back with your parents, stare at a laptop, fiddle with words. But writing felt like a constant dialogue, so there was never any loneliness. I loved it, and I got lost in it. It hadn't previously been an aspiration. I'd enjoyed writing a blog with MSF, but when I got home, I *needed* to do it. I couldn't otherwise articulate what I thought. 'I don't know what I think until I write it all down,' said Joan Didion, an American author, and I felt this. It was partly also my little act of 'witnessing', of trying to render the beautiful moments. Like being at a bedside in a small, torchlit hospital ward late at night, in a region that I hadn't known existed, with a local health worker and family, helping to treat a child. Or even just documenting the sad moments. They'd otherwise be lost. Even if only a few people read what I'd written, it was *something*. The moment hadn't disappeared forever.

Between all this, I completed my rural medical training, spending a lot of time in Central, then Cairns for the Flying Doctors, which consumed a few busy, happy years. There were a couple of great relationships in there, but my constant need to pull out a calendar to figure out when I'd be back sent people running. 'Three nights away together, next month? Absolutely, I'd love to. Oh, wait, I've got training in Cairns. Then I'm in Central for two weeks. Then I've got a mandatory resus course in Sydney. How about July?'

Maya is in the same position. Among the many things we have in common, the flying around and the experience of long-distance relationships are big ones. It's not that we don't want a more settled life; it's just that it's hard to leave this work once you discover it. And maybe there's some guilt at the prospect of walking away and turning your back on all of it. Because now you *know*. You've seen it. You've put faces to the statistics. Stepping out isn't so easy.

The ideal scenario? If a genie granted me a few wishes, or something like that? Easy: to work up north in the day. To sleep in my own bed at night. To wake up next to a loved one. To see things improve for people up there—*significantly*.

Not too much to hope for, right?

I fly back to Cairns. The Flying Doctors crew meets up early in the morning. Again, there's strong coffee in my mug and the smell of aviation gas in the air, and that school bus feeling. We catch up, load our bags and board the two aircraft, heading to communities for the week. When we land, the clinic car meets us and I drop my bags in the dusty doctor's house and get to it.

'I don't know,' says Rose, a patient, when I ask why she's come. 'You tell me. You mob called me.'

'Did we?' I ask, still trying to connect to the internet to find her notes. A cockatoo screeches outside the open window.

'Yeah, the driver come and tell me I gotta be here.'

'Oh, right. Did we give you a letter?'

'Nah. He just said I gotta come.'

We send reminders to patients for scheduled check-ups or abnormal results, but the lists have grown from dozens to more than a hundred some weeks. I can't keep track.

'Any idea what it might be for?' I ask. 'You had any problems recently?'

'Nah,' she says. 'But you probably got it on that thing, yeah?' She points to my laptop.

'You'd think so, Rose, wouldn't you?' I laugh. 'Give me a moment.'

Rose takes off the plastic bags tied over her shoes as we talk, folding them neatly on the desk next to me. 'Too much mud after the rain,' she says. She's the owner of the jealousin' dress, and she's the full-time carer for her husband, who's palliative and housebound.

'What's your date of birth again?' I ask, trying another way on my laptop. There are also two different spellings of her surname. I thumb through her paper chart. There's a separate desktop computer with the state health department's software and notes, but we're not authorised to access it. The Aboriginal Medical Service next door uses its own computers, and we can't access them; they can't access ours, either. But they haven't had a regular doctor for a while, unfortunately.

I walk down the hall and talk with Helen, the receptionist.

'You got any idea why Rose is here?' I ask.

Helen looks through trays. After a few minutes, she finds something: a scan result from weeks ago.

'Got it,' I say to Rose, ten minutes already wasted, and I run through it with her. She fortunately thinks this is funny, but she complains as I try to type the results into the laptop.

'You mob always lookin' at that computer,' she says. 'Not talkin' to me. Not like old days.'

I agree. The system is ridiculous. If a camel is a horse designed by committee, then this is the IT equivalent. And for a population with complex health needs and often poor health literacy, it's dangerous. I'll spend hours going through results later, many in duplicate or triplicate. It reminds me of a short story in which Poseidon, the god of the sea, sits at his desk at the bottom of the ocean, lamenting that he'll never see much of it because he's too tied up with administration. It was written more than a hundred years ago by Franz Kafka. He could've been a doctor here last week.

The clinic is again a whirlwind. I spend much of the day squinting at the laptop. The man who'd contemplated dialysis and declined it is deteriorating quickly, and the strong, ammonia-like smell of urea stays in the room long after he leaves. His body is no longer able to pee it out, and the itch can become overwhelming for him. I discuss treatment with a kidney specialist and get palliative care involved.

Gloria drops in for a chat, and says she's got a new phone number because her granddaughter dropped her phone off the boat. A soft-spoken youngfella ticks like a clock as he sits quietly, waiting for his blood thinner test results. He had a metallic heart valve inserted in a Melbourne hospital because of severe rheumatic heart disease, but if he forgets his blood thinners, his chance of a stroke is significant. A few young people in Central have had this misfortune.

'Ah, Zach, your result is very low,' I say. 'You missed tablets?'

He nods.

'It's so important, mate.' I speak with him at length about the dangers of skipping his medication. I try not to lecture, instead exploring what's preventing him from taking them—but the bottom line is that he *must* take them daily. He's not even twenty. A stroke would be a disaster, even more so up here. These roads aren't kind to wheelchairs. He nods quietly, and I put him on a recall list for next week.

'What the hell did you do to that kid?' shouts Helen to a new agency nurse as I walk out to call the next patient. 'You mucked that kid up! He came in here smilin', he sees you, now he's screamin' and walkin' funny. What did you do?'

But the nurse had only given him his penicillin injection as planned. She looks worried for a moment, but Helen laughs. Helen knows everyone here and runs the show, which suits us because she does it well. A man in the waiting room asks her for a cup of water. 'What?' she says. 'Your arms painted on? That tap's right there. You get it!' The man laughs. 'And you,' she tells me, 'you gotta sign here. Travel form for Edith, the blind woman. And new flights for Paxton. He missed that other one. He said it was too early.'

I do as I'm told, and I trade her for a pathology result. 'You know this fella?' I ask. 'I can't find him on the system.'

'Yeah, I know him,' she says. 'He's stayin' in Cooktown now. He's got some new chicky down there. I know his uncle. Yeah, I'll find him today.'

I'd nominate Helen for head of the department of health, if I could, or at least head of the IT department. People like her are the backbones of these clinics, completely irreplaceable.

A teenager wanders down the corridor sometime late afternoon. 'She just needs a sandwich and a lie down, I reckon,' says Helen. 'She's been smoking ganja all morning, but her Nan wants to see you.' Ganja is marijuana, and the girl does need a lie down. She's glass-eyed, and polishes off the sandwich Helen gets her. But her grandmother is worried that she's hearing voices.

'You gotta tell her straight, Doctor,' she says. Carol is her name. She takes a seat beside her granddaughter in my office. 'She been smokin' too much. You gotta tell her it's dangerous.'

The young girl's a quiet, thin fourteen-year-old, hair tied back and wearing a singlet, and we're not going to get far today. She smiles and looks around slowly, and asks for another sandwich. 'Sometimes she havin' that ice one, too,' Carol says. Ice is methamphetamine, and it's been a disaster in some communities.

'There's ice up here now?' I ask.

'Nah, not here,' she says. 'She goes to Cairns with friends. They doin' it down there.' The fact that the girl is hearing voices is a red flag, but she's not hearing any right now. Carol is clearly supportive, so they're okay to go home. I'll see them tomorrow and arrange for the drug and alcohol team to follow up. 'Town's no good,' says Carol, as they get up to leave. 'Youngfellas not doin' good, not like my day.'

'Oh?'

'Nah, too much trouble now.'

'Actually, Carol,' I ask. 'Could we chat sometime? I'd like to ask you some questions.'

'I'm good now,' she says.

'No, I was thinking when I'm not working. Is that okay?'

'Why?'

'I just want to hear your thoughts. About what you reckon the problems are up here. And maybe about when you grew up and all that.'

I feel self-conscious as I ask, but I've made this pitch before. I'd asked others when I'd first started working at Central. Everyone seemed so open to talking, and they were incredibly honest and blunt. I hadn't expected that. I'd collected the names and details of many who'd said they'd be happy to catch up and I'd sat down with a couple and chatted; but then work got busy, and things here became normal to me. Those moments of 'You won't believe what happened today!' shifted to 'Yeah, I've heard that before.' And people are passing on, too. There aren't many Clancy Number Threes around these days.

'Yeah, I give you my number,' says Carol.

It's a week before I call. 'Yeah, I remember you,' Carol says, 'Tomorrow is good. Wanna go fishing?'

I do. But when I mention these plans to a colleague, she says that's great, but I should probably give Carol some money.

'What?' I ask. 'For fishing?'

'No, for her time.'

'Really? But that's all very transactional, no?'

'Well, yeah,' she says. 'But it is transactional. You're using her time to get what you want, right? Didn't you say you wanted to ask her a bunch of stuff? There's gotta be something in it for her.'

I don't like the idea, and I wonder if I'm misreading this whole thing. There's no chance I'll give money. And chocolates make it feel like a date, so I opt for nothing, then I feel bad, and at the last minute I get her some groceries.

Carol's house is a simple breezeblock building with a 'No alcohol or drugs' sign on the gate. Her little dog yaps and keeps me away. 'He only barkin' at whitefellas,' she laughs. 'You got fishin' gear?'

I don't. She says her son has taken hers.

'You got a blanket?' she asks.

I don't. She fetches one and when she returns, I take the grocery bags out of the clinic car's boot. She looks confused.

'What's this?' she asks.

'Nothing much,' I say. 'I just went to the shop before and got some extra stuff to thank you.'

'What? For yarning?'

'Yeah. Well, I just bought too much for myself.' But the three bags are full, more than I'd need for a week here.

She looks through them. 'Nah, I'm right,' she says. 'I got my shopping. Put 'em in the car. Maybe my daughter will want 'em.' I load the boot, and she looks confused again. 'Why you gettin' this?'

Have I insulted her? I worry now that she feels pitied, something I hate projecting. Interactions can be complicated, and I've seen differing expectations cause difficulties over the years.

Some of my non-Aboriginal colleagues have been 'adopted' into Aboriginal families. Being accepted in this way gives you an immediate 'in' with the community. You're given a skin name, a cultural classification defining your new relationship to others; this woman here will now be your aunt, and that man there your brother. It's a whole new perspective, but you'll now be affiliated with some families more than others, which in health care can create problems. Missteps and resentments can accidentally occur. You may be invited to camping trips and ceremonies, but you'll also need to help out, maybe lend someone money or do an airport run. And why not? It's give and take. I've seen many navigate this beautifully, and some others struggle as various parties feel used.

Carol directs me to the edge of town and calls her daughter. She chats softly on the phone, then hangs up and opens the window.

'I never talk with a whitefella before,' she says matter-of-factly.

'Oh?'

'Nah. Never.' She's silent for a while. I really hope this isn't going to be awkward. I assumed it'd be a casual chat and quick attempt at fishing from the river's edge before dark. 'I mean, whitefella cops and teachers,' she says. 'And you mob in the clinic. But not just yarning, you know?'

'Really? Never?'

'Nah. You first one. Sixty-one years.'

This catches me by surprise.

She directs me past the airport, to a grassy spot under a large tree. We leave the groceries in the car and lay her blanket down, and she sits cross-legged, comfortable in her sky-blue skirt, white T-shirt tucked into it, a pair of white-grey runners. I'm the stiff white guy, outstretched legs, sweating in the mild humidity.

'Yeah, righto,' she says. 'What you wanna yarn about?'

I'd love to know about her background, I say. About how things have changed here, what she thinks the problems are, the solutions, the trouble with the kids, the—

'Too much,' she laughs. 'You tell me about your family.'

I tell her that I grew up in South Africa, and she stops me.

'Africa? But you not a blackfella?' She giggles often. I notice a long, old scar on her forehead, partly covered by grey hair, and a large 'step' in one ear—maybe a roughly sewn laceration. She went to a mission school, she says, then got married young. 'Big trouble for my family,' she says, when I ask about her husband. 'See this?' She shows me the forehead scar. 'We get a big hiding,' she says. She'd been 'promised' to an older man but ran off with her boyfriend instead, going against traditional laws about who could be together. The pair hid in another community but were found. 'We get punished proper way,' she says. 'No grog, no fighting. They have a meeting, and we take our punishment. Two of us, standin' in the middle. Big hiding.'

'And then you broke up?' I ask.

'Nah,' she says. 'We run away again.' She laughs. She tells me that things became more relaxed with traditional law in her community over the years. She now has a handful of kids and a dozen grandkids, but left the marriage. She struggled with alcohol for years. 'Now, no men, no grog,' she says. 'I got church and family.'

We talk about the clinic here, and town, and what works and what doesn't. She says that the clinic staff are nice. She hates going into the city, though, because she gets humbugged by people who recognise her, and the whitefellas don't make eye contact.

'Maybe they reckon I'm dumb,' she says, when I ask why. 'I dunno. I don't talk with them. My reading not too good, so maybe people think I'm stupid, you know?'

I don't doubt her experience. I wonder, too, whether some of us whitefellas are not sure what to say. Younger, newer doctors are sometimes awkward when they arrive, worried about crossing invisible boundaries. Their speech becomes overly simplistic, even childlike. Interactions can become clumsy.

'How should I talk with them?' one soft-spoken medical student had asked Chris.

'Like people,' said Chris, a little dryly.

An older colleague in the region has more strident views. 'We'll never be accepted in these places,' he tells new doctors. 'You'll never understand them. Ultimately, you're the coloniser. This colours all of your interactions, and many will resent you. Don't forget it.' He's historically correct, of course, but I'm not sure the pep talk helps people settle in or find a warm tone. If I'd heard him talk years ago, it may have scared me from ever coming here.

My take is that I can't possibly know all the cultural nuances: the complex kinship systems, which relatives can't be in the same room, the names to avoid because of a death, and so on. Such things vary between regions, too, and individuals. My aim is to be approachable. I smile and hope people will tell me if I'm putting my foot in it, because I'm obviously an outsider. There's no point pretending otherwise.

I ask Carol about this, and she giggles. 'Yeah, I dunno,' she says. 'Maybe we thinkin' too much. Maybe we just gotta talk more.'

I agree. And my legs now have pins and needles. I stand, and we chat for a little longer, swatting mosquitos as the sun drops, and as I drive her home, she tells me that her granddaughter has just run off to Cairns again with troublesome friends. She's got an aunt down there who she'll stay with, but she otherwise does her own thing.

'Parents can't control 'em,' she says, when I ask why this is happening more. Many of the grandparents take in the grandkids, picking up where some parents drop off. Alcohol is a part of it, Carol says, and discipline.

'In the old days, we get a hidin' for disrespecting culture. Now, the youngfellas know if they get a hiding they can go to the cops.'

Maybe boredom is a part of it, I suggest. I remember speaking with two young boys brought into the Central ED by the police. They smelled like a fuel bowser, all stoned and giggly, high on the fumes they'd been sniffing. This was in the late hours of an otherwise quiet night. I pulled up a chair and chatted with them, these blond, athletic, curly haired kids, like little pro surfers in the desert. Why were they sniffing petrol? I'd asked. Did they know the risks? They came and sat at the desk with Sue and I, spinning on the chairs and joking around, making us laugh. They were honest and cheeky. Yeah, of course they knew it was dangerous. But they were bored. And it's what some of the other kids did, and what else was there to do?

Now, Carol shakes her head. She says that her generation had less. They found things to do. 'Sit-down money,' she says, referring to welfare payments. It's what many people call it up here. 'Young kids watch parents gettin' sit-down money, now why they gonna go to school or work?'

This is a thorny issue. An Aboriginal activist whose books I've read speaks often about welfare dependency, about how demotivating it is, and about the importance of creating jobs, and taking away any disincentive to keep them. 'The tyranny of low expectations,' he called it. No one would assume that this was normal in other communities or for other people, he argues, but here we walk past it as if it's just expected of Aboriginal people.

I'd assumed this man would be revered here—he's from this region.

'Nah, he's a coconut,' laughed one of the health workers when I'd mentioned him: Black on the outside, white on the inside. 'He come up here, he gonna get a spear,' she said. 'I like him, but most mob here hate him.'

So this is part of my coping strategy: being comfortable with contradictory information, or at least sitting with it. Accepting that many different things may be true, to some degree, at the same time—even if large parts of what I hear don't dovetail with my values. And I try to choose my battles, because there's little that I can do about many of the deeper issues; being well rested and balanced is what I can bring. It feels a little like giving up, but it's necessary if I'm going to sleep, or avoid ruining a dinner table conversation down south—as I'd done a few times early on, unable to bite my tongue in the face of confident opinions.

'We go fishing next time?' asks Carol, when I drop her back. Her little dog barks at me through the fence again.

'For sure,' I say.

'Did it go well?' my colleague messages me later—the one who'd suggested the whole payment debacle. I flick back an emoji of gritted teeth.

That night, Carol messages. 'When you comin' back?' she asks. 'We gotta yarn more.'

Everywhere I work, these strong women hold these communities together. Or at least work hard at it. Squeezed between our law, their law and complicated family obligations. Between electricity bills and tight budgets, break-ins and humbugging, and kids and grandkids veering off on difficult tangents. Getting everyone to their medical appointments. Filling the fridge. Finding transport to funerals. Hanging on to these frayed, disparate strands around them, weaving a beautiful, sometimes broken community from it all.

11

Misconceptions and Numbers

September, Central Australia

Three new medical students rotate up to Central. One leaves and drives to Uluru after a few days, to go camping with his partner. The expectation is that they're in the hospital full-time, but Uluru is in the neighbourhood—about a seven-hour drive each way—so I understand the urge. He's gone for two of the four weeks, but Chris can deal with sorting out his attendance sheet. And it is a spectacular place to camp, an absolute must-see.

The two other students stick around—on weekends, evenings, the works, but not nights. Safety-wise, they're not allowed. Emily recruits one into her running club, which now has two members. Emily's training for an ultramarathon, so I don't dream of keeping up. I plod a few kilometres up the highway, but she runs right out of town, around old mine sites from the gold-rush days.

This hospital has become a popular rotation for students now. It's an adventure and an eye-opener, and a few have been inspired to train in rural medicine. They also get to do procedures and see patients properly, rather than jostle at the back of a crowded ward round in the city. And we put them to good use—if they're keen.

'You've put in drips before?' I ask one as they introduce themselves in the ED. 'Great. You've done two? Perfect. You're about to double that in cubicles three and four. Let's go ask them. And you, Amir, you've practised suturing on an orange? Hmm, it's a little different. Same principle, though. Let's ask cubicle five if he's happy for you to do his leg. Don't mention the orange, though.'

On the weeks I'm rostered to the inpatient ward, we'll do the round and then go through the to-do list in our small office and divvy up jobs—myself, two students and the two junior doctors. I'll go back to the ED later. The ward nurses and social worker will pop in often with tasks and queries, as will the Aboriginal Liaison Officers and counsellors. The child protection workers and police come to us less, more so to the ED, which gives us time for philosophical discussions prompted by specific patients. All tangents and any ideas are welcome. Students almost always say that they had no idea it was like this here.

'Which aspect?' I'll ask.

Everything. It's worse, better, more complicated, not at all what they'd expected. 'The whole world seems to be going downhill,' one student says this morning. 'It makes you wonder if anything ever works. Chris said you'd both worked in Africa? It must've been so sad. Things just get worse there, too, huh.'

Nope, I say. Not at all. Some of it, yes. But not all. And most of what we read is biased towards the negative, I suggest. It's also easy to miss any progress, because it's incremental and not dramatic, and it's harder for media to report something that *didn't* occur. When long-term, well-thought-out programs actually work, and the efforts of many people pay off, it doesn't make headlines.

There's a hypothetical scenario, I tell them, told often by a famous global health professor, that if you sit a medical student and a chimpanzee at a desk together, then pose multiple-choice questions about the state of the world, the chimpanzee will win—and by a long way. I tell them this with respect, of course, and we laugh. The scenario only works if the chimp has a limited number of options, such as three bananas with an answer sticky-taped to each of them, rather than an actual paragraph to read. And their adversary doesn't have to be a medical student—anyone will do. The point is that the chimpanzee lacks the biases we develop, and doesn't hang on to outdated facts or incorrect ideas. Without these, they're more likely to choose the correct answer at random than an educated person with biased thinking is. The chimp doesn't read the news. It doesn't doomscroll at night.

The professor who'd suggested this was Hans Rosling, a Swedish doctor. He surveyed leaders and global health students, asking the same questions: had the proportion of people in extreme poverty doubled, stayed the same or halved over the last twenty years? Halved was the correct answer, but only 10 per cent got it right. Yet 33 per cent of chimps would've picked that banana. Ditto with his other examples. Was the average life expectancy across the world 50, 60 or 70 years? The correct answer was 70, but that was the option least often picked. And was the overall percentage of the world's one-year-olds who'd been vaccinated against major diseases 20, 50 or 80 per cent? The correct answer was 80 per cent, but my instinct would've been the lowest number.

There are obvious criticisms with his examples. Some said he painted an overly optimistic worldview, but to me this misses the bigger point: that progress has been real for many, and profound, but we consistently underestimate it. And we therefore also underestimate what can be done. That's not to detract from the reality of wars, enduring poverty and other significant problems, or to say that things can't go backwards. But reflecting on the wins is important. Knowing that progress is possible, and real, is more likely to inspire someone to engage. 'Pay attention to what you pay attention to,' I remind myself.

One of the medical students has to write up a long medical case as part of her studies. I suggest talking to Doris, Tyreese's grandmother. She's here for weeks while her leg heals, and she's also diabetic. My suggestion is to focus on the diabetes, and her lifestyle.

'You don't mind?' she asks Doris when I introduce them.

'Nah, you right,' Doris says, playing cards on her phone. Her family visits often, but the weeks here must have got boring. There are only so many *Woman's Day* and *New Idea* magazines from the tearoom to flick through, or hours of daytime TV to endure.

'What sorts of things do you eat in a day, Doris?' I hear the student ask as I stand outside the closed curtains a few minutes later, catching up on another patient's notes.

'Normal stuff, you know.'

'Like Weet-Bix?'

'Yeah.'

'And pasta?'

'Yeah.'

'And tea?'

'Yeah.'

'And fruit?'

'Nah.'

'How about bush tucker?'

'Yeah, sometimes.'

'Oh wow! That's great. We went to a bush tucker night in Alice Springs recently. It was so amazing. Do you eat lots of it?'

'Yeah.'

'Like, do you go hunting sometimes?'

'Yup.'

'Wow! Do you go hunting a lot?'

'Yeah.'

'And do you eat the meat?'

'Yeah.'

'Like, just there, off the fire?'

'Yup.'

'Like what—kangaroos?'

'Yeah.'

'How about other bush tucker, like plants?'

'Yeah.'

'Wow. Like bush tomatoes?'

'Yeah.'

'And what about insects, like honey ants?'

'Yeah, honey ants.'

'Wow! Really?'

'Yeah.'

'And damper?'

'Yup.'

'On the fire?'

'Yeah.'

On this goes, and I get the strong suspicion that Doris is concentrating more on her card game, not so much the questions.

'You don't really eat all that stuff a lot, do you?' I ask her later, when the student had left.

'Nah,' she laughs. 'But you mob always askin' too many questions. Sometimes not even listenin' right.'

Fair point. The lesson for me is not only to ask open questions, but also to not overlay your assumptions. Not that I should throw stones. I'd arrived at Carol's with bags of groceries, *and* I'd been encouraged to take cash by an experienced colleague. I can't count how often I've made the wrong assumptions.

On my last visit to South Africa, I was surprised by the perception the locals had of Australia. A man was talking to me outside a supermarket where he was working as a 'car guard'. This is an extremely low-wage gig that involves standing in the fickle, windy Cape Town weather, keeping an eye on cars for much of the day or night for a tip. 'You have an accent,' he'd said as I looked for change. 'Where are you from?'

'Australia now,' I told him. 'But I was born here, in Cape Town. I miss it.' He was from Zimbabwe, he said, and had an engineering degree.

At this point, people often remark that I was lucky to have left. Many don't and are rightly proud of their home town, but this man clicked his tongue. 'Eh,' he said. 'It is very sad what is happening in your country. I am sorry for your people.'

'What, in Australia?' I asked.

'Yes. All those animals getting burned. All those koalas and kangaroos. And all those houses destroyed. It is too sad. Is your family okay?'

They were fine. That summer's bushfire season had been particularly bad, and millions of animals had been killed or injured and a few thousand homes destroyed. It was a disaster for the affected regions, but most of us lived nowhere near them. Here in South Africa, images of rescued animals were all over the newspapers and TV, along with 'Australia burns!' headlines.

The guard said that he'd like to donate some money. This was an extremely kind offer. *But really!?* I thought. A third of South Africans are unemployed, and crime rates are the highest on the continent. Life is no picnic there—even if Cape Town is the most beautiful city on earth, in my biased view. My sympathy was aimed mostly in his direction.

But maybe it shouldn't be. Maybe mine is a patronising, outdated view. And what I see in the clinics in Australia overlaps increasingly with the problems in South Africa.

When I'd arrived to study public health in London, a senior professor had said that we shouldn't be focusing on rare tropical infections, because many were on the way out. I'd just slid a bank cheque for a few thousand pounds under the cashier's window, barely an hour earlier—the annual tuition fee, and at that point the most I'd ever spent on something—so I'd wished his comments came earlier. More of us should've been studying diabetes, he said, and other non-communicable diseases—the cancers, hypertension and cardiac disease, among much else. Most of the course wasn't focused on rare tropical infections, as it turned out, as fascinating as they are. We covered a lot of other things, including the rise of non-communicable diseases. This was the new reality. The problems I see in remote clinics daily are the same problems that are increasing across much of the world. India now has *one hundred million* people with diabetes, as just one example. This would've been unbelievable a few decades ago.

'Overnutrition kills more than hunger' proclaimed headlines around the time I'd started the course. For the first time in human history, too much food now killed more people than an overt lack of food—specifically, too much ultra-processed food. This was based on extensive data that included every country in the world. I'd read these articles sitting in the university's glorious antique library, lined with old and new books about exotic infections. This new reality of dealing with food and diets and lifestyles seemed far less appealing, and far more difficult, than a disease outbreak. There's now an effective vaccine even for Ebola. But influencing what people eat? Enter the arguments about personal choice, food industry regulation, restrictions on freedoms, advertising, markets and capitalism itself. Running a vaccine program seems far easier—and the results more immediately visible.

We are deeply shaped by our environment and social context, is again the common thread. Our postcode is one of the strongest predictors of life expectancy. We can have all the passionate discussions we want in our little office in Central, beneath some great artwork and photos of staff nights out, but we're ultimately pulling people from the river, late in their course. The bigger social determinants of health lie outside the influence of hospitals and clinics.

There are also our own genetic determinants of health, of course, and our behaviours and cultural influences. And our infinitely wondrous, complex personalities . . .

Carol and I catch up again. I don't bring groceries this time. She's in Cairns to see her granddaughter, and I'm on my way back to a clinic up north, and we overlap for an afternoon.

'Lunch or maybe a coffee?' I suggest, when she calls.

'What, like in a coffee place, or what?' she asks. She's on speakerphone, kids yelling, dogs barking in the background.

'Whatever you want,' I say. 'I've got a work car for the afternoon, but I fly out early tomorrow. Anything this afternoon is good.' I suggest a popular lunch spot near the botanic gardens, and she gives me the address of a relative she's staying with on the outskirts. It's a warm day, but when I pick her up, she's wearing an old fleece jacket and beanie.

We drive to the gardens. It's in a beautiful part of town, along a narrow road that winds past giant fig trees and under a curtain of aerial roots and thick vines. My favourite area, tropical and jungle-like.

'What, in there?' she asks, as we pull up near the cafe.

'Yeah, it's a nice one,' I say. 'You been before?'

She looks around. 'Nah,' she says. 'Not here, I reckon.'

'It's my shout. They've got good food.'

'Nah,' she says. 'People gonna look at me funny. Only white-fellas and tourists in there.'

Damn it, I think. A minute in, and I've made her uncomfortable again. 'How about we get takeaway and go sit in the gardens there?' I suggest.

'What, like a meat pie?'

'I don't think they have them here. We could look, though.'

'Nah, let's go to another place.'

'You sure?'

She is. I ask for any suggestions.

'BP,' she says.

I laugh. 'Really? The petrol station?'

'Yeah, they got good meat pies.'

'We can do better than a meat pie from BP, surely?' I'm wanting a decent feed myself before I fly up north for a few days. 'Honestly, it's my treat.'

'Nah, that one past the airport, they got good pies.'

I look at her. She's serious. We reverse out, and I drive the ten minutes to BP. I'm not thrilled by the idea. She stays in the car when we pull up and says she'd like a beef pie and Coke, so I run in and get the same for myself. 'Where to now?' I ask her, back in the car, because I'm drawing the line at sitting in a service station car park, windows up and air conditioning blasting, listening to bad local FM and spilling meat all over the work car.

'What's this?' she asks, holding up the soft drink.

'Coke,' I say.

'Nah, it's not.'

'You wanted a Coke, no?'

'Yeah. This one's Coke Zero,' she says.

'Same thing, no?' I ask.

She looks out the window. 'Nah, no good,' she says, quietly.

'But doesn't it taste the same?'

She shakes her head. 'Nah, you bring me shame, you know?'

'What do you mean?'

She tells me that she's diabetic, and I've embarrassed her by drawing attention to her sugar intake. 'Like, it feels like you tellin' me I'm sick,' she says, 'like my body not right.'

'Carol, I'm a doctor!' I say. 'I always buy Coke Zero. I got myself one, too. Here. You know how many spoons of sugar in proper Coke? It's no good for anyone.'

'Nah,' she says quietly. 'You makin' me feel shame.'

I apologise. She genuinely looks upset. *Dammit.* I switch the car off, go back inside to exchange them, and now we're set: 60 grams of sugar in a bottle and a fatty meat pie each, a gift from the primary care doctor. She directs me to a shady spot near the northern end of town, and we find a fixed concrete table under a large tree. There are no other people around, just us and two million flies also wanting some pie. We chat, and she tells me that her granddaughter has been picked up by the police and sent for a mental health assessment. Carol's worried that she may get sentenced to juvenile detention. Her back car window was smashed, she mentions later, but she's got to drive a few hundred kilometres to a funeral tomorrow anyway and it might rain.

'Where was it smashed?' I ask.

While visiting her son in ICU, she says.

'Why's he in ICU?' I ask.

'Some big infection,' she says.

I'm shocked, but she shrugs and giggles. 'Shit week,' she laughs. 'You got photos of your family?'

Yet again, I shelve my preconceptions.

12

Offering Apologies

October, Far North Queensland

'Troppo' season is starting. Heat and humidity climb. Mango trees begin to swell with fruit, and antiperspirant gives up working. It'll be a while yet before the heat peaks, and longer before the wet season brings relief. Our aircraft don't have air conditioning when they're parked, so if we're stuck waiting for an ambulance or a clinic car to arrive, we fan ourselves with notes, sticking to the chair, and aim the little battery-powered fan at the patients. Loading people becomes damp, sweaty work.

The upside is the storms when they do finally come. They're spectacular. We fly around an early season storm on the way to fetch a stroke patient one afternoon, picking a slim corridor of perfect weather between kilometres-high clouds that strobe and sizzle with lightning beside the windows. I watch it from eye level and send a clip to Maya. She pings back a screenshot of the weather in Vancouver, where she's visiting an unwell relative: five degrees.

I'd asked a pilot once what would happen if we had to go through one of these storm clouds. 'Those things?' he'd asked, pointing to the red spots on the radar. 'They'll rip the wings off.' And he said it with a straight face. So we load extra fuel for possible detours, and we'll sometimes land in another community and wait for the system to pass. If bad weather sets in heavily, we're sometimes unable to fetch a patient for a day or two.

The change in weather will also bring a change in the types of jobs we're called to. Roads to remote communities will become flooded and closed, meaning we'll have fewer call-outs for car accidents, and less sly grog will make it into communities, resulting in fewer of its attendant problems. There'll be more sepsis due to infections, though, and the occasional jellyfish stinger case.

There's also more birds. They come out in force as wetlands flood once more. We fly up to Cape York one morning after an early season storm. Large brolgas are bathing in puddles beside the runway, looking like feathered surface-to-air missiles as we come in to land, nervous and skittish and ready to launch. Airport staff fire 'blank' dummy rounds to scare them away, but these ones look unfazed. Maybe it's their little morning espresso-shot of energy. They at least stay put.

The driver meets us on the tarmac. We load our gear and drive to the clinic, where a shirtless young man is pacing at the front entrance. Nurses and family members are nearby, and two police officers are behind them. 'I really hope he doesn't kick off,' says Julie, the flight nurse, and I nod. He's well built and looks highly agitated.

We park nearby and walk over. 'G'day, Ryan,' I say, trying to sound lighthearted and nonchalant. We introduce ourselves and suggest going inside, or sitting in the shade for a yarn and cup of tea. An older man, presumably Ryan's father, tries as well. 'C'mon, fella,' he says. 'Gonna be way cooler inside.' But Ryan eyes me up and down and drags deeply on his cigarette.

'Nah,' he says. 'I'm not goin' anywhere.'

This could get difficult. His family called police after finding him wandering with a rope, talking to himself and saying that he wanted to die. He's got a challenging mental health history, and his partner recently left him and took the kids. He's been on a drug and alcohol binge for days. The on-call psychiatrist has 'sectioned' him, meaning that he's considered to be at significant risk to himself or to others, and needs an urgent assessment. It's our job to now get him safely to Cairns—whether he agrees to go or not. Easier said than done.

Ryan paces, barefoot. His eyes are bloodshot.

'Come on, Ryan,' says a woman who is presumably his mum. 'This mob gonna look after ya, come talk with them,' she pleads. She looks exhausted.

Coffee and tea are offered, but he stops and looks us up and down again, his arms and legs jittery. 'Why the fuck you mob here?' he asks.

I tell him honestly. 'We just wanna make sure you're okay, mate. We wanna help. People here are worried that your mind's racing a bit. We just wanna do a check-up and help you feel a bit better, make sure everything's okay, you know?'

'What, I gotta go to Cairns?' he asks.

'Yes,' I say. 'But just for a bit.'

He swears loudly and shouts that he's not going.

'I hear you, Ryan,' I say. 'And I don't wanna make your day harder. I know you've had a difficult time. But mate, we need to make sure you're okay.'

He stares at me and starts pacing again. 'You not listening,' he shouts, and kicks over a nearby bin. 'I'm not goin' anywhere.'

The police step closer. This will now likely go one of two ways. Ryan may give in soon, exhausted by the days of psychosis, his racing mind and lack of sleep, and take the oral sedation we hand him. This often happens—people just take the tablets. You talk, you make it clear there are no other options and that you're on their side, and at some point, they give in. They welcome a way out of their crisis. If Ryan takes the tablets, we'll insert an IV and give stronger sedatives via injection, then place him on monitoring and fly out.

Alternatively, he'll escalate. He may run off or lunge at us. The police will try to restrain him, and we'll give an intramuscular injection—I've got two syringes drawn up in my pocket, and I'll give one straight through his shorts if need be—and he'll yell and scream that this is assault, that he has rights, maybe also that this is racist and we're only doing it because he's Aboriginal. We'll wait long minutes for the injection to work, then get an IV in.

The third option, the nuclear one, is a general anaesthetic and ventilator. Agitated patients have lunged for the pilots during flights previously, so it's safety first.

All of this is my least favourite thing to do as a doctor. It's distressing for patients and their families, but we have a duty of care.

'How about we just yarn out here,' I say. 'I'll sit there, and we can get you a chair.'

He starts shouting. We go in circles for another couple of minutes. ‘The sooner we get down there, Ryan, the sooner you can get back home,’ I tell him. ‘And your family can fly down tomorrow.’

He escalates again. I nod at the police. It’s time. They step closer.

‘Ryan, listen,’ I say. Time for me to be tough cop. ‘There are only two options right now. We head inside and get you nice and comfy, and you take those tablets and have a good rest. That’s one. Or else these officers hold you down and I give you a needle. That’s the other. There’s nothing else, Ryan. Understand?’

He yells at me.

‘Come on, mate,’ says Julie, playing good cop. The actual cops stand quietly beside Ryan, ready to intervene. ‘I’ll get a cuppa and those tablets,’ she says. ‘How many sugars?’

He yells again. I repeat the options. Calm but firm is the aim. ‘Tablets or needle,’ I tell him. ‘There’s nothing else, Ryan. It’s your choice. Come on mate, let’s get that tea and you take those tablets, we get you comfy.’

He’s wide-eyed and clenches his jaw. *Here we go,* I think, and he stares at me. A long moment passes. I still can’t read these moments. I’m ready to step away quickly. A few weeks ago, a patient in a similar state calmed down as we chatted, and sat beside me in front of the ED. He agreed to take the tablets but suddenly threw them away, then bent his iPhone and shattered the glass in his hands, all the while staring at me. I jumped away, but then he picked up the tablets, swallowed them and came calmly into the ED. He was fine after that. That was a good outcome.

There have been more difficult ones. Chris and I had to chase a half-sedated patient up the road one night. We’d given him an intramuscular injection a few minutes earlier, but he suddenly 'woke up' and took off, past security and out the ED doors, still bleeding from his earlier injuries. We ran while someone else called the police and ambulance, all of us aware of the disaster it'd be if he became unconscious and we couldn't find him. So there were two whitefellas chasing an Aboriginal man, yelling after him—for his own safety, to be sure, although a terrible image for the health service. Fortunately, we found him a few minutes later, and he was tired and willing to come back.

Sedating someone is never to be taken lightly. Neither is 'sectioning' them. Stripping a patient of their autonomy, of their right to refuse treatment, is strictly regulated, and we use it for as short a time as necessary.

Ryan stares at us.

His parents plead.

The cops ask him to please make this easy.

He looks at me, then Julie. Something suddenly gives.

'Yeah, you right,' he says, and walks inside.

A million tonnes lift off our shoulders.

He walks to the treatment room and the clinic nurses are great with him. There's a male and a female police officer, and they're also good with him. Their presence in these situations seems to either escalate or dramatically settle them, depending on personalities and dynamics, but we rely on them for safety. An officer takes Ryan's mum to fetch clothes and toiletries for him.

Ryan lets us put a small IV into his forearm, and we tape it down securely. We'll put a second, larger one in when he's asleep. He takes the oral sedation and slowly settles.

I don't like the dynamics of all of this: a whitefella doctor threatening a blackfella patient, sometimes holding them down.

Of course, it's only ever for their own good, and not all the mental health patients I deal with are Aboriginal or Torres Strait Islander people. I've had to do this elsewhere, many times, but in remote areas it's an increasing part of the job. Especially among Indigenous people, mental health crises are becoming more common, along with suicide attempts and violence.

We head to the plane and board. We roar down the runway and the birds stay put. Another urgent job has come up—a motorbike accident on a remote property. We discuss whether to land with Ryan still in the plane, or to make a detour and drop him first. Neither option is ideal. I call coordination to discuss it, and as the phone rings, I wonder how long I'll keep doing this, how many more cases like Ryan's before I take a quieter job, one without the moral injury of other people's trauma so raw and on view constantly, and where my role in the whole equation feels easier.

Health outcomes worsen as the distance from a city increases. Potentially avoidable deaths are two to three times higher in remote areas—the so-called tyranny of distance. With a heart attack, time is muscle, and the sooner the clot can be dissolved or removed, the better the outcome. It's the same for many strokes. And with trauma or severe infections, adequate treatment during the 'golden' first hour has a huge benefit. Delays cost lives.

Telehealth has helped to bridge some of these gaps, and some of our shifts are now allocated solely to answering calls or dialling into clinics.

'Did you get that photo, Doc?' a man asks, calling from an old mining town, concerned about a skin infection.

'Not yet,' I say.

He tries again. 'The reception out here is bloody awful,' he says.

But other calls are queuing up, so I confirm the phone number and tell him I'll call back.

'Got it,' I say, a few minutes later. 'That's your leg, yeah?'

'Nah, forearm,' he says. The photos are blurry, so he sends more.

'That's not your knee on the left?' I ask, looking at the new batch.

'Nah, elbow,' he says. He sends more through.

He's got cellulitis, so I give him the name and dose of some oral antibiotics he'll need to get. But the keys to the pub are the next problem. Many stations or businesses in remote areas have a large Flying Doctors medical chest, extensively stocked with medications that we need to authorise. In this guy's town, the publican keeps the chest key. But the pub doesn't open for a few hours.

'You got his mobile?' the man asks me.

'The pub owner's?'

'Yeah.'

'No, sorry. It's not on our system. You know where he lives?'

'Yeah, he's a bit out of town.'

'Sorry, we've got nothing on file here.'

'Ah, righto,' he says. 'Maybe I'll try up at the servo. Ronnie there would probably know his number.'

The servo sounds good. It's better than anything I can suggest.

This service is a lifeline for these remote places. The Royal Flying Doctor Service was the world's first aeromedical rescue service, founded in the 1920s to provide a 'mantle of safety' for the outback, with an aircraft borrowed from Qantas. These days, there are about 90 aircraft around Australia. It's a long way from the days of horse-drawn carts pulling up to wood and canvas planes, or using a pedal-powered radio transmitter to call for help.

'No births on the plane,' a pilot had told me when I'd started, although I needed no convincing. Doubling the number of patients on a plane, in an instant, wasn't an ambition of mine. But their concern was that amniotic fluid is corrosive to the airframe. If it spilled, the engineers would have to strip the cabin and clean the structure—an expensive undertaking. Who knew that a bodily fluid could be good enough for a baby to grow in but no good for aircraft metals? We use medications sometimes to slow the mother's contractions in early labour, and if her cervix has dilated beyond a certain amount, we'll weigh up the possibility of delivering at the site before we board the plane.

There are plenty of calls for injuries. And in the efficient lingo of emergency services, these are often summarised as two opposing and usually non-compatible objects: car versus tree, croc versus leg, propeller versus forearm, stinger versus thigh, bull versus arm, tooth versus knuckle—also known as a 'fight bite'—and other objects, among an ever-growing variety of combinations.

My colleague got the croc versus leg job. Not many people survive a croc bite, and I'd wanted to shake the man's hand when I heard the story. The propeller versus forearm was a call that I took, but it was more logistics than medicine. The patient was on a fishing boat dozens of miles off Cape York, and the closest community didn't have a pier. They found a natural harbour, and a clinic ambulance drove out to meet him, and then we flew up. He was lucky—the laceration was huge, and if it'd been even a few millimetres to the side, he'd never have made it. His trial of life had been passed—with flying colours.

The stinger versus thigh was on an expensive island resort nearby, and I could hear the patient yelling in pain in the background. We couldn't land on the small island, so coordination tasked a LifeFlight helicopter—they're the other flight retrieval service in the region, and they tend to do the closer jobs, and lots of them. We usually do the longer flights, since our aircraft have a greater range but the downside of needing an airstrip.

Coordinating all of this has become more complicated. Partly this is because patient numbers are rising and the population is aging, and the complexity of managing medical conditions is increasing. It's also not helped by the growing number of services involved in care, and the constant staff turnover.

'Tell them I'm going to make the bloody medical decision myself,' said Matt, the pilot, one night when we were diverted multiple times by the coordination centre, 2000 kilometres to our south. 'Have they looked at a map?' he asked, listening in to a call. 'Do they understand fuel? And aerodynamics? They know we can't just pull over and idle in this thing, right? Tell them to leave it to us!'

That was a bad night. Most aren't like that.

There are other times when having a specialist to run things is essential. A remote clinic nurse sends me details about an unwell child one morning, then a short video of the patient.

'She's struggling with her breathing,' she says, when she calls a moment later. 'I think she's got a viral infection, but she's also got congenital heart disease.' She reads a summary of the heart abnormalities the girl was born with. They're rare, and severe.

'We'll get there as soon as we can,' I say. 'I'll call back shortly.'

The pilot and nurse start preparing the plane. I call the coordination centre, and they contact a paediatric ICU specialist. 'We can put them on a jet from Townsville,' the coordinator says, 'but you'll get there quicker. You go, and we'll support the clinic via video. We're getting them online now.'

We board immediately. Air control gives us priority, and we pull out in front of commercial liners and take off. We've got an hour before we land, so Mel, the flight nurse, and I make plans, calculate and draw up drugs and infusions. The doses are tiny, everything in little syringes.

As we start to descend, I call the coordination centre for an update. They say the little girl is worse. Getting an IV in has been difficult, so the nurses have put a line into the bone marrow instead, a great option, and they've given her key medications. This would be a stressful case for a specialist team in an ICU, never mind up here. We prepare for landing, and a few minutes later our satellite phone rings again. It's the coordination centre.

'How far away are you?' they ask.

'On the ground in fifteen.'

'She's deteriorating fast.'

I tell Rob, but we can't descend any quicker.

A couple of minutes later, the phone rings again. 'They're starting CPR.'

Damn. Mel and I look at each other. This isn't going to end well. Not out here. We've still got to get them back to a hospital down south, which will be at least two hours—if this goes well.

Hydraulics whine and flaps extend, and there's a *thunk* from the landing gear. Flocks of birds scatter. I've written all the doses on my forearm and tucked the syringes into my pockets.

The clinic's LandCruiser ambulance is here to fetch us. As we climb out of the plane my phone rings.

'CPR's been going for around fifteen minutes,' says the coordinator. 'We're about to call it. It'll have been going for twenty minutes by the time you get there.' They've had the whole team on video link with the nurses and agreed this was now futile. There's nothing else that can be done.

Mel and Rob listen in. It's terribly sad.

'Will they want to leave the body in the community for now?' I ask the coordinator. Family would normally be given time to grieve with it, and the clinic would follow up with the coroner.

'Yes,' he says. 'But we think it's best if you two go in. I think the family need to see that we've tried. It'd be good if you could talk with them, and if you could do a debrief with the staff afterwards. They're going to be devastated. And talk to the community. You know how these things can go.'

I do. A death in Central had been blamed on doctors a few years ago, and they'd needed to be ushered out and to leave town. I've witnessed a few moments when I've felt that grief could turn violent due to misinterpretations and misunderstandings.

We get into the ambulance and bring some equipment—maybe to feel as if we're still trying. Rob stays with the plane. The coordinator calls back. 'CPR is ceasing, just so you know. We've made that call, so you won't have to.'

We drive the short distance in silence. A crowd is gathering outside the clinic. There's soft weeping already, but nothing like what's about to unfold.

The driver swipes us into the treatment room. A handful of nurses and some family members stand around a bed. Medications and syringes and equipment are lying around it. Faces are sombre. We introduce ourselves. There's a little body on the bed. I spend a minute or so listening to her heart and her breathing, and looking at the monitors. I shine a light in her eyes and close them. The family surely knows. CPR has ceased, but I suspect that there's a perceived thread of hope, a glimmer that this isn't final, not real, until it's been formally declared.

I look at them and gently shake my head. 'I'm very sorry. There's nothing more we can do.'

The sobbing grows.

I remember the first time I'd seen this, in Angola, how the wailing rippled through the entire community that night. I'd heard it from all directions in the distance. I'd thought that people were more used to it in such places, that grief would become muted through exposure and repetition. It doesn't. I think it amplifies.

Family members look at me. They look at the body, and at the nurses, and I look at each of them, meet their eyes. Everyone's now crying.

'I can see the team here have done everything,' I say, trying to reassure them. I don't want the family to feel that their child was dismissed. 'The doctors on this big screen,' I say, 'they're the specialists for sick children. The best doctors from the big hospital in Brisbane. And they said the nurses here been doing everything. Everything right and proper, all the right medicines. But it sounds like she had an infection, and it made her heart too crook.'

My voice cracks, and I say it clearly, because it's kinder than euphemisms or weak language: 'I'm so sorry. She's dead. There's else nothing we can do.'

Someone asks if we brought better medicine, and I say sorry, there's nothing else. The nurses have given everything.

It begins. Wailing. Holding each other. Flailing arms. Pacing. It washes through the walls, and I can hear it from those outside, too. I step out to talk with the bigger group gathering. It's important for them, and for the ongoing functioning of the clinic, the trust in this place, and the safety of the nurses, that the community feels everything realistically possible was done today. That they weren't ignored. A chain reaction of grief is about to tear through the region, for days. Misunderstandings are best offset immediately.

A few dozen people are gathered. I stand on the veranda and look them in the eyes. I explain what I can. I tell them about the specialists on the screen and that we flew as fast as we could. And I make it clear that she's dead.

'True, Doctor?' asks an older man. 'She gone?' He wipes tears.

My god. I usually don't cry at work. But here I go. 'True. I'm very sorry. I'm sorry for your family, sorry for all your mob.'

The wailing floods through the group.

I head back inside. The nurses are devastated. We make cups of tea in the kitchen. No one can really drink, but we stand around and hold mugs anyway. We have an informal debrief, talking through the events since the patient arrived, what had happened, what went well, what didn't, what could be done better; but it's a hot mess emotionally, and it's as much a cry together as anything. These nurses have to keep on living here. They have to staff the clinic this afternoon, and tonight, and get some sleep, and be back tomorrow morning, get on with a job that's difficult enough without this. They sometimes deliver babies before we land. They manage heart attacks, and get out of bed at 2 am because someone wants Panadol for a slightly sore knee, or is critically injured. They stay and do all this despite occasional break-ins and sometimes widespread community violence, and still they arrive the next day. Every day.

We go. There are other jobs we can still fit in.

It's a sombre flight back.

13

Psychology and Sore Backs

October, Central Australia

'Fill your cup before you can fill someone else's.' It's a self-help cliché I'd never paid much attention to, because I'd never seen any reason to. I always did fine. I get to fly out of these places and head home to an easier life. But as I spend more time up here, the importance of refilling my own cup starts to become clear. I've heard plenty of cautionary tales over the years as others have burned out, and I've started to feel similarly at times.

'Memento mori' is another phrase I've come across often—remember death, or the inevitability of it. It's an invocation to remember the transience and fragility of life, and to appreciate it. Remembering death isn't something I need reminding of, but, like many healthcare workers, I've learned to separate a patient's predicaments from mine. Illness and disease are things that happen to patients, not us. They happen over *there*. At least this is what I'd come to believe, on some level at least. You empathise with people at the bedside, but when you walk out, you leave that emotional weight at the door. You have a quick debrief with a colleague, then recall a lighter story from earlier and share it, and head for dinner. How else will you show up to work for another couple of decades—hopefully somewhat well adjusted?

But as the sad cases accrue, and some of your friends and loved ones become patients, too, the line can start to blur—for me at least. The separation of home and work begins to dissolve. An elderly patient on a trolley in the ED corridor is not just another patient to be found a bed, not just an inconvenient Friday afternoon 'granny dump' by tired family members or an understaffed nursing home; it's the beloved grandmother you watched as she descended into frailty. Even deaths such as the one on that nutrition ward in Chad are easy to forget—as Sébastien had said, they're far too common—but watching relatives grieve hits me harder these days. Maybe I'm also just getting older. For a while, most of my patients were far older than me but, in remote communities especially, they're often my age or close. Again, the line blurs. But empathy needs a boundary. Where exactly that boundary is, I still don't know.

When I left South Sudan, I felt burned out. I didn't want to manage another patient. I couldn't see things improving, and at times in the Northern Territory I've started to feel the same. I've caught myself being the cynical person when talking to newer staff, thinking things like, *Oh, that'll never work here*—an attitude that serves no one. So I now actively work at the cup-filling.

I signed up for a ten-day silent retreat recently. Two friends had been on it. 'Best thing I've ever done,' said one, 'but you couldn't drag me back there. It's hard. You go deep.' But another person I knew had loved it and returned every year. I'm not overly spiritual, and I'm fairly sceptical of the alternative healing crowd, but this sounded like a good reset, a ctrl-alt-del for the mind. I was in.

On arrival, we had to lock up our phones and any reading material and take a vow of silence. This suited me well. Getting off-grid and away from emails and distractions was my aim, rather than any enlightenment. The schedule was tough. Up at 4 am, lights out at 9 pm and ten hours of sitting meditation a day. Meals were taken at communal tables in silence, with fantastic vegetarian food cooked by volunteers, and lots of it, but trying to avoid eye contact with others was its own battle. I desperately wanted to hear their back stories and debrief about the sessions. The bus trip there had been a teaser: I'd met a 40-year-old lawyer who did this most years, she said, and a twenty-something-year-old music student who'd never been before, and a 60-something-year-old widow who was coming back to this after decades. A hundred other souls were balancing on cushions in the hall with me, presumably—and hopefully—also coming to the realisation that they had no apparent ability to concentrate.

My first day was marked by back pain and a deep regret for not having snuck in a book. Then came an intense phase of irritation: an inability to get comfortable on any possible combination of cushions, no matter how high I stacked them. Then an annoyance at the guy in front with his constant sinus clearing, and then the guy to my left who couldn't sit still for more than a minute, and who had what was clearly the world's noisiest blanket. Random sneezes were like gunshots. My leg went numb. The one-hour sessions felt like three hours. Surely the clock was broken—no single hour should take so long. *I should've gone to Bali and rented a surfboard instead*, I thought.

On the morning of the fifth day, I packed my bag. I was done. 'Everyone feels this,' said the instructor's assistant, a carpenter who volunteered here a few times, a seemingly lovely guy. 'This is classic,' he said. 'Stay. It passes. You're over the hump.'

By the sixth day, I was back on the hump. My lower back was on fire. I decided again to leave. There were restaurants and mates in the outside world, and the weather was great.

'It's all just sensations,' said the instructor, regarding my back issues and my desire to leave. 'It'll pass. This is part of the process, of letting go. Just observe it. Don't react. Just see it for what it is, all transient.' I did. The pain was still there.

In the evening sessions, we had to occasionally repeat mantras, but I kept quiet. The chants made it feel a little cult-like to me. Still, my mind wandered incessantly. I could focus on my breath or 'scan' for sensations as we were instructed—up my feet, up my legs, across my lower back, or feel the breath enter and then exit the nostrils—but for seconds only, maybe a minute. Then my mind wandered again. 'Bring it back to the breath' was the exercise; losing focus was fine, but recognising that and coming back was the key. Still, my brain was a restless monkey. *Back to the breath*. It wandered again. *Back to the breath*. It wandered again. My job in the ED rewarded this pattern, with the constant disruptions and task-switching being an inescapable part of the work. A necessary skill, even. Undoing it seemed impossible.

Stories meanwhile grew around me. The meditation instructor walked slowly across the front of the hall at the start of each session, once we were all seated. He wore a robe, and we sat solemnly in silence, and as I watched him over the days, he looked increasingly like a boxer entering the ring. I wanted 'Eye of the Tiger' to blast. I wanted him to shadow box as he dashed out, drop the robe, break character and punch at the air, show off his footwork and ding the bell, and say, 'Just kidding, everyone! What's with the serious mood in here? Beers are down the back and the DJ will be here in ten. And no more sinus clearing, either, please.' This became a fixation, him breaking character. Not giggling became my goal.

Then I worked through shopping lists. Relationships. What I should've written to an ex when she'd slept with a colleague in a small rural hospital. *Back to the breath.* My first-ever kiss, with Tiffany at a school dance in Cape Town, before we migrated. What was the song that was playing? *Back to the breath.*

I started sitting outside and skipping a few sessions. It was spring, and the gardens on the large property were blooming, bees doing their thing. I lay on my back for hours watching clouds, something I hadn't made time for in years.

When the retreat was over, I felt almost euphoric—whether from the meditation, or because of being off-grid, or because I could now finally talk and leave the place, I couldn't tell. But I hadn't felt as clear in years. I had a few main takeaways: intense lower back pain; a deep reluctance to ever open my inbox again; the realisation that you *did* have control over what you fixated on, even if momentarily; and an overwhelming feeling that life was ridiculously short. This latter point was an obvious thing for a doctor to realise, but the last of my grandparents had recently passed. I'd thought about them a lot during the retreat. Their house had been sold and now demolished, and my grandfather's meticulously kept books and sports memorabilia and neatly labelled bottles from his days as a compounding pharmacist were things to be cleared away. Once-treasured items were now mostly rubbish. My parents had both had significant health scares, too, and by Northern Territory standards, I was well and truly at the halfway mark. So, spend your days well. And pay attention to what you pay attention to.

Cliché, yes. But still important.

This is navel-gazing, I realise again; I'm not the one who needs to cope with the difficulties my patients are facing. But self-care seems a sensible investment if it means that I'm not going to flame out—or throw a computer monitor across a busy ED, as a colleague up north did after a bad week of call-backs; or fling a surgical instrument across an operating theatre, as I've seen more than one surgeon do; or berate junior doctors for mispronouncing medical terms, as one boss often did. Another colleague pulled me aside after a difficult week and confessed that they didn't want to be a doctor anymore, that they didn't feel cut out for it. Ironically, they were probably perfect for the job: questioning and humble, rather than brimming with misplaced confidence.

I've had my own intense frustrations over the years. I've had a few run-ins and strong disagreements with management, sometimes speaking angrily, but over issues of patient and staff safety, I'd like to think. I've sent a few emails up the food chain, and then thought, *Uh-oh, definitely should've slept on that.* These days, frustration is the prevailing sentiment, though, not anger. And exasperation—aimed at systems and attitudes that aren't helping.

⊕

Back to Central Australia. A dinner in Alice Springs. Wine with friends under that wide, glorious, starry sky, and a morning trip up with the Flying Doctors. The sun's rising over the MacDonnell Ranges as we take off, lighting the long, east–west ridges in warm reds and oranges and browns. According to the Arrernte owners, they were formed by giant caterpillars moving under the earth; from up here, I can see it. Further north, we pass over salt lakes, then dried-up watercourses that tendril and fan out over baked earth, before we descend.

The always-chatty orderly meets us at the airport. The town's noticeably hotter and there are still no clouds. We stop quickly for fuel. The *NT News* headlines, usually fixed in steel grilles outside the servo, are worth looking out for while filling up. 'Bloke Nearly Loses Left Testicle' is a past standout—oddly specific about the side yet vague about the mechanism—and 'Man Stabbed with Fish' was another head-scratcher. The paper lacks the depth of the *Guardian* articles Maya sends me from London, but I love both equally.

At the hospital, I pick up my unit keys and take the ward handover. Back into it.

A smoking ceremony is held at the dialysis unit on Sunday morning. Since the successful resuscitation a couple of months ago, there'd been another collapse, and a death, both unrelated to dialysis but traumatic for the other patients. 'You treated a couple of them people before,' says Angela, one of the interpreters. 'You should come. Maybe you got bad luck now or something,' she laughs. The thought has occurred to me, but I know she's teasing. 'We wanna purify that place. Clean 'em out, you know? Clean all of us. Make it okay again.' I'm more than happy to attend.

A lot of health workers start to believe that they're 'shit magnets', that the bad cases increase when they're around. I'm not superstitious, and I realise that it'd be borderline magical thinking to assume I could influence anything much beyond what's in front of me, but I've heard enough comments like 'Oh my god, we haven't had a shift that bad for ages!' when I've started in a new place to have some mild concerns.

We meet in the front dialysis car park. It's a little after nine, sunny and warm, and flies join us as well. There are about 30 of us, a mix of staff and patients, and Chris is in the ED alone for the half-hour to cover me. I'll do the BP coffee run on the way back.

We chat and introduce ourselves, and we're asked by an older woman to form a semicircle around small piles of leaves. Fires are lit in four empty metal paint buckets. A male Elder greets us, and expresses gratitude to the renal team and hospital staff. He speaks of the deceased person but avoids using their first name; as is the custom, the name won't be used for a long period, and those who share the same name will be addressed by an alternative. In some communities, the deceased's house will have to remain empty for several months, and residents will need to live elsewhere.

'We gotta work together,' says the man. I recognise him from the Aboriginal council. 'We gotta keep our mob strong and healthy.' He's tall and dressed in a brown jacket, flannel shirt and jeans. Two female Elders speak afterwards, a little shyly, thanking us all for coming, and we wait for the fires to burn down to coals.

One of the new trainee doctors is here, wide-eyed and soaking it in. 'Settling in okay?' I ask her, once the welcome is over. Alice is her name. She's older than most trainees, having been a nurse for years prior, and she wants to do rural health—not the top pick for most graduates.

'So amazing,' she whispers. 'The town, though. Oh my god.' She asks if I've been to these ceremonies often.

'Second one ever,' I say. The first was on the ward, years ago after a revered Elder died, but the smoke alarms went wild and the manager at the time didn't allow further ceremonies indoors.

Sue from the ED is here, too, and a few ward nurses. It reminds me of the staff catch-ups we used to have when the hospital was smaller. It's a diverse group this morning, too; among us are people born in Kenya, Zimbabwe, South Africa, Botswana, the Philippines, the Democratic Republic of Congo, China, India, New Zealand, Nepal, Sri Lanka, and even a couple who were born in Australia.

'Doctor,' says Faith, one of the ED nurses. 'Are you engaged yet?' Faith never calls me by my name, only ever 'Doctor', perhaps because of her Zimbabwean healthcare background. It feels very formal. Faith wants to know when I last saw Maya, and why I'm working out here if she's elsewhere. 'You are getting too old to be alone. You must marry her,' she says.

Alice laughs. 'Ouch. I *guess* that's a compliment?'

'Nah, marriage is overrated,' says Sue. 'Been there twice. Having a boyfriend in another state is much better. A girlfriend overseas sounds perfect,' she laughs.

Faith laughs and grabs my hand. 'But Doctor, really. You must start a family. It is much more important than work. You can find work anywhere. You are not getting younger. Alice, are you married?'

She isn't, and I'm happy to deflect the scrutiny. My cheeks burn as I laugh, roasted first thing in the morning.

The fires burn down to coals. We gather around. The women place handfuls of green leaves into each bucket. Thick clouds of blue-grey smoke funnel out, carrying a strong smell of eucalyptus. We stand back for air—so do the flies—and one of the women calls us over, one at a time. She reaches down to gather the smoke and pour it over each of us. It's a delicate gesture, making curls of thick smoke, repeated many times. It's soothing to watch. The smoking buckets are then topped up with leaves and picked up by women wearing oven mitts—brand new, and presumably purchased for this morning—and we follow in single file, walking slowly around the perimeter of the unit.

'A really obvious question,' I say to the unit manager, just ahead of me, 'but you did turn off the smoke alarm, yeah?'

'Yes,' she laughs, 'but you can never be too sure. Two of us have checked.'

We file inside. Thick smoke quickly fills the room—'The fire alarm is *definitely* off?' people ask—and we snake our way around the unit, then the offices. I feel a little buzz. I love seeing this: an ancient ceremony—muted and diluted in a concrete car park, but still practised—hinting at another view of health and illness and death. It's a contrast with the sixteen dialysis machines here, these expensive, highly calibrated devices that'll run a person's blood volume out of their bodies and back in, several times each session, but that can never properly replace the work of even one kidney. A striking juxtaposition of worlds.

None of this was here a few decades ago, but there was no need for it. This unit is a nod to closing the health gap in remote Australia, but it's also a marker of this evolving disaster. This is all treatment after the fact, commenced only when kidneys fail completely, as a result of health problems that have usually been simmering for years.

We pass the chair where Sam had collapsed. Smoke is poured on it. This is where he'd gone through those rounds of shocks. Three generations of Aboriginal people are here—older women in colourful skirts and tracksuit tops, young girls beside grandmothers, mums and aunties, the future of all this, and we move slowly, sore backs and hips causing limps—

Loud screeching. Lights flash.

'My god, the alarm!'

We dash outside. 'The side office is on a different circuit,' someone calls out, looking at the fire panel near the entrance. Smoke pours out the door.

'Can you reset it?'

'No! And the fire crews get notified automatically!'

There's a lot of laughter and embarrassment. We stand outside, giggling, lights flashing on the roof as smoke continues to stream from the buckets. Someone calls triple-zero and tries to get them to stand down, but the fire crew arrives a minute later, horns blaring. The fire station is a block behind us so at least it wasn't a long journey. I'd last seen them watering their lawns with a hose from one of their trucks last night.

'Yeah, righto,' says one, climbing out in full, heavy gear. 'Smoking ceremony, I take it?'

'Yeah. Sorry.'

'Fair enough. We'll do a full check anyway,' he says, and pulls his visor down as he heads inside. Which is my cue to get to BP to pick up coffees.

There's a bigger universe here that I skim over. Cultural dimensions are largely lost on me. A woman presented to the ED with chest pain a while ago, and after some initial tests I reassured her that her heart looked okay.

'Yeah, I know,' she said. 'I just wanted a quick check-up. I'm goin' home now.'

I explained that we needed to do another test in six hours, and that this later test was the important one. But she insisted. I tried again. 'You've only got one heart,' I told her, as I often say here, 'and there might not be a second chance. Let's just be sure.'

'Nah, Doctor, this is blackfella stuff,' she'd said. 'I just want check-up quickly.'

I asked her what she meant, and she started crying. 'I been fightin' with someone and they put a curse on me. Whitefella medicine not gonna help,' she said, and leaned forward. 'I been sung.' She looked despondent, utterly frightened, and left the unit.

To be sung is to have a spell put on you, I'm told. I've asked Aboriginal staff about this, here and up north—specifically, how people knew whether something was a curse, or an illness that they believed needed Western medicine.

'You just know,' an Aboriginal Liaison Officer once said to me. 'You feel it.'

I've heard many variations of this, everywhere remote that I've worked. Traditionally, illness and death were attributed to curses and spirits. Here in Central Australia, I've heard the word 'Featherfoot' used at times, or other local words referring to a type of sorcerer, or enforcer, or avenger. Kids in the ED, and some adults, have occasionally been scared by the prospect of admission overnight because this person may visit. 'Pointing the bone' is another phrase I hear sometimes, which means to curse someone.

Not long after I'd first come here, a middle-aged woman was found in the bush outside town. She was brought in by ambulance in a critical condition and blood tests showed that her kidneys, liver and electrolytes were dangerously out of balance. She wanted us to leave her alone, she said, and she wouldn't tell us what had happened. I'd feared it was a sexual assault and got an Aboriginal health worker to spend time alone with her, but they came to another conclusion. 'She's been sung,' they said. 'Someone pointed the bone at her. She believes she's gonna die.' And so she'd wandered into the desert, to accept her fate and fulfil the curse.

Dying on Country is important. It's not just about having family close; the land itself is vital, I'm told. Easing death is something we do a lot. We're guided by family and the palliative care doctors in Alice Springs, and we do our best to make the process smooth and less traumatic.

Two dying patients are on the ward at the moment, in private rooms at the far end. There's an older Aboriginal woman, whose many family members are always coming to visit, and a homeless non-Indigenous man with end-stage cancer, who's declined treatment. Last year there was a 21-year-old palliative patient admitted here, too.

I meet with the woman's family in the first room. It's a bright and airy space that opens to a back courtyard, where children are playing and yelling—the patient's grandkids. Many of the visitors have come in from remote communities, which is no small thing. Cars must be borrowed or lifts found, breakdowns dealt with on desert roads and fuel money cobbled together. Accommodation has to be sought with relatives in their already crowded housing, or in expensive motels. The alternative is long-grassing—possibly for weeks. The social worker and Aboriginal Liaison Officer do what they can. Then there'll be what's known as Sorry Business afterwards, a prolonged period of ritualised grieving involving ceremonies, family time, maybe church, and sometimes self-inflicted injuries—occasionally severe, like stab wounds. Increasingly, we deal with fighting, too, especially if there's suspicion of a curse—the death of a younger person, maybe, or an unexpected event.

'Do you have any other questions?' I ask, after examining the woman. She's sleepy and not in obvious discomfort. They do. Lots of questions. Different family members arrive often and want to clarify everything.

I've got this wrong before. I've spoken to the wrong family members first, or misjudged timelines and prognoses. The latter is difficult in the best of circumstances. When I was a junior doctor in Melbourne, with all the benefits of ample tests, I'd asked a family to come in quickly during the night. They raced in bleary-eyed, only to find the patient, a grandmother to the kids, sitting up and asking for breakfast. 'She definitely didn't look like this a few hours ago!' I apologised. *Still, better to have erred on the more cautious side*, I thought.

Years ago, a well-known and highly respected Elder was admitted up here, and his family decided that we should treat on Country rather than transfer him. He was clearly dying. His blood tests showed that multiple organs were failing. We stopped testing and I clarified with specialists that we'd tried everything we could reasonably do. Twice daily I gave updates on the front lawn to a growing crowd of relatives—some in camping chairs, many staying with relatives in town or nearby, keeping vigil outside the hospital all day and much of the night. 'Tell 'em true, Doctor,' a few would shout, imploring me to be honest.

'Always,' I'd say. 'I promise. Right now, his kidneys are proper crook. They're not working anymore.'

'We can't hear you this side!' someone would shout.

I'd yell the bad news in the other direction. 'His kidneys aren't working anymore!'

'True?'

'Yes. And his heart is very weak.'

'We can't hear you this side.'

'His heart! It's very weak! He also has an infection now, it looks like.'

'True?'

'True. I'm sorry.'

For him to die in an ICU hundreds of kilometres away, alone, wasn't worth risking, they'd said. His passing in coming days seemed a certainty, but I couldn't give the family any more honest information. Who could predict these things accurately?

Days later, though, I was told off. 'You not tellin' 'em true,' a relative said to me, as I passed them in the corridor.

'Oh? How so?'

'He sittin' up before, asking for water. He lookin' much better.'

Incredibly, he was. And over the coming days, his sepsis resolved and his kidney function stabilised, and he even got well enough to go home with his family for a few weeks. But he did pass after that.

'I'd never have survived all that,' I said to my colleague, shrugging. 'No chance. Did you see his results? Three organs had failed. Would you have done anything differently?'

They also shrugged.

People here are *tough*.

14

Qantas Lounges

October, In Transit

Chris tries to sell me his medical director job at Central. We're on the same flights, from Alice Springs to Melbourne, via Adelaide. I'm going home for a few days and then to visit Maya, and he's doing a life support course.

'It's made for you,' he says, as we get a beer at the first airline lounge. 'You'll love it. You get a management allowance, and the bosses in Alice Springs are supportive.'

'No chance,' I laugh. 'You've shown me your emails.'

'You haven't seen the half of it,' he says, caving.

Probably not. But I've seen enough. Managing doctors is like herding cats. I remind him that he told me about the doctor who wouldn't come to Central unless there was a yoga studio in town, and another who refused to work any weekends as they'd promised as much to their partner. And the vegan doctor who demanded that their share house not include a meat eater; and the meat-eating housemate's reply that this was discriminatory, possibly even racist, as their background meant that meat was important for them. Then there were the sudden resignations, the personality clashes, the ill-advised hook-ups, the time two male staff got into a physical tussle after a stressful resuscitation . . .

'No chance,' I say again. I'm flattered he'd ask, but I'd have to give up the Flying Doctors work, and I'm far too blunt and not diplomatic enough when dealing with management issues. 'You've seen me,' I say. 'I'd ruffle too many feathers.'

'Perfect,' he says. 'The last thing this place needs is a shrinking violet. What do you think I do upstairs?'

Maybe so. But I've had enough run-ins with management over standards of care in the past, or with the occasional locum doctor who'd come for quick money and to do as little as possible. And then there are endless police reports and 'victim of crime compensation scheme' forms, the periodic court appearances on the hospital's behalf, the child safety reports and dealing with complaints. I've done some of that previously. The clinical work is plenty.

Chris needs to be replaced, though. His family is leaving town after a break-in. Intruders stole wallets and car keys, then sped around town and dumped his car, all while Chris and his wife slept through it. They were probably kids, but it spooked everyone. Weeks earlier, another colleague's family had been threatened by teens who'd pulled out a knife. Chris's family will relocate south, and he'll go back to FIFO like me.

His phone rings every few minutes, undermining his job pitch.

'Hello? You're kidding,' he says. 'He slept in and missed the plane from Darwin? But he's just had a week in Bali. What?

He wants to wait until next week for the cheaper flight? But he's working tomorrow night, yeah? No chance. Tell him to get his arse down there now. He can rent a car and drive if he has to.'

A new job applicant calls a few minutes later. 'She's got an amazing resumé,' he tells me afterwards. 'We'll definitely sign her. The problem will be finding her somewhere to stay. We've got no more housing. Nursing are struggling, too.'

We get up to fetch another beer, but a few minutes later, there's another problem, this time with a patient. 'Hi, it's Chris. What? He's still demanding a separate room? Seriously? Tell Jack this isn't 1955 anymore. White people don't get separate rooms.' Chris rolls his eyes. 'No. Tough. He'll have to share with them. My god. Like Damien told him this morning, if a separate room comes up, Billy gets it. Not Jack. He can walk to Alice Springs or get the bus there if he doesn't like it. It's not going to happen. Okay, cheers.' He hangs up. 'My god,' he says to me, and downs the beer. 'Sorry. You want another?'

Back to the bar.

Jack is tricky. He's an 80-something-year-old whitefella I saw on the ward this morning, and he's openly racist to blackfellas. He's also increasingly frail and lives alone. He gets scared when he's unwell and insists on being admitted for days. I do my best to see him with no judgement each time, to start from scratch, but I've also had to be stern with him and tell him that he'll need to leave if he keeps it up. He's charming with the staff, though. There can be a difficult balance with behaviour in Central. Certain lines should never be crossed, racism obviously among them, but we also have a duty of care. There's no other hospital to go to. People of many backgrounds will sometimes say that they don't want staff from certain other backgrounds attending to them—they'll hint at it, or even yell it—and we'll make it clear they'll be asked to leave if they continue. But that's difficult to enforce if they're genuinely unwell. The last time I told Jack that he'd have to leave, he wandered into town and came back with a bag of sausages. 'Cheese kranskies, Doc,' he said, handing the warm plastic bag to me. 'They're me favourite. You'll love 'em.' This was his apology, I supposed, or his attempt to knock me off. I didn't brave them.

These issues often remind me of South Africa, of the small farming town where my maternal grandparents lived, and some of the rusted-on attitudes back then. Not that my grandparents were like Jack. Both spent time volunteering, raising money for projects in the local African townships; but my grandmother would still occasionally make dinnertime statements that'd stop us chewing, and prompt my mum to nudge me under the table, as if to say: 'Please, I know! But don't start an argument!' Like Jack, they grew up in a society that saw racial hierarchies as the natural order. Even at their more subtle, there was a little of the David Livingstone to the attitudes—he was the Scottish explorer who'd wanted to bring his Three Cs to Africa: civilisation, commerce and Christianity. This is what my grandparents' government had taught, and their schools, even their church. That's not to defend it; I certainly don't. But this was their reality, and it presents a glaring contradiction for me: I loved my grandparents dearly, and they did a lot of great, kind things and raised a loving family—and they held deeply problematic views. Both things are true. Neither fact diminishes the reality of the other. Like a lot of things up north.

Chris's phone rings again. 'Dammit, sorry, Damien. I'll switch this thing off after this. Yeah, hello? He doesn't want to do nights next week if she's also on nights? Since when do they have a problem with each other? They had a fling? And now it's over? Already? For god's sake. Okay, let me get out the roster.'

I shake my head. 'And still you ask me if I want the job?' I laugh.

In Melbourne, we go for dinner. I come home to rescue my house plants and work on my relationship via FaceTime. He heads to his course.

My tax return is overdue. I see my accountant, Les, for what feels like an annual State of the Union Address. His questions delve deep. They're a checklist of inner-city, middle-class progress. I need a hug and a therapist afterwards. An old friend from university is in the waiting area, having just finished his appointment, and we chat and vow to catch up soon. He's a surgeon at a great hospital now, but I remember him sleeping on the floor after a house-warming party back in the day, shoe missing, shirt discarded, an empty pizza box like a half-finished book beside him, having won a dance-off the night before. His suit this morning doesn't fool me—I've seen his caterpillar-crawl move. It's outstanding, but I'm grateful we grew up before social media.

The office is on a high floor in central Melbourne, with plain walls and a view of a nearby park. I make small talk with Les for a couple of minutes. Then he walks to the whiteboard and takes out his marker. It's business time.

'So, just bring me up to speed again,' he says, preferring to start at the beginning each time. 'Married?'

'Nope.'

'Divorced?'

'Nope. Never married.'

'De facto?'

No. Maybe? I think we'd need to live in the same country for that to be a consideration.

'Kids?'

'Nope.'

'House?'

'No. But I do have a unit.'

'Paid off?'

'Fair way to go still.' I give him the figure. Eyebrows rise.

'Assets?'

'An old VW Golf. Drum kit. Lots of books. A huge didgeridoo.'

'Artwork?'

I think about this. I've purchased two dozen canvases at the ED door in Central and in various communities. 'Love Story Dreamin'' was the last, from a woman named Andrea, and she'd written the story neatly in Sharpie on the back at the triage desk. It was about a forbidden relationship under traditional law, she said, the dots and lines in warm, earthy colours depicting a man who'd 'sung' a woman to fall in love with him. As punishment, they'd been turned into a stone formation nearby. I didn't have cash, so transferred the money by phone as she gave me her account details, checking over my shoulder. As for Gloria's art, I haven't asked for a commissioned piece yet, but I'm told that it's one of those 'if you have to ask how much, you can't afford it' scenarios. A couple of other artists I've met also fetch hefty prices from international galleries, but cheap and cheerful pieces at the ED door are good for me.

'A few canvases,' I say.

'And you've finished your training, right? What's your speciality again?'

'Rural and remote medicine.'

'Oh, is that a speciality?'

It is. Not so much in the city, of course. I explain it, and I again feel like an outsider in my own home town. I can see Les trying to account for the missing zeros on my totals, but they've been spent happily on airfares and studies and time off to work elsewhere. There are no pity parties here, though; even my patchy income stream represents wealth for most. It's just that Les didn't completely rub out a couple of numbers from my surgeon friend's appointment before, and I can see them, and to me he's still a drunken breakdancer—an outstanding one, for sure—not a highly respected surgeon and father. And it reminds me that I'm living halfway between two worlds, neither completely here nor there. If only my photos were an asset, Les! Tax deductible, ideally.

I do catch up with a therapist afterwards. Not specifically because of Les, more as an ongoing debrief. It took me a while to decide whether I needed to see a therapist. It also took me a while to find one I wanted to talk to again. The first had insisted that I never ask how they are, even by way of greeting.

'Ah, sorry,' I'd said.

'Hmmm,' they said. 'We don't do that, either. We don't apologise in here.'

'Oh right, sorry.'

They corrected me again.

That relationship clearly wasn't going to work.

The second asked me about my first sexual experience—within the first five minutes of the consult.

'Oh, nah,' I said, 'it's more because of work that I'm here.'

'It's all connected,' he said. 'Why don't we start with any sexual experiences you've had at work, then.'

'I work with the Flying Doctors,' I said.

His eyebrows rose. 'Do tell,' he said.

We didn't finish that session.

The guy I see now, though, Colin, is great. He's older than me, dry, funny and blunt. He asks me this afternoon what I'm reading. It's our usual warm-up—either this or what we're watching—and I like it. He's got great recommendations, although at the private specialist rates I'm paying, it's the most expensive book club I've attended.

We circle back to work, and some persistent themes: getting frustrated with standards and a lack of progress up north, and choosing which battles to fight. Managing sick patients is easy compared with these other issues.

'One of my colleagues,' I tell Colin, 'told a new medical student last week that "This is like working in Africa, except that you get paid a lot!" My colleague and I had a talk afterwards. I mean, I get it. It's different and resource-limited and all that, but there's a big dose of cowboy, devil-may-care bravado in there. It's a red rag to me. Someone made the comment when I started that the coroner's jurisdiction ended at the town's outskirts. As in, no one really cares what happens up there. It was a bad joke, I guess, but it underscores an acceptance of lower standards by some. Occasionally, a doctor will arrive and do their own thing. They won't discuss plans, and they'll practise in a way that they wouldn't dare try in a bigger hospital—one where there are more specialists and a constant level of scrutiny. They'll prescribe drugs they have no experience with or try procedures they shouldn't. So am I meant to be the Zen-like, water-off-a-duck's-back bloke with all this, like some in management have suggested? Or do we always demand a certain standard, even if that ruffles feathers?'

Colin is all for the latter, he says. So am I, even if it's nicer to just be everyone's mate. But patient safety comes first. Chris runs a tight ship, although he's away increasingly for family reasons or training, or for fatigue leave. And the vast majority of my colleagues are hardworking, and practise at a great level. Some are even too hardworking. A few will drive patients home or go to the supermarket to buy them things with their own cash—items like nappies, infant formula or new bedding. One even paid for a pouch of tobacco in return for the patient agreeing to finish their antibiotics, a creative but less-than-ideal approach to health care, not yet in any guidelines. And for many colleagues, the issue is getting them to go home on time—and to look after themselves.

My bigger query today is how long I can keep working up north. What happens when the compassion isn't replenished by a couple of weeks away anymore? Like a rubber band stretched too far. And what if you've been out of mainstream hospitals for too long to be able to return to a more 'normal' practice somewhere—skills-wise or personality-wise? I've seen this with field workers. 'Disaster junkies' I've heard them called, when a normal life becomes unthinkable, or unachievable.

'Define "normal",' says Colin.

I laugh. 'You define it. I'm paying you for answers.'

'No,' he says, with a slight smile. 'There are no right answers.'

'Okay, maybe this,' I say. I tell him about the university friend I ran into at the accountant. Married, three kids, walks into the same workplace every day, with the same people. There's none of the relentless turnover I see up north. I imagine he has a barbecue every Sunday with the same good mates. My parents did this. Every weekend in Cape Town was a small event: school sports on Saturday morning, a drive to the harbour to get fresh fish, a long *braai* with the same close friends.

'You're not a barbecue kind of person,' Colin says. 'What, with the same people? Every week? No longer flying to work somewhere difficult? You'd die of boredom.'

This is part of the issue, I suggest. Surely it should be normal to want routine? To not be in tricky places year after year?

'Normal?' he asks again. 'I can tell you, after three decades of this work, I can't define "normal". Do you know how many people I've seen who feel nothing about their work?' There's a drawing on his wall of a human-shaped tape measure, looking towards another tape measure. *Comparison is the thief of joy* says the caption. 'Look how passionately you talk about your work.'

'Or frustratedly,' I say. And either way, I'm increasingly unsure whether we're making much progress up there sometimes. Providing a safety net, yes. But helping things shift? I'm not so sure.

I feel more like a bent cog in a broken, rusting machine at times. A colleague used to say that working in these places is a young person's pursuit—the job *of* a lifetime, not *for* a lifetime.

The session's almost over. Colin has another Netflix recommendation. 'How's Maya?' he asks, as we get up.

'Great. Amazing. Perfect. On another continent, though.'

But a few days later, I'm hugging her at the airport in Bali.

Two glorious weeks is what we've got together. We fly in within hours of each other, then sit in a taxi in an endless traffic jam. It doesn't matter: we're teenagers holding hands in the back, her normally straight black hair curling wildly in the humidity.

'Wait, this is your tribe?' she asks me, as we wander the crowded Kuta waterfront briefly. 'You show me this, and then you want me to move to Australia?' She laughs. Noisy bars broadcast Aussie football on their TVs, as sunburned blokes in Bintang singlets prop up the bar counters, a few with cling wrap covering new tattoos. It's an outback town exported en-bloc to Asia. We go for a cheap massage the next day, and as we wait in the front of the salon, a group of Aussie women light cigarettes while getting mani-pedis.

'Sorry, loves,' says one of the women, to the staff, then us. 'You don't mind, do ya?'

The staff smile, too sweet to say anything. Maya smiles. I bite my tongue. 'Your tribe,' giggles Maya under her breath.

One of the women laughs. 'We're bogans, and we bloody love it!' she says.

I suddenly like them.

Maya's tribe has its own idiosyncrasies over here, too. We spend the second week in a guesthouse beside lush, terraced rice fields. For hours we watch ducks and farmers, and Balinese women laying out colourful little offering trays, lighting incense, waving delicate hand gestures in the smoke. They place the offerings everywhere, even in intersections.

'You're all so *ammmaaaay-zing*,' says a North American yoga instructor at a class one morning. 'You're all so *brave* for coming here. For visiting Bali! Give yourself a hug.' She begins a chant, and I tap Maya's foot.

'*Your* tribe,' I say, and she giggles. This is ground zero for the *Eat Pray Love* crowd. Afterwards, our waitress at brunch is a heavily pregnant Balinese woman, ferrying plates and drinks up and down stairs in the heat, being corrected at times by patrons that they're keto, or palaeo, or vegan, or no, please, oh my god, this plate has carbs on it.

'How much longer have you got to go?' Maya asks her when she serves us.

'One week,' *she smiles*. She's tiny but her belly is huge, as if she's post-dates with twins.

'So close! And you're still working?'

'Better to save money before the baby comes,' she says. 'If you need a caesar, you must pay more. Better to have the money before. Otherwise, your family must find it.'

Maya says later that we could probably leave the entire surgical fee as a tip. It'd be a few hours' work for us, we suspect. We don't, but I do love her concern. I love that she's spent her career doing what she does. But therein lies the problem: it'll be our jobs that keep us apart. We both want to live together, and have kids, but our centres of gravity are far apart. She has an unwell relative in North America, and nieces and nephews there. My world's on this side. And we both love our jobs—most of the time. If she didn't do what she does, we'd never have met anyway. I couldn't ask her to give that up. I haven't been prepared to give up my work for anyone in the past, so it's not fair of me to expect the same.

Our two weeks together fly past. We'll see each other soon, we vow. Hopefully around Christmas in about two months.

We share a ride to the airport. A long, bittersweet hug. Moist cheeks.

'Call me from Singapore?'

'I will, I promise.' Voices crack.

Another flight.

Another airport lounge.

FIFO work, and now a FIFO relationship.

I fly back to Melbourne, to get ready for work.

Back to Melbourne airport the next day, to head north. I queue with well-dressed businesspeople, holidaymakers and families.

Back through Alice airport that afternoon, beside families, backpackers, FIFO crews in high-vis gear, and two people I recognise from Central.

Back to Central airport a little later, which is basically just a room. The always-chatty orderly meets us again, and we drive past a town camp, past the dialysis unit, and pull up near the mob sitting on the lawns outside the hospital, an IV pole beside one.

They're like a diver's decompression chamber, these airports—a staged transition between worlds, socio-economic gradients, opportunities and cultures. Or maybe they're a recompression chamber, because I'm increasingly unsure which place is the reference point—or which way of life is. Which context is the yardstick, the up or down, the more 'normal' or the more like home.

15

Remote Seafarers

November, Arnhem Land

The Northern Territory is vast. A quarter of a million people live across an area bigger than the UK, France and Germany combined. If you like being outdoors, or alone, this is the place. It's also a good place to *not* be alone. Almost a third of people here are Aboriginal or Torres Strait Islander, by far the highest proportion in any part of Australia, and a third of Territorians were born overseas. It's also the youngest population in the country. A friend in Melbourne once mentioned that most patients on his ward that week were in their late sixties.

'That's a lot of older people,' I'd said.

'No,' he'd corrected me. 'It's young! We'd normally have mostly 80- and 90-something-year olds on our ward.'

In the Northern Territory, most of our patients are under 50. Not many people make it to Clancy Number Three's 80-something years.

The population is spread widely, with 500 or so tiny outstations or homelands, some with only a couple of families. Providing health care for everyone is complex. There are a lot of flights and a lot of small, very remote clinics. I've worked at most of the hospitals and a few of the clinics over the years, and none is more beautifully located than Gove Hospital, in north-east Arnhem Land. A couple of times a year I try to come up to cover leave.

This region feels different. You need a permit to be here. Traditional languages are spoken widely; when I pick up my rental car at the airport, Radio Yolŋu is on the preset. People are proud. A few words of Yolŋu will get you far. Once I'd asked an Aboriginal man I'd met near Central if he was from there. 'No way, fella,' he'd said firmly. 'I'm Saltwater Mob! Not that Desert Mob.'

Nhulunbuy is the main town, situated on a peninsula with plenty of white-sand beaches and long, flat, turquoise bays. This is the land of Yothu Yindi, Dr G and Baker Boy, and it's where the iconic David Gulpilil films were made. The *yidaki*, or didgeridoo, originated up here; I was lucky enough to get one handmade by a master, a man named Djalu. 'Please just make one that you'd love to play yourself,' I'd said, when he asked what I wanted. He did. It's huge. I visited him to pick it up—he'd chiselled and shaped it from a termite-eaten log of stringybark in his backyard, his long awls and sawblades and sheets of sandpaper scattered around. It's taller than me and weighs a ton, and it was tuned to blow a low D. I'd sat for hours to get the circular breathing right, practising with a straw and glass of water. The problem was getting it home.

There's a local surfing club, somewhat unbelievably given the saltie and stinger population. Stand on any beach, and most days you'll see a croc or three. I watched a handful of surfers one evening after work, off the point at Yirrkala, the nearby Aboriginal community, riding the wet season swell, and I couldn't understand how this'd be possible.

'Stinger suits, mate,' one of them told me when he came in. 'The box jellies won't get you through 'em.'

'And your face?' I asked. His wasn't covered at all.

He shrugged. 'Small area.'

And the obvious question then: 'The crocs?'

'Nah, they can't be arsed chasin' ya in the swell,' he said. 'It's too tiring for 'em. They hate it.'

All of them hated it, though? Every single saltie in Arnhem Land? For sure, not one could be arsed? Just one spirited creature is all it'd take. Living here for a while clearly altered people's concept of risk and reward, and I was obviously still the soft inner-city guy.

I haven't been flown up here to contemplate surfing, though, or to learn the *yidaki*. I'm here to cover anaesthetics. I pick up my keys, do my grocery shopping and get reorientated to the 30-bed hospital, then start the on-call shift.

The adage that giving an anaesthetic involves long periods of boredom, interspersed with moments of sheer terror, also applies here. I'm a GP-anaesthetist, though, not a specialist anaesthetist, and I'll sometimes go weeks without giving an anaesthetic. My boredom is less, the anxiety slightly greater. The operating theatre at Central closed years ago, so to keep up my skills, I spend a few weeks in a large Melbourne hospital every year and cover gaps here, or at Katherine Hospital. The rule is to stay out of trouble—especially in these places. Help is a while away. Never start cases that are likely to be problematic, unless it's an emergency. Always have a backup plan. Things can turn quickly. In an operating theatre, boring is good. Boring is to be encouraged.

A large part of keeping things safe is to screen patients in pre-op clinics in the weeks before surgery, via telehealth or in person.

'Look, there's a doctor on TV!' says a mother, sitting with her five-year-old son in a remote clinic. They're on Groote Eylandt—'large island' in old Dutch—just a short flight south of us in the Gulf of Carpentaria.

'Morning,' I say. 'Can you hear me?'

There are thumbs up and waves. A few other kids jostle to be on camera, too, and a clinic nurse helps. Mum's comfortable with English. 'Yeah, he had one operation before,' she says. 'He went crazy when he come into that operating room. They gotta hold him down,' she laughs. 'He was fightin' hard.'

This I don't doubt. Five is a tricky age. I write up a good dose of oral sedation to be given here before he comes into theatre.

The next patient is from Gapuwiyak, a small community west of here, but the young girl has a chest infection. I apologise that we'll need to postpone her surgery and change the flights, because the risk of an anaesthetic problem is higher.

A teenage boy in Numbulwar is our next patient, south of here on the mainland, then a young girl in Gunyangara, a small island nearby. Then we call someone in Angurugu. These calls are as much a primer to the region as a medical chat; I'd never heard of these places before working here, not even in passing. And all this is just in our corner of East Arnhem Land. West Arnhem

Land is different again, and beyond that are the vast wetlands and plateaus of Kakadu—and this is only part of the Top End.

The more you know about these places, the more you realise you're only ever scratching the surface.

The telehealth clearly pays off the following week. 'Ah yeah, you that one on TV!' a few kids remember, creating instant familiarity. We start on Monday morning, as soon as the ear, nose and throat surgeon flies in. Most of the kids arrived yesterday. The good telehealth vibes don't always last once they enter the operating theatre, though, with its intimidating overhead lights and trays of instruments.

Our first little patient marches in happily, looking brave and defiant. This is encouraging. He stands on the bed and looks out the window, and Rowie, the anaesthetic nurse, cues up a Yolŋu music playlist on her phone. We're in business.

The next patient has crumbs all over his mouth, despite having needed to fast.

'Did he eat breakfast?' we ask Mum. He's been on the ward overnight, and everyone knows the importance of fasting him.

'No way,' says Mum. 'I been with him. He was hungry, but he didn't get anything.'

We ask the patient. 'Max, you had any food?'

He nods. Mum swears. 'I didn't give him anything,' she says, and I don't doubt it. But the empty biscuit packet in her bag suggests he managed a snack. 'Ah, shit,' she says, as she pulls it out. 'He musta done it when I went to the toilet.'

Max nods proudly. He did. So he will now be last on the list today, and watched constantly until then.

Our fourth patient is nervous. She walks in gingerly, holding Rowie's hand, barefoot in a theatre gown, curly black hair cascading from beneath her hat. Rowie cues up the Yolŋu playlist again and banters with her in language. This is the secret: a good anaesthetic nurse, like a good flight nurse. They're two steps ahead in an emergency, and you don't know how reliant you are on them until you're without them.

'Big, deep breaths,' we tell the patient. 'Blow up that balloon! Try to make it pop!' The balloon is on a circuit full of oxygen, and Mum stands beside it, looking on. I mentally double-check the drug doses, three syringes ready to go behind me. We try to make this situation feel calm and fun, although occasionally this part becomes a bit of a wrestle with a forcefully held mask—always with the parent's permission, of course. But internally, I'm focusing hard. Drifting a young kid to sleep and managing their airway is not to be taken lightly. And many parents cry around this stage, too, as they kiss their precious child goodbye and leave them unconscious in an intimidating-looking room. It can be touching to see, but I need no reminders of the stakes of all this.

'Some special wallaby milk now,' I tell the two, and I run in the white propofol medication through her drip. Down south I call it penguin milk, but there aren't many penguins up here.

She twitches a little. 'Big, deep breaths,' we tell her again. She looks at Mum. Her eyes close. I give another drug and then switch on the anaesthetic gas, through the mask, and the theatre tech escorts mum out. We'll take good care, we promise. Everyone's quiet and focused. As the muscle relaxant takes effect, we gently intubate her, then connect tubing from the anaesthetic machine. We watch closely for a minute. She's good. The ventilator's now breathing for her. We check her vital signs and tape the tube firmly, and only now does my tension ease.

'Great,' says the surgeon, stepping in. 'Pass the prep. Music up! We'll do the right ear first.'

The large microscope swings over her ear canal.

All health workers should go through this occasionally, I think—be surgical patients for a moment. It'd do us good. It's a vulnerable, scary thing, to lie on a hard table, trays of steel instruments being set up, gossip in the background, while you wonder whether you'll wake up. I'd had a chest lesion removed a few years ago, and while I was lying on the table, the anaesthetist showed me the tube he'd use, then the surgeon explained how he'd get behind my lung, and I thought, *Just tell me you've had a good sleep and you're on your A-game. I'll pay you double. The rest, I don't need to know.* Never underestimate the value of a good theatre tech or cleaner, either. Their small talk can do as much for an anxious patient's nerves as drugs will.

This feels very different to the public health work I've done. Maya's in Ethiopia right now, working on long-term policy; here, I can control the depth of anaesthesia moment to moment, but there'll be no effect afterwards. The surgeon's work will patch the patient's ears, improve her hearing and language, but this is reactive, not preventive. There's nothing we can do in here about the underlying health drivers. It's still satisfying, though, and it means these families don't have to travel to Darwin. There's an elegance and satisfaction in immediately fixing something surgically, too.

A hole in an eardrum? Patched. Done. I'm envious of that finality at times.

Obstetrics is my favourite part of the anaesthetics work. You arrive for one patient, and then there are two. It's almost always a happy outcome, but the emergencies can be dramatic. Twice this week I'm called to put in an epidural late evening, which often means a subsequent caesar late at night. Epidurals are satisfying, though: like a little card trick.

See the pain? I think, as I set up and explain the process and the risks to the woman, who by this stage is usually moaning through frequent contractions, and doesn't care at all about the consent paperwork, she just wants the drugs to work yesterday. *Now watch the pain disappear*, I think. I guide the needle into the thin space between a ligament and spinal canal covering, then insert a thin plastic catheter and leave it in place, the needle safely removed. Often the woman will disagree that it's all set up and working properly when the first trickle of local anaesthetic runs in. 'It's not doing anything!' she'll say. But fifteen minutes later she'll be lying down, sleeping between contractions.

Problem fixed.

And here, a few hours after the epidural goes in, a little Yolŋu baby is born. Happy staff, and a very happy family.

Too often on these trips there's no time for exploring. The hospitals book the flights, rostering me until I leave. But in the last couple of years, I've made a point of booking a side trip on the way home when I can: a week of camping near the wetlands of Kakadu, a drive through the western Kimberley with a mate, and a few days with a friend who was working near Uluru. These visits otherwise pass in a haze of shifts and musty old hospital flats and noisy motels. Fly in, fly out, see little else.

Fishing and camping are the big things to do up here, and one guy, Jonno, has a particularly good set-up, I'm told. He's a teacher in a nearby community, and our schedules line up on my last evening. 'Bring a few others if you want,' he messages me, and then: 'Can you drive a tractor?'

I assume this was a typo.

We meet along the foreshore in Yirrkala, which is about twenty minutes from town. There are four passengers—three colleagues from the hospital are coming with me—but Jonno's running late. The sun's already setting by the time he arrives with the boat, the Arafura Sea shimmering in deep reds and pinks. The aim was to have left hours ago, but he'd said the boat's engine 'needed tinkering with'. It's now that I remember some others declining the trip. 'Loose,' they'd laughed. 'Things get loose. Once is enough. You'll see. But you'll have a blast.'

I wasn't sure what they'd meant, but as the boat pulls up at the top of the ramp, towed by a tractor, I get a sense. The boat is huge—as in, somewhere between a backyard cruiser and a small fishing trawler, to my eye. Jonno jumps off the tractor and directs us. We pass the eskies and fishing gear from the cars up to the boat, then board and get ready for Jonno to reverse us down the ramp.

'Actually, Damo,' he says. 'You happy to reverse the tractor?'

I laugh. 'Oh, for sure.'

'Sweet,' he says. 'Just back her in. I'll guide you from the boat.'

'You serious?' I've never driven a tractor, I tell him, and this boat may as well be the *Titanic* for ease of practising with. Two of the other three guys volunteer, but Jonno's already back in the saddle, starting the tractor up, the rest of us on the boat.

'Hop in the water and guide me back,' he yells to me. 'Watch out for rocks.'

'Isn't this place full of stingers?' I shout back.

'Nah. Yeah. Sometimes. It's only for a minute. It's fine.'

'And crocs?' I yell.

'Shine a torch first,' he shouts back.

My other colleagues are laughing. 'You boys don't wanna jump in?' I ask.

'Nah, you're gonna do great,' they lie, opening beers. 'He asked you. He seems to trust you.'

I stay in the boat, and we guide him from there.

It's pitch dark by the time we're on the water. It's a moonless night, thick with stars, and Jonno opens the throttles. We fly. I get a little buzz. I'm thrilled to be out here—this region seems boundless, almost completely unknown, at least to me and most outsiders. You visit a rock-art site and some waterholes, but then you're told of a dozen better places. A family invites you to their homeland, and a colleague stumbles on an incredible campsite. Traditional life and history here are rich, and on display, far more easily visible to *balanda*, or white people, like me.

For hundreds of years before Europeans came, Macassan traders sailed here annually from what's now Sulawesi in

Indonesia, setting up seasonal camps along the coast and fishing for sea cucumbers. Some of their words are still used, and a few Elders still smoke long, thin clay pipes in the style used by them. For Europeans, though, much of this region was impenetrable early on, or unwanted. This kind of land wasn't good for cattle, there was no obvious gold, and it was a long way from the southern colonies.

We slow and drop anchor. The rods go out but there aren't many bites. Jonno fires up the little barbecue on the back of the boat, and we have another round of beers. 'Which esky's got the food?' asks Dave, one of the doctors.

'Blue one,' says Jonno.

'Nah, that's beer,' says Dave.

'Green one?'

'Beer.'

'Light blue one?'

'Uh, nah. Also beer.'

'Galley fridge?'

'Also beer.'

Four containers full of beer are what we've got. No dinner. Fishing is more of a priority now. Up comes the anchor, on goes the GPS and fish finder, and we race off into the dark. We'd have slammed onto a reef without the GPS by now, I'm confident—the outboard engines roar, and even with lights we can't see far in front—and I think about the people who navigated all this in dugouts, for tens of thousands of years, and later with dingoes from South-east Asia, and how they found food and survived storms. This is the probable region of the original migration into Australia, around 50,000 to 75,000 years ago—or so says a book I've read recently. On the clock of migration, this was the fastest out of the gate by a long way. The ancestors of Aboriginal people left Africa and walked across the Middle East and Asia, then crossed via land bridges and kilometres of open ocean to get to the Australian and Papua New Guinean landmass. In comparison, Europe wasn't settled until 40,000 years ago, and the Americas about 15,000 years ago. By any measure, the movement to Australia was incredible, and far ahead of others.

Yet here we sit. Not a nibble. A few beers in, completely lost if that GPS fizzles out. Hungry but having a great time.

Jonno suggests croc-watching instead. They're apparently breeding and highly territorial at the moment, he says. We pull up anchor and speed for another half-hour, then come up towards the shore, along mangrove swamps, to the opening of an inlet. A low moon rises and the bush hums with insects. We idle gently, lights off, scanning the banks with the four spotlights he hands us. Bright red circles glare back.

'That's a female,' he says. 'The alpha male would be near, for sure.'

The distance between the eyes is how he can tell, he says. An alpha male would dominate this stretch. There'd be a few females with their nests of eggs. I think of the crocodile farm at the end of the runway in Cape York, and the worker there who'd explained that the sex of the hatchlings can be chosen by regulating the temperature of the eggs. Keep them cool, they'll be female; warmer, they'll be male. Luxury Hermès handbags is what some of them will become, either way.

We motor up to a narrow point and almost get stuck. A ten-point turn is needed to get the boat around, as we duck under branches and throw off broken bits of mangrove. Finally facing the right way, we cruise back to the entrance. Engines off, we watch for the big male out here. I admire Jonno's sense of adventure. I'm not sure I'd move to a remote corner of Oz, buy a boat and figure out where crocs hang out. I'm impressed. A doctor I'd met years ago had spent months living with a family in this area, learning the language. This was incredible, I'd said to him, but why Yolŋu?

'Why French?' he'd asked me. I loved his attitude.

We see a male. He's dead still and facing us, not a ripple in the water, maybe five metres away. A literal chill runs through me. He and I know he's king out here: my neck and back feel it. Soundlessly, he sinks, no ripples, no trace. He'll hold his breath for a few hours if need be.

'Fuck. That,' says Dave.

We wait a while for him to resurface, scanning the water, enjoying the isolation. I always wish I made more times for these things, and for visits with people like Gloria. It's too easy to get stuck on call and caught up in admin, and never-ending roster and hospital issues. We open another round of beers.

'Hey Jonno,' I say, a while later, sitting on the back of the boat. 'Your engines are almost touching rocks here, mate.'

'Oh?'

He peers over. The relaxed vibe evaporates. 'The tide's going out,' he says.

He starts the engines and angles them up, away from the rocks, then revs hard but the boat doesn't move. Plumes of water spray behind us, but the boat still doesn't budge. He looks worried.

We're an hour by sea from the nearest small community, no mobile reception, and stuck at a salties' breeding ground. Not good.

Jonno directs us to the front of the boat. 'Maybe bounce on the front?' he says. 'I'll rev again.'

We do but nothing happens.

'Try hopping,' he says, and revs hard.

Nothing.

'Righto,' he says. 'Two of you stand this side, two over there. Jump alternately, as hard as you can.'

Nothing happens.

'This is serious,' he says. 'We'll tip over when the tide gets too low. Righto, you three, you're gonna have to get into the water and push us off. Damo, keep an eye on the crocs. If any get near, use this. Hang on.' He goes into the galley and emerges with a shotgun. He loads it and hands it to me. I laugh.

'Uh, mate, nah,' I say. 'You serious? I've never held one of these, let alone shot one.'

He nods. He is serious.

'But I'm more likely to shoot your boat,' I say.

The conversation becomes more sober. Two of the guys aren't keen to jump in. We rock, paper, scissors for the roles. I get the shotgun again. Unbelievably, the others climb into the water. The reef is at least shallow and visible. I get handed the gun and a spotlight. 'Keep the shottie on that one's eyes,' Jonno says, fixing the light on the male who's now come up. 'You know how to take off the safety?'

I don't, and I remind him that I'm more likely to accidentally shoot the hull or one of the boys. 'I'll fire a warning near him, how's that?'

But Jonno's all business now. 'Safety here, trigger there,' he says. 'Let us know if he submerges. And don't hesitate if he comes near. Righto, you boys ready?'

They say they are. There's an air of giggly disbelief and bravado, like we're naughty schoolkids about to pull a prank. It's infectious but I can't believe they're going to do this.

What follows is ridiculous. Ten minutes resembling a Steve Irwin doco set to Benny Hill music, with the *Jaws* soundtrack behind. They jump in and rock the boat hard. The croc submerges. I shout, they jump out. We wait, they repeat. I'm not game to shoot at the water. We see the croc rise in the distance, maybe moving away. They go in again and rock us hard, and the boat starts to shift, and I hold on, worried I'm going to fall with gun in hand and shoot someone. But the boat slowly moves. The croc sinks. I shout and they jump back in the boat. Jonno revs hard and the engines howl, and we very slightly scrape across the rocks. We go to the front and bounce. The boat shifts some more.

Jonno asks Adam to go downstairs and check for leaks. He can't see any.

I go to hand the gun back to Jonno, but he says to hang on to it.

The engines howl. Gradually, we clear the rocks with noisy, painful scraping and more revving. *This is going to be an expensive repair*, I think.

But then we're free. We move out of the river mouth and back into open water. There's another check for leaks. We're good. I put the shotgun downstairs, the engines open up, and for an hour we fly under a half-moon, bouncing on the ocean. No one says a word. I'm not sure if we're angry, tired, thrilled, hungry or all of the above, but if I wasn't leaving tomorrow, I'd probably give

Jonno an earful about safety—and then ask to do the trip again tomorrow night.

In the early hours of the morning, we pull up at the boat ramp, noisily, outside the quiet little community. The tractor's headlights are still on. They look to be dying.

'Hey, Damo,' says Jonno. 'You happy to wade out and jump-start it?'

16

Testimony

November, Central Australia

Billy's here. He has an 'open bed' now, which means he can come and go as needed from the ward, rather than waiting in the ED when he needs admission—which is often, these days. There's no *Top Gun* mask needed this morning; instead, he's getting an infusion that tries to squeeze as much fluid from his body as possible, via his failing kidneys. This eases the burden on his failing heart. It should help his breathing.

'Where you bin, Doc?' he asks as we start the round. His roommate today is Jackson, a lovely guy who's had two below-knee amputations and struggles with alcohol-related complications. Jack must have been discharged.

'Up in the Top End,' I tell him. 'In Arnhem Land. You ever been?' It'd be a two- or three-day drive from here, but some head to Borroloola at the bottom of the Gulf for fishing.

He shakes his head. 'Never been. Good?'

'Beautiful,' I say. 'It's supposed to be good barra fishing, but we didn't get anything. Not even a bite. I know, right?' I show him a few photos on my phone, and my respect for this Desert Mob grows as I do. The Saltwater Mob have an 'ocean that's like a supermarket', as I've heard it called, and water everywhere to swim in. Here, it gets ten to fifteen degrees hotter and the riverbeds are dry. They say that when you've seen the Todd River flow three times in Alice Springs, you're a local, but it's still too early in the season for any good rainfalls. Bright green grasses will spring up quickly after the first, a gorgeous contrast against the red earth. After a few more downpours, the insect population will explode, making the bush sizzle and hum with life like a wet high voltage cable.

'You campin' there?' Billy asks.

'Nah, too hot for this baldy whitefella,' I say. 'I'd cook. But I've been once, in the dry. I loved it.'

He nods. Camping is one topic we overlap on. He's proud of his old LandCruiser with its snorkel and sand tyres, and shows us photos. I'd embarrassed myself when he asked what car I drove. 'A Golf,' I'd told him, and I could see his disappointment. But Chris bought a fancy new LandCruiser with all the upgrades and took a few of us for a drive on a rutted backroad to an abandoned old mine, near a remote community. While he fiddled with traction control and aircon and boasted about how well it handled, we were overtaken by a couple of overcrowded old sedans heading to community—back sagging, a window or two missing, dings everywhere, sailing past us. Us: all the gear and no idea.

'You go campin' with your missus?' Billy asks me, and I say that Maya doesn't really enjoy it. 'No good,' he chuckles. So if Maya and I don't manage to make this work, I've got Billy's endorsement.

'You going to stay in tonight?' I ask him.

'Nah, home. With family.'

'You sleeping okay at home?'

He gives me the thumbs up. But the pile of pillows behind him suggests that he can't lie flat, another sign of his deterioration. His thumbs up are relative. A glass-very-half-full outlook.

Stepping into the ED again, past the furnace blast of hot air from the entry doors, I wonder why I hadn't stayed in Arnhem Land these past years instead of here. Or any of the prettier or less isolated towns and communities. There's something about this place, though. It gets under your skin. And this is where I'd started. These are the people I'd first met. Part of it may be habit, and familiarity, but maybe I also like that this region is the underdog, the hardship post. And who doesn't have a soft spot for the underdog?

But the underdog can bite. And this one does, increasingly.

A colleague is assaulted. Severely. It happens in their accommodation at night. Details are deliberately withheld, but it'll be life-altering for them. It's a dreadful scenario. To compound the distress, they have to recount it to some of us, because we have to treat them initially. The Flying Doctors retrieve them, and detectives attend, and the victim is the one who apologises. 'Sorry for taking up all of your time,' they say. 'Please, don't worry about me. I'll hopefully be back at work soon.' But they won't. No one could possibly be expected to come back after that.

A period of fear and anger follows. Some staff quit. Housing isn't safe, a few say. Most of us have slept in that same house, too.

Some management up the chain are fantastic and supportive, others not. 'It happens everywhere,' says one, shrugging. 'No need to overreact.' But there are tears, and emails, and meetings, and raised voices, and competence prevails. The staff compound now becomes uglier, though, as many trees and bushes are removed. High fences go up. New floodlights are installed, streaming through gaps between the blinds all night. Female staff will be given accommodation on site as a priority rather than rentals in town, and a security guard will escort people on late shifts home. The alleged attacker evades capture for weeks, adding to the unease, but after a while is caught.

This is what local people in the town endure—and often. The rate of murder here, and attempted murder, is *50 times* the national average. Try burying that statistic if it was a Melbourne suburb. Victims are almost exclusively Aboriginal. Domestic violence rates here are *ten to 50 times* higher than down south, depending on the source of data, and rates of hospitalisation for violence-related injuries are significantly higher for men as well. There are five times more police here than the rest of Australia, per capita. Little of this is in the newspapers. The news outlets that I do read, the progressive ones, seem to avoid the topic. The prime minister flew out for a few hours following a particularly horrific sexual assault, but that was quickly forgotten.

The difference now is that it has happened to one of us. Crime has almost always been among local people in my time here. I wouldn't work here otherwise, to be honest. Not even an MSF posting comes with a 50-fold higher risk of violence or death, at least not that I'm aware of.

I've had a few mildly close calls, aside from that whitefella grabbing me. A couple of times, someone had tried to force their way into my accommodation, in another town, as I lay in bed. Another evening, we were asked by police to stay inside the ED as kids sped up and down the road outside in a stolen car, sounding wildly out of control. Police apparently had to wait for them to either run out of petrol or crash, rather than risk causing an accident if they intercepted them. So there we sat, listening to tyres screeching, braced for a major trauma at any moment. A colleague in the Kimberley was roughed up by kids with a crowbar when she went home for dinner, and another was pulled from his car and beaten at traffic lights. 'Control your kids!' said a handwritten sign stuck outside a Cape York clinic when I'd arrived one morning. 'Because of last night, today we'll see emergencies only.' The clinic had been broken into, through an outer wall, and car keys and some other things had been stolen. The football field that morning had some impressive circles and skid marks from the ambulance, now on its side and out of action.

None of this is a specifically racial problem, I'm very sure. It's a problem of intergenerational trauma and the upheaval due to colonisation; of unemployment and welfare dependence; substance abuse and broken homes; and of energetic, athletic kids who catch and ride wild horses bareback in Cape York, and then do the equivalent with cars in Central Australia, egged on by TikTok videos. It's a problem of popular media that avoids the topic, or just rehashes simplistic right–left tropes rather than examining the underlying drivers; and of a justice system that constantly adjusts the settings when Aboriginal men already represent the most imprisoned population on the planet. If Carol can't steer her granddaughter from trouble, for all the concern and support she offers, something bigger is happening. I don't excuse all this, though. I hate it. Behaviour needs limits.

And anyway, I'm getting on my high horse, which is my issue, increasingly. It's not that I care too much to be here, as Chris says sarcastically of others. Maybe I've just been here a bit long, or I'm getting to that point. I've seen the same patterns, over and over; the same disengagement by leaders in our cities. There's little detail or specifics for solutions, just broad, woolly statements. I keep most of this from Maya, because I've debriefed enough with her. She'd bought me a Mr Grumpy T-shirt after I'd spent half our recent time together venting about this place. She'd laughed, but there's truth in it. And I keep almost all of this from my family. I definitely keep this from the dinner tables in Melbourne; I've been lectured enough by people who've never been here. There's a general consensus that a person's certainty about solutions to problems is inversely proportional to their distance from them.

This is my growing issue, though: how can we hope to address a problem if we don't talk about it more widely? And calmly, and in good faith, and with specifics?

Anyway, dinner at Chris's tonight. He's back to being a FIFO, and it's my turn to buy drinks again, so I've gotta park that NT Government car outside the bottle-o, chat with a cop at the door and hope I don't get seen by patients—especially the ones I've counselled regarding alcohol.

'We'd love to hear your thoughts,' says Lee, a medical student who's arranging a conference. We'd arranged this FaceTime a few weeks ago, but it's now days after the assault. Things are still raw. 'It'd be great to have you do a talk,' she says. 'You know, someone who's worked in Africa and up there, to come and share all the amazing stories and really inspire us.'

Uh-oh, I think. I'm flattered, of course. There's the impostor-syndrome aspect, but more than that, this is a national med student conference, and there'll be a lot of keen, bright, impressionable attendees. The trick will be to get the tone right. To walk the line between being honest about the reality—for the sake of the local people—and the challenges we see at work, versus a more appealing, 'you can fix this if you just care enough!' talk. I don't want to deliver some kind of TED-style, feel-good, Insta-worthy speech, but I don't want to deter people, either—I want everyone to come and work here. I'm also wary of yet more people arriving and saying, 'Oh my god, I had no idea,' which also serves no one.

I agree to do it. They fly me down, and I opt for a good slideshow. Lots of photos and a few stories, like Baz and an exciting landing, some good-news statistics, descriptions of some of the difficulties, and some worthwhile articles and books to read.

The questions are always interesting, too:

'How do you apply for MSF?'

'Do they pay well?'

'How do you balance all this with a relationship?'

'Would you recommend a career like this?'

All great questions and easily answered. Click on the 'apply here' button on their home screen. Nope, volunteering doesn't pay well. No, I don't balance this well according to my ex-girlfriends, but here's hoping. Yes, I'd recommend it—if you want to do it. But I wouldn't recommend it if you don't want to do it.

A more memorable question was asked quietly, in person, after a previous talk. I'd assumed at first it was a prank by Chris or another mate. 'How do you have the confidence to work in these places,' a guy asked me, 'even though you're bald?' I'd laughed. Turns out it was a genuine query, though, and I'd upset him with my reaction. I apologised, even though I was confused. Was he worried about sunburn? Being able to find a good hat in a market in South Sudan? He never said. Not speaking another language properly was my actual source of embarrassment in the field.

No hair-related questions at this talk, but there's another that takes me by surprise. 'I'd love to do Aboriginal health,' a student says, 'but I'd be too ashamed. I don't know if I could look those people in the eye. How do you manage your guilt?'

I'm speechless. An inelegant, 'Uhhhhh . . .' is what I manage. I look around. What to say? 'I guess my question for your question,' I say, after a long moment, 'is how does that help the roster? If there's no doctor for the night shift, because they're 1000 kilometres away feeling bad, what good does that do? Or if a remote clinic can't get a doctor for a week, or a month, as happens often, what then?'

He takes this well. He'd not thought of it that way, he says, and we move on. But I mull over his question later. Do I even have guilt? I don't know. Not enough of it? Or is it all still unexplored? I don't think about it much these days. What good is guilt anyway if it doesn't motivate you? And if you're trying to act in a good, useful way, what does it matter what your motivations are? I really don't know. This isn't a well-thought-out philosophy I've grappled with, just a gut reaction to a surprise question.

When Billy presents at 3 am, does he care why the doctor is there? Results are what matter, surely. And honestly, I'd rather the reaction of some close friends back home: 'Glad you do it, but I wouldn't. Keep the stories coming, though. Anyway, more wine?'

I don't mean to pile onto this student. No doubt they're well meaning and they'll have a good career. But I'm still upset about the recent assault, and the seeming lack of urgency elsewhere about the ongoing crises up here.

I'll try to write a book, I decide. I need to get some of this down. I'd tried to start a few years ago, partly because I'd wanted to capture some of these moments before they were gone; many of the Elders I've met have passed, and things are changing. I'd sorted through a box of notes that I'd kept—comments on the back of X-ray forms during ward rounds, or in a notebook, or emails to myself, often just a phrase or two:

'Fifty-two. Dreadlocks. Chatty. Living in Dry Camp to get away from town. Former ranger, keen to chat.'

'Grandmother. Grew up on mission. Happy to discuss. Contact is via payphone at outstation or visiting nurse.'

The arts centre in Pormpuraaw, on Cape York, has published a book of photos and recollections by many Elders. I'd picked one up on a recent trip. One of the women writes that she's the last singer of her language: 'If I gone, then nobody,' she says. The clinic manager tells me that a few of these Elders are still easily contactable, but timing my visits there to catch up with anyone will be the trickier part.

An interpreter in Central puts me in touch with her uncle. He's got an incredible story, she says, and he's keen to talk, but he's an eight-hour drive from Central on a rough track, in a remote homeland. A flight there on the small, weekly charter plane is almost as expensive as getting to Europe. Clancy Number Three is also happy to chat, but when I sit with him, his memory is fading. And Gloria's phone is offline again. Carol's happy to tell me her story, she says—thrilled, actually, and very proud—and I wonder if Billy may be, too. Between shifts and in the evenings, I cobble together a brief book proposal. I write a couple of chapters, then contact a freelance editor to test the waters. We don't get past the first line.

'No,' she says, when we meet via phone. 'You can't use this draft subtitle, for starters.'

'What's wrong with the subtitle?' I ask.

'You can't use the word "Dreaming".'

'Really?'

'No. It's an Aboriginal concept, and you're not First Nations.'

'Of course,' I say, surprised that I've tripped up already. 'But I'm saying that I *don't* have Dreaming. So I'm punching myself, right, not others?'

'Maybe, but it's still problematic,' she says. 'The bottom line is that you're speaking about other cultures.'

This I'm mindful of, but I'm not speaking *about* them, I defend. 'I'm speaking about working *alongside* other cultures, as someone who knows he doesn't get it. I'm not hijacking anyone's story, surely?'

She's still uncomfortable. A section with Billy she likes, but the conversation with Carol is problematic, despite Carol's consent.

'She feels like a token Aboriginal person that you've shoehorned into the story. It's as if she's a mouthpiece for how you think they are. Is her situation representative of others'?'

'Very,' I say. 'I mean, obviously not all of it. But yes, I've heard a dozen similar views during consults. A hundred, actually. Nothing Carol said to me would provoke even the mildest response up north. And in terms of the problems with her granddaughter, honestly, I hear of struggles like this a lot. I'm also not saying that she's the exemplar. Most Aboriginal people live in the city, anyway, not out there, and I'll discuss that stuff.'

I'm in Melbourne as we chat, still half-unpacked from my last trip, sitting at my desk, watching people wander past with rescued greyhounds and full-price goldendoodles. The vanity of pursuing a book about remote work sits uncomfortably, no less when I'm doing it down here.

'I hear you,' says the editor. 'But the reader may suspect you're cherrypicking people to fit your own narrative. That you're using them to project your own take on things. The question will keep coming up. Have you ignored people whose accounts or views didn't fit your narrative?'

I get a little defensive. 'Not at all,' I say. 'I have no narrative other than this is complicated, and we need to engage with more depth, and urgency. Ignoring all this because of our discomfort seems the bigger sin, surely?' I mention one of MSF's foundational principles, 'to bear witness', to speak up about injustices. 'And yet here I feel like I have to actively avoid talking about my work,' I say. 'Not to equate it with a war zone. Not most of the time, anyway. But surely more voices are better, no matter how imperfect? Anything that stokes the conversation respectfully is an improvement, no? I mean, everyone up north would need their own book to do their stories justice,' I say. 'That's very clear. And that's not what I'm trying to do.'

We talk for a while longer. 'Ever scroll around on Twitter?' she asks. She cautions me about wading into this space. 'You'll be misconstrued,' she says. 'And the thing is, the story has to be centred on you. This is memoir, after all. It's what readers will respond to.'

This I'm not keen on: a middle-class doctor writing about themselves, surrounded by people who're actually doing it tough. 'I can't,' I groan.

She laughs. 'I know you hate the idea. It's a balance, though.'

By the end of the conversation, I've binned the manuscript. *Maybe I'll come back to it one day*, I think. Or not. It's easier to just go to work, see the issues, bury them when I fly home, and take the salary. These beautiful, troubled places can stay an open secret.

Chris emails. 'What the hell is it with you and not earning money?' he writes. 'First overseas and now on your arse at a desk? Get back here! We're short.' He's still the part-time director as no one else has taken the role, and he's got a distraction for me, he says. 'We've got a big week ahead. Get back up.'

17

Under the Rug

December, Central Australia

Christmas in the Northern Territory is different. Last year I'd been with Maya, rugged up on cold evenings under the festive lights above London streets, pavements full of shoppers. There's none of that here. In Katherine, up the highway, the Rod N Rifle outdoor store has a large, brightly lit Santa on the roof. He's hooked a big fibreglass barramundi with his rod, all of this above the giant fibreglass crocodile. It's lit up beautifully. And here in Central, an inflatable Santa is watching over our ED waiting room from the corner, and the wards are outdoing each other with tinsel and Christmas-themed scrubs. Given where we are, it's very festive. Christmas is still a couple of weeks away, and I'll be lucky enough to fly out and spend it with my family, then Maya in the New Year.

'Another gift,' says Kate, one of the paramedics. She wheels in a patient and stops at the ED Christmas tree, opens a garbage bag and tips out the contents. A large brown-black snake lands on the floor. It glints under the flashing lights. 'Merry Christmas,' she says, as two kids rush over to investigate and prod it.

'You're sure it's dead?' asks Jo, the triage nurse, holding the kids back.

The patient looks down from his trolley. 'Pretty sure,' he says. 'I got 'im good with a spade. But I felt a snap before. Like a rubber band, you know? Maybe he got me. I don't know.'

Either way, we'll go through a full assessment. He'll get blood tests before we take off his pressure bandage, and we'll repeat them over the day. Most of these cases are fortunately stick bites—a branch or twig scratches someone and it feels like a bite—or the patient sees a snake nearby but wasn't bitten. And if it is a snakebite, many are dry bites—no venom has entered the body. It's rare for us to get a severely envenomated patient. But most of Australia's deadliest snakes are around here, so when it does happen, it can be dramatic. I also quickly confirm that we've got antivenom in stock. A few years ago, a locum doctor gave our entire supply to a dog and forgot to tell anyone. 'Oh yeah, oops,' she'd said, when a human came in with a possible bite. 'Didn't I tell someone? I thought I did. Didn't I?' Nope, so the Flying Doctors raced up to fetch the human and leave us some vials. I'm not sure what happened to the dog.

This week, our bigger problem is the roster. The night shift has no doctor. Trainees usually work these, and I've done my years of them so I'm reluctant. Chris asks anyway, but I'm not keen. 'Why me?' I ask.

'Why not you?' smiles Emily. 'I did them last week. Chris is on next week.'

Fair point. My turn then.

'Oh, wait,' says Emily. 'Chris told you what week this is, I assume?'

Chris shakes his head and grimaces. 'Sorry. You got the short straw.'

This can mean only one thing: it's Mining Royalties Week. The town is about to erupt.

A few times a year, mining companies pay the Traditional Owners and their families for the use of their land. I'm all for it—this is Aboriginal land, Aboriginal peoples' resources—but it's poorly executed. Hundreds of thousands of dollars of cash, possibly millions, will suddenly be available, and more people drive in from out of town. The car dealer will truck up four-wheel drives to sell for cash and the bottle shops will be even better stocked. Extra police will be sent up, and another ambulance crew put on. And in the hospital, we'll have to make do. *Eighty* assaults were reported in three days during a past Royalties Week—and those are just the documented ones.

Of course, most people in town will be at home, looking after their families. Many even leave town to get away from it all. A lot of the money will be spent on power bills, or paying loans or getting a new fridge, I'm sure, but we won't see that in the ED. We'll only see the problems. And there are many. The effects will reverberate through town, through families and kids, whether they want to participate or not. I'd previously doubted the correlation between cash flooding a town and subsequent violence, thinking it too simplistic. But it's real here. I've seen it. The cash is like fuel on an already simmering fire.

The next morning, I sleep in as late as I can. In the afternoon I nap again, then head in at 8 pm. No extra caffeine needed.

Two police cars are parked out the front. A woman is talking on the phone, others smoking. Grasshoppers are everywhere this week, dozens clinging to the entrance doors. In a couple of weeks, it'll be winged termites and bugs of every other shape and colour. Rainfalls have revived the region. Inside the ambulance entry doors, the bug zapper is sizzling and popping, and beneath it, three women and two men are waiting to be triaged. Tea towels and gauze and icepacks are pressed against injuries, extra chairs put out.

'No beds left in the hospital,' says Ruth, the afternoon doctor. 'Flying Doctors should be here in an hour or so. Five patients need to go down. Want to pull an ankle?'

I do. She introduces me to the man in resus whose foot is twisted far further to the side than should be possible. It's an incredibly painful injury.

'Tommy?' I ask. 'Ouch, mate. How'd you do that?'

'Ah yeah, Doc,' he says. He extends an unsteady hand to shake mine. He's incredibly drunk. He's a friendly guy and a talented artist, here often, usually in a bad state. 'I got 'em stuck in that big hole near the shops,' he says, explaining that he twisted suddenly with his foot still in place.

Not many injuries make me wince, but this does. I explain that we'll need to pull and twist his ankle back in, urgently so that the blood flow isn't compromised, and that it'll hurt. He's highly intoxicated so won't need a lot of sedation. It's also riskier with alcohol on board, but this is the one upshot of this week: alcohol is an excellent pain reliever.

'You right, Doc,' Tommy says. 'Just pull 'em straight, I'm right.'

'It's gonna really hurt,' I tell him. 'But only for a second. After that, we'll put a cast on it and you'll have to go to Alice, probably for surgery.'

He nods and asks for a before photo. We get a few extra hands and give him fentanyl to take the edge off. Ruth holds his leg and I grab the foot, where the skin of his ankle is pulled tight. In a firm movement I pull his foot down, hard, then over and back onto the ankle joint. There's a loud *clunk*. This is what I'd expected with that shoulder at the rodeo.

Tommy shouts. 'You fu—!' The words ricochet around the department. A kid comes to look. Tommy calls me a few names, then giggles, then shouts at me again, then smiles when he sees his foot.

'Hey, you fixed it!'

'Mostly,' I say. 'Sorry about that. But you still gotta go to Alice for surgery, I reckon.'

'I didn't mean to be rude, Doc,' he says. 'That was a big bloody pain.' He high-fives us and takes an after photo, then asks for a group pic. We oblige.

One patient half-sorted.

If pain relief is the medical upside to alcohol, honesty is the endearing attribute. People here don't lie about quantities. Down south, patients will tend to under-report their consumption. Delicate questions can be more revealing: 'Do you ever feel you should cut down? Do you feel guilty?' Up here, there's no need to be indirect.

You ask upfront and you get an honest answer—sometimes an astounding answer. Alcohol tolerances can be high.

'Pain where?' I ask the woman in cubicle four, who's next to be seen. She points to her upper belly. The paramedic's notes said that she's been drinking since this morning.

'You weren't hurt or anything like that?' I ask.

'Nah.'

'And you didn't trip or fall?'

'Nah.' She shakes her head.

I ask a few more questions about her medical background. 'Did the pain start after the grog, or before?'

'After,' she says.

'How much have you had today?'

'Big mob.'

'Big mob of which one?'

'Box wine, box beer.'

'Full box of beer?'

She nods. That's 24 beers and two litres of wine. This is the daily maximum that any one person can purchase with the restrictions in town, although there's also the black market with its eye-watering prices. Previously there were no restrictions and things were far worse, and even now the laws change often. Boxed wine used to be called simply 'a lady', or 'lady in a boat', because the popular brand's logo was that image, so a reply was often 'one lady' or 'two ladies'. Mosel is another popular drink, and occasionally the answer to 'What happened today?' Port is currently banned because the sweet taste made it too appealing. It was sometimes mistaken for blood when vomited, so an upside for us in the ED is less confusion.

As for this woman, we'll work her up for cardiac pain, gastritis and pancreatitis, among other things.

The Flying Doctors arrive, and we stand in the middle of the department and discuss, then bargain.

'Thanks, guys,' I say. 'Maybe take the heart attack in resus two, and the tibial fracture in the side room. And possibly the eye injury?'

'Where am I going to sit?' asks the flight doctor.

'With the pilot?' I ask. 'The patient with the eye injury can use your normal seat. The other two are reasonably stable.'

'What about the groin abscess?' the flight nurse asks.

'They've settled. I reckon we can drain it here in the morning.'

'And the fractured jaw?' she asks.

'Bus to Darwin Hospital.'

'No, I'd prefer the doctor in the back with us if we're taking the heart attack,' says the flight nurse. 'His numbers were bad earlier.'

It's a very fair decision. I'm being pushy to clear beds, and the shoe's now on the other foot. Their safety is paramount.

'What's going on, anyway?' asks the flight doctor, looking around. There's yelling from the waiting room and police arrive again. 'You guys got a footy final on? A big funeral or something?'

Royalties Week, I say, and they commiserate. But they needn't. They're in it with us.

'I'm really sorry,' I say, 'but we've got three more for you after this.'

'Four,' says Ruth. 'I've got another probable transfer, but they can wait.'

It's like a game of Aircraft Tetris, I think. Round one of *Who can fit where?*

Ruth will stay until midnight, she says, but she should've left hours ago. Lucy, another trainee, has also kindly stayed late. Chris is here but he needs to go, and Emily left because she's my backup tomorrow. These night shifts used to be sixteen hours when I'd first started here—4 pm to 8 am—but now they're a saner twelve hours. It's still not ideal.

The department limps on. We find space. No one dies. And then it's 3 am, and then it's 5 am, and at some point, I pee, and I have a muesli bar and coffee with Sue in the kitchen. She's my favourite nurse for a good debrief. We laugh and say holy hell, when are we going to get out of this town for good. We both giggle, and she tells me she's been looking at property in South Australia, in a small beach town, and that she can't keep doing this, even though she's one of the kindest and best nurses I know. And then suddenly it's light outside, and I've sutured two lips and a forehead and stapled a scalp. I haven't made it to the ward to say hi to Billy yet, nor review the others, but I finally get to the elderly woman in a chair at the ambulance entry door with a green tartan tea towel on her forearm.

'I'm so sorry,' I say. 'Barbara, is it? Oh my god. You've been here since I came on. I'm really sorry.'

Many of the others had left without being seen.

'Nah, you right,' she says. 'Town's no good.'

'True,' I say. 'I'm sorry, though. That your granddaughter?'

It is. The young girl's next to Sue, watching her mix a medication. A little apprentice in shorts and old T-shirt, barefoot, although this is definitely a closed footwear environment, what with hastily cleaned vomit and blood around.

Grandma nods. 'Yeah, Shaniah,' she says.

'She's very sweet,' I say. 'Very inquisitive and smart. What's going on with your arm?'

She burned it cooking a few days ago, she says, and now it's infected.

The Flying Doctors come back and clear three more patients, just before the day shift staff arrive. 'You guys are legends, thanks,' I say.

Warm morning light streams through the ambulance doors. Dead insects create a mat under the bug zapper. The Night Patrol—a service started by some Aboriginal Elders that gives people lifts after hours and tries to defuse situations on the streets—arrives, and they take a few people home.

Two patients go to the ward.

Two other patients abscond, leaving a neck brace and an IV discarded.

The social worker and an Aboriginal Liaison Officer arrive. They take details from the domestic violence referral book. There are nine names and numbers from last night, no other information needed. The system is that efficient for violence.

The cleaner comes through. Now it's sparkly and shiny, no bugs.

Chris and the juniors arrive.

'Looks like a quiet night in the end,' Chris says.

'You're kidding me,' I say.

He smiles knowingly.

Bed.

My sleep is broken by leaf blowers. I have a cool shower and a hot moment of denial: *Tonight is going to be a great shift!*

TV comedy and a bowl of cereal are my pre-match preparation, then leftover pasta, but it doesn't sit right.

There's a half-moon in the sky when I head over, the last shades of purples in the western sky, palms silhouetted behind me. It's almost idyllic. On the lawn embankment in front of the hospital, a few ward patients are sitting quietly, alone or with family members. One has her IV pole beside her. Cockatoos squawk and a camp dog limps past. A few years ago, blood was spattered around the ambulance entrance when I'd showed up to work during one of these weeks: fresh red spurts along the driveway and an arc across the glass doors, narrowing to droplets around the buzzer, and a trail to resus. A 'this way to your next patient, please' installation. Tonight, there are no spurts. A good start.

Ruth's still here. So are Chris and Emily. Not a good start. The department is full. Emergency medicine is often said to be 'disposition over diagnosis'—working out where you can safely send the patient, in order to clear a bed, rather than coming up with a specific diagnosis. Here, both are problems, because admitting a patient too quickly, without a clear plan, just postpones the problem. There'll be no fancier tests or sub-specialists to sort it out tomorrow, or ICU doctors or surgeons to deal with issues tonight. It'll be one of us.

'Cubicle five,' says Sue, as we go through patients on the screen. 'Where's she going?'

'The laceration?'

'No, the forearm fracture. Police have finished with her.'

'Partner in custody?'

'Yeah, but he's in cubicle one. He needs to be seen.'

'Women's shelter?' asks Ruth. The shelter is funded by the Aboriginal council, for women leaving unsafe situations.

'She's too intoxicated,' says Sue.

'Sober-up shelter?' I ask. It's open a few nights a week as a refuge for intoxicated people. 'Night Patrol could take her.'

'She's too drunk,' says Sue. The catch is that you need to be drunk to be eligible for the shelter, but not so drunk that you're a danger to yourself or others. The police also won't take people who're dangerously drunk. They'll drop them here, even if the patient doesn't want to stay. The ED has to try to manage them. Sometimes we'll insist the police stay if patients are aggressive, but sometimes they can't. Sometimes other services will bring in travellers who've run out of money and need somewhere to sleep. Sometimes people come in and won't even tell us why. This is the ED: if no one knows what to do with someone—be it due to a social, medical, psychological or financial crisis—they bring them to the ED. It's society's increasingly overloaded safety net. Humanity's catch-all.

'What's the woman in cubicle five blowing on the breath-o?' I ask.

'She couldn't blow,' says Sue. 'But I'll try again.'

A minute later I hear Sue with the patient, the two of them giggling. 'No, blow,' says Sue. 'You're sucking. It's a breathalyser, not a straw.'

They giggle wildly.

'No! Blow! Like this! Fffff. Ffffffff!'

But there are sucking noises and laughs only.

'No chance,' Sue says to me. 'She's too drunk for the ward. She'll have to stay here.'

This is how it goes: see one patient, two others arrive. Do a quick assessment, forget about the reasons. It was the same ten years ago, and six months ago. The cycle continues.

The Flying Doctors come back, and we again try to prioritise patients. Another round of Aircraft Tetris.

'For god's sake,' says tonight's doctor, an intensive care specialist from Sydney. 'Sort this out. We can't take all of them. You've referred too many.' She looks annoyed.

'Oh? You do know that I didn't assault them myself, right?' I say. 'I'd also rather not be dealing with all this.'

She has another go at us and Sue walks away.

'Yeah, I get it,' I say. 'I also do the job. Be nice. We're on the same team. Their notes are over there. Help yourself. I'm going to keep moving.'

There's an attitude that rural hospitals and their staff are inferior, and my fuse for this has become short. 'Fucking Central,' I'll hear sometimes on the phone when I call a bigger centre for a referral. Everyone needs an underdog to kick, I've heard it said, and medicine is full of this behaviour. ICU craps on ED, and ED craps on GPs. GPs work hard in their offices alone, managing complex, undifferentiated problems with no fancy tests down the hall, and they get crapped on by some colleagues and the public. General practice is the hardest of any of the jobs I do. Surgeons and anaesthetists have their own little thing going on between them, and most sub-specialities also have their pecking orders. The younger doctors generally have a far healthier attitude with all this, though, and it's great to see. Most do, anyway. Change is coming.

This doctor and I bond a few minutes later. She's had a bad run of shifts, she says, and we both shrug it off and apologise. And now that she's onside, I tell her about the three other patients we've got lined up for them . . .

'No, wait,' says Sue. 'Four.'

And then it's 3 am, and then it's 5 am, all of it a blur. At some point, I pee, and I have a muesli bar and coffee with Sue in the kitchen, and we laugh, and say holy hell, when are we going to get out of this town for good. And then it's light outside, and I still haven't made it to the ward to say hi to Billy, or review the others there, and I finally make it to the elderly couple sitting near the ambulance entry. She's got a fever, he's got a dialysis session in an hour.

'I'm so, so sorry,' I say.

There's not even a hint of denial on night three. *Get people through to the morning, alive.* The rest doesn't matter.

From now on, everyone and everything are just acronyms. Or organs, or conditions, or two non-compatible objects listed together. Names and contexts won't get much attention. In no particular order, cases seen over the next few hours include:

FOOSH: Fell on an outstretched hand.

PFO: Pissed and fell over.

DAMA: Discharged against medical advice.

TOL: Took own leave.

NFI: No fucking idea. They said chest pain, then leg pain, then left after a sandwich and cup of tea. I don't write this acronym in the notes, just mutter it as I type.

ISQ: In status quo.

RSI: Rapid sequence induction, for intubation. This may need to happen if this man with a head injury doesn't improve. His conscious state is fluctuating. It's likely just due to alcohol and concussion, and he'll probably be fine and walk off in the morning, but we don't have a CT to be sure. There's a small chance there's bleeding on the brain. If we decide to scan him, it'll mean a ventilator and a flight to Alice Springs, and that's going to tie us and the Flying Docs up. Chris is already here to manage him while I keep going.

LOL in NAD: Little old lady in no apparent distress—an acronym popularised in the medical novel *The House of God*. Actually, there are two of these tonight. I'm fairly sure they're escaping bad home situations. One complained of chest pain, another generalised 'total body pain'. When I'd asked if things at home were bad tonight, they cried.

A probable ORIF: Refers to the orthopaedic procedure that'll likely be needed, an open reduction and internal fixation of the patient's fracture.

TTFO: Told to fuck off. Actually, he told us to fuck off, so security escorted him out.

Fight bite, or tooth versus knuckle: What it says on the can. He punched someone in the mouth, he admits, and his knuckle wound will need to be washed out in an operating theatre before infection sets in. Alice Springs by bus.

LRTI for IVABs: lower respiratory tract infection for IV antibiotics. Ward. Easy fix.

TV versus forehead: I have no idea how this happened. Neither does the patient. A trip and forward stagger? Staples fix it after I remove the shards of glass.

Crowbar versus scalp: another staple gun job tonight, and another sticker in the domestic violence book. By now, the ferric, rusty smell of blood is all over this place, mixed with the sickly sweet alcohol on the patient's breath. I wear a mask, but it does nothing when I'm sitting centimetres from someone to suture their face.

A Westpac slip at the door is next. I'd laugh if it didn't illustrate the tragedy of all this. An elderly man is swaying, drunk at the ambulance entry, waving a Westpac withdrawal slip. He wants cash. 'This is a hospital, not a bank,' explains Sue. 'And you gotta wait until the sun's up.' He knocks louder, still waving the slip. 'Hospital!' shouts Sue. 'Not bank!' She points to the sky. 'Wait for the sun!' We call the Night Patrol to take him to the sober-up shelter. Then we laugh. But we shouldn't.

And then, once again, it's 3 am, and then it's 5 am, and I'm nauseous and headachy from fatigue. At some point, I pee, I have a muesli bar and coffee with Sue in the kitchen, but we don't laugh. The ambulance brings a woman in the early hours. She's been terribly assaulted. We call others for help, and she flies out for urgent surgery.

A shower.

A sleeping tablet.

Bed.

One to go.

18

Visual Fields

December, Central Australia

It's an unusual start to my last nightshift for the week: the ED phone rings, and the caller asks if I'm one of the doctors. 'I know this is gonna sound weird,' he says. 'Are you bald?'

I look around. It's not Chris pranking me. I can see him. 'You offering a cure?' I ask.

'Nah, sorry,' he says. 'I'm one of the new paramedics helping this week. We're just on our way to the hospital, and the patient says he doesn't want to see the baldie doctor. I'm just quoting him. Is there someone else he can see?'

'Is it Luke?' I ask.

'Yeah, that's him. Sorry, I don't mean to sound rude. He wants his foot looked at, but he won't see you, he says.'

Fair enough. Luke was abusive with the nursing staff, and I'd told him that he'd need to apologise to them or wait to see the day staff. I get tired of the way hospitals put up 'no tolerance for abuse' signs but then fail to enforce them. We receive enough abuse from intoxicated or severely unwell patients that we have to endure—in every hospital, and from all groups—so if they're not urgently unwell, and it's not a head injury or a severe medical issue causing their behaviour, they can come back later. Or apologise.

'Oh my god,' I laugh, when the paramedic arrives. 'You didn't have to write it down, surely?' He's quoted Luke in his typed notes, and it's now forever in the file.

The next patient is extremely polite. He's handcuffed, and the police bring him for a fit-for-custody check. This is an assessment to confirm that a person's medically safe to be held in custody for the next 24 hours. He's the healthiest-looking person in the hospital, staff included. This is often the case when the police bring in young men.

'Town's kicking off early,' says one of the officers. 'We really need to get out of here. Any chance you could see him quickly?'

Sue looks over. 'The others are stable,' she says. 'Flying Doctors are taking out the two resus patients soon. Go for it.'

Sue triages him, and I take the man into a room on the side. I ask the officers to stay outside and shut the door behind me, because I prefer to talk with patients alone, to give them their privacy. He'll have none for a while.

'Hi, I'm Damien,' I say to the man. 'Any health troubles?' He's wearing a football T-shirt, shorts and sandals. He speaks softly.

'No. I'm right, Doc.'

'Any injuries?'

'Nah.'

'You got paining anywhere?'

He shakes his head.

'No heart troubles, diabetes, anything like that?'

'Nah, I'm right.'

'Any medicines you normally take?'

'No.'

'Any medicines that make you crook?'

'Nah.'

I realise I've forgotten the custody paperwork that I need to fill in, so head out to get it. One of the officers whispers to me as I come back. 'Probably the guy responsible for last night,' he says.

'For what?'

'That rape. That young woman. Heard she flew out for urgent surgery.'

This stops me. I shouldn't know. I don't ask, they don't tell. That's how it usually goes. I need to be neutral. The woman had life-changing injuries, and it's one of the few times I've seen nurses cry up here. I'd asked Ruth to come in to do an initial exam on her—having a man look at her wasn't appropriate—and she was shocked. She's done a lot of these forensic exams. We've all had to do some: multiple swabs, detailed sketches, intimate examinations, strict chain-of-evidence rules and scrupulous attention to detail, as the samples will undergo DNA analysis. It takes us at least three or four hours. On a busy night shift, the time alone creates its own problem. We sometimes need to fly the victims to the forensic medicine specialists in Alice instead.

'Wait,' I say to the officer. 'Doesn't he need a forensic exam, then?'

'No, he'll be transferred to Alice tonight or tomorrow morning,' he tells me. 'We just need an initial clearance.'

I take a deep breath. *Be neutral.* I step in and shut the door behind me. 'I just need to do a quick exam,' I say to the man, 'and then we're done.'

He sits on the bed. I do a once-over for injuries. He rests his heavy cuffs on his lap. Prisoners sometimes have leg chains as well, making an exam more awkward. There's a lower security work camp just out of town, as well, and they usually arrive uncuffed in distinctive yellow T-shirts.

'I didn't mean for trouble,' he says, as I listen to his heart.

'Hold on,' I say.

'I didn't mean for trouble,' he says again, quietly.

'Hang on,' I say. 'I can't hear your heart when you're talking.'

'I can't remember, you know?' he says. 'I been drinkin' too much.'

'I'm not the cops, mate,' I say. There's a snippy tone in my voice. I'm not neutral. 'I'm just the doctor. You can explain it to the cops after. I'm just making sure you're right, yeah?'

He starts crying.

I ask him to lie down so I can feel his abdomen. I help him lie back, supporting his back and holding one of his hands. The cuffs are heavy and solid.

'She right?' he asks.

'No,' I say. But what I should say is, 'I don't know.' Or just ignore the question.

'I don't even remember, I didn't—'

'Mate, quiet. Let me finish the check-up.'

I don't want to hear it.

I don't want to contemplate his side, his backstory, her future, the situation in town, the relentlessness of all this. That her life will never be the same, and that there'll be another Aboriginal person jailed. One of us working tonight will probably have to give testimony in court about this, and sound professional and dispassionate. The woman will need multiple surgeries and have long-term medical issues, to say nothing of the psychological trauma. She's young and otherwise healthy and had a whole life ahead. This is a loss for everyone. Her family and community will suffer as well. His, too. I don't believe that a person who grows up in a stable, functional environment, and who sees a useful place for themself in society, chooses to act like this. Maybe some do. This happens everywhere, yes. But not at these rates. Not even close. This is a wider failure of the system and the conditions here.

On and on this goes.

Where's the outrage?

There'd be protests if this happened in the cities.

Here, it won't make the papers. It's not noteworthy. Or it's too uncomfortable.

I finish the paperwork. The police take him. I head back through the waiting room. I'd punt that inflatable Santa if no one was around, send him sailing across the waiting room, across the Territory and into Canberra, with a big sign strapped to his chest, saying, 'For fuck's sake, people! Get angry about this! And send help!'

I walk out to find Sue. 'Quick chat?' I ask. We head into the small tearoom. Two extra nurses are rostered on tonight, so there are four, and the others can hold the floor for a moment. I tell Sue what the officer had said, and she gasps. 'Oh my god. He was so polite with me. My god. He was in that little triage room with me. That gives me chills.'

It's awful, but both of us have seen cases as bad as this. Some even more graphic. This will be the only debrief we have.

But I'm angry. This week will pass, and we'll never talk about this again, and I'll enjoy my break in Melbourne and come back reasonably okay. The anger will have ebbed, mostly.

And this is again part of the problem.

Where's the wider conversation?

Maybe we just don't know what to say.

Sue makes herself a tea. 'Want one?'

I do. There's leftover cake on the table, too. 'This for us?'

'Deb's birthday today.'

I open the lid and wave off the flies.

'Still good?' I ask. It's warm, with clumps of cream sagging on top. She peers in and the flies settle back.

'Probably,' she says.

Hell yes! How good is this now? A debrief, a piece of cake, and a cheap teabag in a paper cup.

Sue and I chat. We've said it all before, but it helps. Shrugged shoulders, angry venting, a good swear, gossip, a laugh.

'The bigotry of low expectations' is a line I've heard spoken by a few Aboriginal activists. This wouldn't be allowed to happen elsewhere, we agree. It'd never be dismissed if it was happening to other people. 'Don't confuse this with culture,' I've heard another Elder say. 'This is dysfunction.' But then I've had colleagues elsewhere say, 'Oh well, there's violence everywhere. It's not fair to talk about one place.' But who does that serve? The deflection undermines the people here.

'Go see the eye patient,' says Sue. 'See something nice. Have another piece of cake first.'

The inflatable Santa's about done in the waiting room, too. Face down, flat, needing a resus cubicle. A few patients are sleeping on the plastic chairs. Others are waiting quietly. The woman with the eye pain follows me into the side room. It's the same room I'd just examined that man in.

'I'm so sorry for the wait,' I say.

'Nah, you right,' she says. 'Town's no good.'

We make small talk for a minute.

'So, what's happened with your eye?'

She thinks something may be stuck in it. I ask some questions and do a brief exam, then guide her to a chair on one side of the slit lamp: an upright, microscope-like device we keep in this room. She rests her chin on the guard and I sit on the opposite side, adjusting the scope's lenses to focus on her cornea. There's a small piece of debris stuck near her pupil. It's an easy fix. She sits back and I drop local anaesthetic onto her eye. I reassure her that I've got a steady hand as I open a needle. She laughs nervously. We both sit forward at the scope again. With the needle, I approach from the side and gently scoop the foreign body off her eye's surface. It comes off easily. Metal foreign bodies will often rust onto the eye and break up as you lift them, requiring a few gentle attempts. This one is probably wood.

'Almost done,' I say. 'Blink a few times if you need, and then I'll check the rest of your eye. I think I got that dirt.'

She sits forward again and I focus. The scope has a joystick for control, and as I manipulate it, the surface of her eye skates past in minute detail. The smooth, transparent dome of her cornea is magnified many times, her pupil behind it. Both of us are silent. I slow my breath to reduce my movement. She can't feel anything—this is just a light shining across her eye—and as I zoom forward slowly, the image passes through her cornea, then focuses on part of her iris, the coloured part surrounding her pupil. It's almost like a kelp forest at this magnification—an intricate, mesh-like structure. It reacts to the light, constantly adjusting the pupil's size, its three-dimensional network beating and waving, never still, and I steal the moment. It's meditative, like watching the Milky Way on a clear night. 'Cosmic insignificance therapy', I've heard these moments called: a reminder that things around us are more awesome than we remember when our day-to-day life drags us into its problems or trivialities. What I'm watching is a small triumph of biology, chemistry and neurology. One visual pathway regarding another; an elegant symmetry of neurons and receptors and feedback loops and brainstem nuclei and consciousness.

'All done,' I say, sitting back 'This was the piece.' I show her the tip of the needle.

'True one?' she laughs. 'So small.'

'It is. But the front of the eye is so sensitive. Would've felt much bigger, I bet.'

'Yeah, I wasn't gonna sleep tonight if I didn't come.'

I give her some drops and a patch for the numb eye, and she's good to go. 'Sorry again for the wait.'

I should've been an ophthalmologist, I think. Problems that you can fix with your skilled hands. Fewer police reports. Fewer issues that we're powerless to address tonight.

The Flying Doctors land. They try to clear three beds. 'We need a high-speed rail to Alice,' we all half-joke.

The Night Patrol arrives to pick up someone. 'You mob want coffees from BP?' the driver asks, limping in. He's a lovely older guy with a bad back. It's very kind of him, we say, but we're good for now. He says hi to a few patients and tells a youngfella who's shouting drunkenly to behave, then hits the road again.

I'm called to the ward, where a child's fever has spiked. Constance, a long-term nurse who's originally from Southern Africa, is walking up the long, dim corridor with a bedpan when I pass. A patient with dementia is yelling at her. She smiles at me. 'Doctor, how is it in emergency?'

'It's my last night, Constance. And just as well. How are you going?'

'Very well,' she says. She's just booked to go home to see family for the first time in years. She asks how Maya and I are going, which is very kind. These long-term nurses have hearts of gold. They put up with a lot.

'That febrile child,' I say. 'Is it the bronchiolitis patient? Or that new boy, just before?'

The new boy, she says. He came in under the care of the Department of Children and Families. An assigned carer is in the corner of his room, but doesn't know him well—they only met late yesterday. Like this man, many of the child safety workers here are migrants, some of them very recent arrivals. It's a high-turnover job. I can't imagine it'd be easy. Very few people come from the cities for these roles. Why would they? Trying to reconcile the needs of children versus the rights of their parents, and all against the backdrop of injustices and culture and history, including the Stolen Generations, among so much else. There's no chance I'd do it. One of my medical colleagues volunteered as a short-term foster parent up here. She took in a child for two-week crisis care, and she'd had to hide him; the mother was furious and reportedly looking for him in town. I spent a little time with the child and my colleague, helping her out a little with cooking, but we felt terribly guilty and conflicted about the whole thing. There was no question the child's household was in a state of chaos, and he clearly needed urgent care, but that's the thing here: you have ideals, but they may not hold up. So you need to change them.

You arrive with a notion of helping, of doing the right thing, empowering people. But your ideas of what will help and empower people can become muddy. You query your opinions. You come up hard against the reality that you have to do things that you'd previously never considered, or that people elsewhere will disapprove of.

I frequently report men and women for domestic violence. By law, I have to. We all do. It's a streamlined process: we just put a sticker in the book. I also encourage people to press charges for assaults, even if they're not domestic, because I want the damage to stop. But this means that I'm part of a system that imprisons First Nations people at the highest rate of any ethnic group in the world. What should I do? My obligation is to my patients. The broader impact? I'll ponder that during public health discussions, in a nice room, 3000 kilometres south of here, with all the time to talk, no patients waiting to be sutured and a cafe in the foyer.

People gotta work, I hear myself saying. Like Carol had said. And most people I've met up here want to. Structure is good, and necessary. No one can flourish with long, unstructured days, surely. Old ways are gone but new ways are unclear. A friend of mine gets deeply upset when I make a comment about the need for work, though, as we chat over dinner in a nice restaurant. 'What?' she asks, taken aback, and goes from zero to 100 in a moment. 'You want to make people work? And what then? Reduce welfare and *force* people to work? What, and starve them if they don't? Like a war camp?'

Nope. Definitely not. I just hear constantly that people here want jobs. And those who have good jobs really appreciate them. Some say that it altered a difficult trajectory they were on.

A trial policy was introduced for 'problem' drinkers in the Northern Territory, to have them undergo mandatory detox in a locked hospital unit. Many doctors here refused to do it, but I didn't—rightly or not. One patient was pregnant and drinking heavily. A study of some remote communities in the Kimberley found that around 15 per cent of kids had FASD, which causes lifelong disabilities—incurable, but entirely preventable. So yes, I agreed to manage her in here. I agreed to manage other patients, too. I'll try anything that helps. What's more important: an adult's rights or a child's future?

I honestly don't know.

'But everyone has the right to drink,' I often hear in the southern cities. 'We just need to provide enough support so that they can seek advice to cut down, if they'd like.'

I'd agreed. But that was years ago, before I came here. Now, I just want a handbrake applied, urgently, to reduce the harm. Alcohol misuse is a symptom of trauma, and it's a cause of even more. It becomes its own vortex of destruction, a self-perpetuating and accelerating one. This town shouldn't be a battle zone.

I once spent an afternoon at a drug and alcohol rehabilitation centre near here as the guest speaker at a men's health yarning circle. Thirty or so men sat around, and we chatted about heart disease, STIs, consent, grog, sex, prostates, check-ups—all the good blokey stuff. There were some great questions, and some worrying ones reflecting fundamental misunderstandings, and I couldn't leave quickly enough afterwards. I felt sad, and angry. I'd talked with a few individuals about how they ended up in there. It was heartbreaking: the same stories, over and over, as with the hospital here. None of the men wanted things to turn out that way. The ones who'd been sentenced to attend the program were ashamed. They felt they'd let their families and culture down. Most hated grog, and ganja, and being drunk, and didn't recognise themselves on it. This wasn't their culture, they said, but there was an ingrained social pressure to drink in these towns, and long days in which to do it. They felt obliged. Family drank around them. In communities where alcohol was banned, the outskirts and bush camps were littered with empty cans and bottles. Payday was to be spent drinking, and funerals often involved drink. 'Thirsty Thursday' is what they used to call the bans on takeaway on the days Centrelink released payments, to postpone the chaos a day. A book written about this town by a celebrated Aboriginal author, *Grog Wars*, details the fight by many Elders who foresaw this trouble, and who didn't want this. Grog was never a part of culture. Even the word 'grog' echoes the early colonial days, coming from the name of the watered-down rum served by a British captain.

So what now? What does one do with all this, seeing and hearing it repeatedly?

I have no idea.

'Moral injury' is a term I hear increasingly. It describes the psychological impact of having to do things that go against your long-held values or beliefs. Like reporting parents, or kicking abusive people out of the department despite their background, or doing a chemical takedown on a mother who the police brought to us in a state of psychosis in front of onlookers, or advocating for policies that are by definition discriminatory. But then there's harm reduction.

The standard you walk past is the standard you accept, said the Australian of the Year a few years ago. I agree wholeheartedly. I'm not sure what long-term good many of us are doing here sometimes, other than applying band-aids.

And soon it's 3 am, and then it's 5 am. My head is fuzzy, and at some point, I pee. I have a muesli bar and another piece of warm, too-old cake with Sue, and we laugh, and say, holy hell, when are we going to get out of this town for good, and we both giggle. And then it's light outside, and I still haven't made it to the ward to say hi to Billy.

An elderly man knocks on the door with his wife and an old shopping bag of clothes. 'Chest pain,' he says. 'Big mob.'

Sue walks him to resus. She does an ECG and calls me over quickly. He's having a big heart attack. 'He walked here with the pain,' Sue says to me, as she inserts an IV. 'Paddy, you're a tough man!' She smiles at him.

Paddy's wife sighs. 'I been tellin' him,' she says. 'But he didn't wanna come in. All night, he complainin' he got chest pain.'

'I'm right,' says Paddy.

He's another cowboy hat wearer, along with a lovely old checked shirt tucked in, well-worn trousers and black runners.

We do a quick work-up. I explain the treatment, a clot-busting drug—thrombolysis, the process is called—and tell him that there's a small but real risk of it causing a stroke or critical bleeding. It's hard to explain this quickly, without making someone worry even more about the heart attack you've just told them about, while still getting 'fully informed consent' for all risks.

'You understand all that, Paddy?' I ask. 'It's totally your decision. But it's almost certainly gonna help your heart. It's what I'd want for myself or my family, if that helps.'

The cardiologist in Alice Springs agrees. I'd sent a picture of his ECG a few moments ago. Paddy agrees, too. 'You right, Doc,' he says. 'Treat 'em. I trust you mob.'

Paddy's wife is keen, too. 'All night, he been complainin'. I told him!'

Sue starts giving the drugs. There's a strict sequence. We've put the defibrillator pads onto Paddy's chest, too, as nonchalantly as possible. Sue has it figured out. 'Think of it as a good chest wax,' she teases. 'We pop them on to be careful.'

Paddy's jovial. 'Never had so many people fussin' over me,' he says.

We do our best to seem lighthearted, but really, we're watching closely. This is the risky time. Sudden bad heart rhythms may need a shock.

We give the drugs and start the clock. Minutes pass. Paddy jokes. We watch. Police bring in a heavily intoxicated person who's yelling and swearing, and they want to hand them over to us.

'Sorry, not yet,' I say. 'We're gonna be a few minutes more.'

Another fella takes off his neck collar and heads home.

The cleaner comes through, then the social worker.

Chris and the morning team arrive. 'Looks like a good night,' he says, but he knows. I hand Paddy and the rest of the patients over to them.

Head home.

Shower.

Nap.

Then stay up all day, to flip my body clock back to dayshifts. Maya calls with nice news from the other side of the world, and I don't talk about last night, because there's no need to spread the angst. My anger will dissipate soon, anyway.

By the time I'm in Melbourne, I'll have mostly forgotten.

The sense of urgency ebbs.

The cycle repeats.

19

Working with XY Axes

Two Years Later, Here and There

The comfy leather armchair invites confession. Outside the window, oak trees are in full foliage, shading a small group of students resting on the nature strip. February sunshine streams into the corner of the office. A man with a moustache and neat mullet passes on a scooter, his bright white T-shirt catching my eye. There's a major university not far from here.

'You've never watched *Game of Thrones*?' asks Colin.

'Not yet, but it's on the list. I know, I know.'

'What else did you talk about in tearooms during those years?' he smiles. 'Please tell me you've at least seen *Mad Men*. Or *The Sopranos*?'

I have. We're now about twenty dollars into my therapy session, still in the book and movie club phase. He's sitting across from me in his armchair, in this smallish, book-filled room in the inner north of Melbourne. He's a picture of neat academic dishevelment, smart casual, with an air of 'I overslept and had to run with food in hand': shirt partly untucked, waistcoat and brightly coloured tie, socks in a wacky green, yellow and pink pattern, and a small stain on his vest—from the pho he just had for lunch, he'd said. On the desk beside him is a framed cartoon picture of Dr Marvin Monroe, the therapist character from *The Simpsons*. The resemblance is striking.

'You've seen *The Wire*?' I ask him.

'Not yet,' he says. 'I've heard it's good, though.'

Great drama and characters, I say, but it's also the best examination of systemic barriers and entrenched disadvantage that I've come across, better than any article I've read. Someone could make a compelling Aussie reboot with only a few tweaks.

'Did you get to *Normal People* yet?' he asks me.

Sort of, I tell him, but I had to shelve it. 'I think you recommended it, no? So, I started it with Mum when she was visiting recently, but I don't remember you warning me about the sex scenes. Pretty spicy ones, too. Got a little awkward. We scrambled for the remote and switched to *Law & Order* reruns.'

We're now 30 dollars into the consult. We move on to books; I make a point of reading most of what he recommends. And then we talk podcasts. I like this, and I imagine that this is 'rapport building', bringing up ideas and themes in a less direct, intrusive way. My take on therapy is that much of the work is done by just showing up. The finding of the parking, the trip to the office, and the thinking of *Oh my god, I need a story quickly, what the hell am I going to unpack today?*, and then the parting of ways with cash. What comes out can feel useless more often than it does useful, but sometimes the penny drops months later, when he'll circle back to what I'd said, and it'll be an insight I'd never have come to myself.

Today, though, there are plenty of things to unpack with Colin. I'm just back from South Africa. It was the first time I'd returned to my birth country with my parents and sister in decades, and the first time that our extended family had ever been together, coming in from all over the world for a cousin's wedding.

Colin asks about it. Where to begin? Everything there is so evocative, even just the arrivals hall.

'How about we go get a bite now?' asked my aunt, after all the excited hugs. She'd kindly met us at the Cape Town airport. 'Let's drop the bags and go for lunch.'

'What, *right now*?' asked my cousin. 'Or *now now*?'

'No, *just now*,' said my aunt.

In South African English, 'now now' means 'soon', and 'just now' means 'a little later'. 'Right now' is what it sounds like. Just saying 'now', alone, can be too non-specific. I'd forgotten all this. My old accent immediately seeped back, too. I'd shed it within months of moving to Australia, very deliberately, because fourteen wasn't a good age to stand out in school, but it returns whenever I come back. I like it. And I love the sound of the 35 languages spoken there, twelve of them official, and the words that are borrowed and swapped among them. '*Ja-nee*,' replied a man at a kiosk when I asked if this time of year is busy. 'Yes-no' is the translation, a happy overlap with our Aussie 'yeah, nah'.

The entire trip was like this, the feeling of finding buried treasures everywhere. In the morning I woke up to the sound of cape doves cooing in the garden. They're unremarkable there, but I immediately thought of my late grandmother making porridge in the mornings, windows open, doves outside, a life-shortening knob of butter bobbing in the middle of it and a layer of salt and sugar glazing it all. Her false teeth fell out once when she laughed while dishing it up.

It's a bizarre feeling, being back. Foreign but familiar, like an old movie that I'd once loved but long since forgotten. But these visits are invariably 'greatest hits' albums with little resemblance to real life. We visited the Kruger National Park and saw baby zebras, then woke up to elephants breaking branches in the garden. We headed to wineries, wild beaches and my cousin's wedding. It all felt like home—the birds sounded like they were supposed to, the accents were familiar, and my grandfather's name was still stencilled on the rugby awards board of his old town, gold letters peeling and faded. Many of our family members are buried in the nearby cemetery.

But it's clearly not home anymore.

Wandering in the Cape Town city centre one morning, I got mugged at knifepoint. Not badly; quite gently, actually. It was in broad daylight, with others walking past. The man faked falling over, stumbled into me and said, 'Look down. *Ja*, see that? I'm crazy, I'm crazy, I'm on tik and I need money. I'll go crazy if you don't give it to me. Give me your wallet.'

'Tik' is local slang for methamphetamine. He looked dreadful and wild-eyed, so I believed him, and told him that I'd give him cash if he stepped back and dropped the knife—although really, I wasn't in a position to bargain. I'd have been happy if all he took was cash, and my pants stayed dry. A moment later it was over. I called for police, but he was gone. I resented the interaction—now I was going to be one of *those* people who crossed the street whenever a person with a certain vibe was nearby.

'What, *just now?*' asked my aunt, when I told her.

'*Ja*, just then,' I said.

'But why were you walking in the CBD? We never walk there.'

'*Ja*,' said Dad, having reverted to his original accent, too. 'We never head to that part of the city, no?'

'Well, you told me not to head to *any* part of the city, in fairness,' I said.

'What? Really *just now*?' asked Mum.

'*Ja*, right now.'

This wasn't much of a story—not by comparison to everyone else's. But it did burst the bubble of my rosy views. Crime rates in South Africa are among the highest in the world—80 murders each day, on average, give or take. My friends in medicine there work hard, under difficult conditions and for far less money than in Australia; one told me that he sees more major traumas in a week than he had in a full year in a large UK hospital. Apartheid ended three decades ago, but socio-economic divides still persist for the majority of people. By any measure, my life in Australia is a breeze compared with what I would experience in South Africa.

I still hadn't closed the book on my birth country, though. Not yet.

'You probably never will,' Colin says, shifting in his chair, adjusting his waistcoat. We discuss this for a while. 'It's an upheaval, moving countries,' he says. 'That sense of dislocation will likely persist.'

And yet we did it as middle-class migrants, who spoke the language and looked like most people around us. We weren't complete outsiders. Being teased for my accent was as dramatic as things got, along with having to make new mates as a teen. But the move did shake the family in unforeseen ways, and for years.

The dislocation is partly why I enjoy the Northern Territory and remote communities, I suspect. The appeal of the work is obvious, but there's community among the staff, too, both in the work we're doing and in a shared experience of being an outsider. And maybe I also like the sense of slight unease—of things feeling a little uncertain. And that you can't not empathise with those around you. You can't not feel that the chance distribution of melanin, your birthplace and a random foreign visa allocation account for much of your lot. Here in Australia, I get to work and travel as I please. I live as I choose; I don't need to struggle in a Joburg hospital, or wander Cape Town with a knife, unemployed, stoned on tik, stumbling into tourists.

Colin looks at the clock over my shoulder. He shifts and gives me a small look. Our time is up. 'We didn't even get to your new job,' he says, 'or Maya.'

'No new issues,' I smile. 'Just the same old ones.'

He walks me to the credit card terminal in the hall. 'You're working near here now?' he asks.

I am. A stone's throw away, no flights needed.

My new job is at an academic facility nearby. It was time to get back into the bigger picture stuff in health. As of a few weeks ago, I sit at a beige office desk and don't do on-call. I've started public health specialist training, the next step up from my Master's, but a step down in pay and responsibility. I'm employed as a junior office worker now, not a mid-career clinician. I'll still fly to Central for a week each month, but I've decided that there's little point in criticising the system from the outside. Throwing stones is easy. It's better to be on the inside and try to understand the system, and maybe try to advocate from there. Next year, the plan is to continue the public health work with MSF, and to live with Maya. After that, we'll both come back to Australia—we hope. What could possibly go wrong?

The short answer is Covid.

No one wants to relive too much of the pandemic. It's like reliving a root canal.

'What do you get when you mix science and politics?' asks one commentator. 'Politics,' their answer. This sums up many decisions, to me at least.

'An exponential rise in the use of exponential graphs,' another journalist quips. Predictions and strong opinions are everywhere.

A few other things stand out for me. Firstly, just getting to Central. This becomes difficult.

Secondly, my public health role. This is either the best time in history to have started training in the speciality, or the absolute worst.

And thirdly, the globalisation of bad ideas. No good will come of that.

Getting to Central becomes a whole thing. What took one day now takes three, requiring two letters from government departments, a small fortune in airfares, evidence of multiple negative tests, and explaining myself at police checkpoints.

Melbourne airport is a ghost town. A departure screen lists two flights when I arrive, not the usual dozens, and most screens are blank. Shops are closed and stock stripped. There are about ten check-in staff I can see, outnumbering us passengers, and on the flight to Sydney, the only route I could get, almost every seat is empty. In Sydney, I overnight in an airport hotel, and a day later fly to Alice Springs, where there's an even higher level of scrutiny. Federal police examine my documents on landing, and I'm again swabbed. Outside the small airport, dozens of large aircraft are parked in rows on the orange-red earth, many of them from major international airlines. The dry desert air is good for the airframes, I've read, so this is a prime storage area.

Emily picks me up. I'm thrilled for the company. On the way back into town, we're stopped at two police roadblocks. 'Papers, please,' we're asked, like we're crossing a divided Berlin in an old film, and then: 'What's the reason for the travel?' I explain and hand over my documents, but the officer steps back. 'Whoa, mate. Bloody hell! You come up from Melbourne? It's all over the place down there, no?'

My Victorian ID now reliably gets this response everywhere. I may as well pass them a dirty tissue. I'm heartened by the caution, though. As much as all of this is a hassle, Covid would be a disaster up here. The crowded housing and high rates of chronic disease would almost guarantee bad outcomes.

The following day, I rent a car and pick up another doctor, Jason, and we drive to Central. There couldn't be a better time to travel, economic disaster aside. No slow caravans to get stuck behind, and not many road trains shuddering your car towards the highway edge as they pass. The sense of vast, wide-open space is even more heightened than normal.

The hospital itself is bizarrely quiet. Patients are avoiding it, which will create its own delayed health issues. For now, there's not much to do aside from prepare. Two ventilators? *Righto,* we think, *we'll charge and test them, then buff them nicely. With two of these, we'll last fifteen minutes when this virus hits.* More are on order, but we at least have plenty of PPE.

'Uh, I don't wanna scare you guys,' says Jason, a couple of mornings later, sneezing into his mask at the work bench. 'I've got a bit of scratchy throat today. Actually, it's pretty sore.'

'Uh-oh,' says Sue. 'Weren't you working in a Covid testing centre before? In Sydney or something?'

'Yeah. But I was tested heaps.'

We test him heaps again, then shuffle him out like a plague patient in the Middle Ages. He's not to leave his unit, he's told by management, and we'll drop food to him. One supervisor is angry—this has screwed up the roster, they say—but Jason's fine with it. He'll get paid anyway for the whole block, and binges as much Netflix as his data plan can manage. It turns out to be a common cold.

This becomes an unfortunate theme. You sneeze, you leave. If you're a contact of a case, you're out. But the definition of contact changes often. How close? Three feet. But for less than fifteen minutes, right? Who knows. Someone decides to add nausea to the list up north: if you're nauseated, you're a suspect case. But then you're not. Wait, now you are—there's a new email this morning, didn't you see it? As if staffing these hospitals and clinics wasn't going to be difficult enough. But, of course, no one wants to be responsible for an outbreak. Not with the likes of Billy, with his fragile heart, and the dialysis patients coming in, or the kids in town with congenital heart disease, among many others.

In the following months, I manage two more trips to Central. Chris and some others stop coming, unable to risk being stuck away from family. But then there are no more travel exemptions. Cases in Melbourne climb. My permission to come is revoked, although I have some surprising conversations in Central before then.

'Nah, it's a whitefella disease,' says a man in the ED, when I ask him to wear a mask. 'I seen it on TV. Whitefellas in Europe gettin' it. Not blackfellas.'

'Well, for now,' I say. 'But we gotta keep it that way.'

'Nah, we don't get that disease,' he says. 'Only you mob.'

An older woman shows me a Facebook clip on the cracked screen of her mobile phone. 'You know this one?' she asks, sincerely. She's wearing a brightly patterned beanie, old dress and no shoes, and the video is of an American guy in his basement, wrinkled curtain and a US flag for a backdrop, talking to the camera. He seems like a standard flat-earther, end-of-days type, and he's talking about 5G, Bill Gates, DNA and all that.

'You can't really believe this stuff,' I ask.

But she looks worried. And why wouldn't she be? This man's message has a gravitas that the dry, sometimes poorly delivered public health messages don't. It offers up a secret, and implicit in all this is membership to an exclusive club—you're among the people who really *know. You're lucky.*

'You don't reckon it's right?' she asks.

'I promise you it's not right,' I try to reassure her. The truth is far more boring, I say. But this globalisation of bad ideas is striking. There's no crazy yelling on a street corner anymore, reaching a dozen people; now a guy like this can get a million views in a few hours, even in remote outback communities.

'Are other people watching this stuff?' I ask the woman. Janice is her name.

'Yeah,' she nods. 'We all seen it.'

We chat longer. Us staff would be happy to come have a yarn with others, I offer, but the public health teams here are already out and about, getting the standard information across. And the buy-in from most communities is strong. They've embraced precautions and often led the community closures themselves.

Sometimes the messages are taken very literally. 'You okay there?' I ask a man sitting on the grass outside BP. He looks a bit worse for wear, alone with a carton of iced coffee and a loaf of white bread. He pulls his mask down to take a sip and a bite, then puts it straight up as he chews.

'You don't have to wear your mask out here,' I reassure him. 'Only inside, or close to others. You're okay out here. You can relax and enjoy the fresh air.'

'Nah,' he says, 'he keepin' me safe.' He taps the mask. He's worried about getting sick, he tells me, and he's going to stay long-grassing, laying low, because he doesn't want to get stuck somewhere due to all the roadblocks and checks.

In Melbourne, my public health job had officially started a few weeks before the pandemic. The plan had been to look at the impact of chronic illness in remote communities, but this was quickly shelved. I was transferred to a large infectious diseases institute to help with Covid modelling—creating a series of scenarios for the government, in part to estimate how hospitals would cope. This felt like an exciting front-row seat to government advisory work, at least in the early months—the science part. But then the politics part dominated globally.

The team was incredible—passionate, highly trained, open to new ideas—and I wasn't sure when my boss slept, or if she slept. She sent emails at midnight, and by 5 am was editing documents online, then doing national media. The director and many others seemed to be doing the same, often getting up during the night for online meetings with European colleagues. There wasn't a lot of ego in the meetings that I could see, either.

'Lovely to meet you,' said the Nobel Prize winner who the institute is named after, when we first met. He introduced himself warmly, but I knew well who he was. The large portrait on the wall behind us was of him—he looked genuinely uncomfortable when I pointed that out jokingly—and the multistorey building bears his name. He'd tried to google the opening hours for a Dan Murphy's liquor outlet at home during lockdown, but he'd mistakenly tweeted the question instead. Media outlets picked up on this and it went viral, but he laughed it off and left the tweet up. Tens of thousands more people followed him as a result. I loved this.

Once the Northern Territory closed completely, my public health work became my only outlet. As a researcher, I had to work from home, as Melbourne descended into winter and dragged itself towards the 'world's most locked-down city' title. Maya was stuck on the other side of the world, doing much the same, but at least we were employed, and we didn't have a houseful of kids to entertain and educate. It was all very solitary, though, with only one friend allowed in my 'visitor bubble'. So when I received an offer to continue my public health work in the Northern Territory at the end of my Melbourne contract, I jumped. I'd need to spend two weeks in a quarantine centre, they cautioned, but after months in my little unit, this was a cakewalk. I booked the earliest flight I could. Weeks later, I was having dinner with friends in the first restaurant I'd been to in months. It was pure bliss. At work in a Darwin office, I was tasked with chasing up a mud fever outbreak on cattle stations—I didn't previously know what mud fever was—some Covid work, and a day a week in the TB clinics.

Carol called. She was now living in Cairns. 'You outta Melbin' now or what?' she asked. 'When we gonna catch up?'

Very soon, I hoped.

Blocks of clinical work came up everywhere. Katherine, Gove and Central hospitals were nearby—by Northern Territory standards, anyway—so I took work between the office days. It was great to be back, if cautiously so. The same old challenges existed, but I'd at least had a break from hospitals. I'd missed the interesting patients, the conversations and an occasional tricky on-call shift, but an old pitfall loomed: saying yes to too many shifts. I started arriving at the next job still tired from the last. Everyone was short, though, and staff were exhausted. Where do you draw the line?

And again: how to help things improve in the longterm?

20

Zebra Dung

Another Year Later, Far North Queensland

The start of a night shift. A strong breeze is blowing off the Coral Sea. I stand at the large hangar doors, looking at the rainforest-covered hills to the north of Cairns. The sun's setting behind them. Even after all these years, this is hard to beat as an office.

'You've definitely told me the right destination?' asks Baz as he calls the refueller. He smiles.

I hope so. This will be a tricky landing, even if everything goes well.

Baz starts the little tug and pushes the aircraft back. The refueller arrives and I take a quick toilet break and fill the coffee flask. We soon take off, banking into the last light of a tropical sky, climbing gently over sugarcane fields. It's a clear night and the moon's low. After an hour we descend and loop past the cattle station below, for what I'm hoping will be my first dunny-roll landing. Toilet rolls have been soaked in kerosene and laid out along the sides of the dirt runway below us, we think, and they're about to be lit—or so goes the plan.

'It may only be half a dunny-roll landing,' says Baz, tempering my excitement. 'I think they've got some battery lamps down there, too.'

'Mostly dunny rolls, though?' I ask.

'Yeah, I reckon.'

'I'll count it then.'

Dunny-roll landings are the Rolls-Royce of outback improvisation, the you-beauty of outback landings. After years of never experiencing one, I'd started to assume that they were a myth, like the 'bucket of KFC for a bucket of fresh lobster' swap at the Torres Strait airport—which I'm still yet to see.

The cattle station's homestead lights become visible, a little island in the blackness. The runway slowly reveals itself as orange dots light up around its edges, and Baz makes a quick call to someone down there. 'They're making another sweep for wildlife,' he says. Some of these properties have tens of thousands of head of cattle on them, as well as roos and other curious creatures. Hopefully none are tempted to come out and see the pretty orange lights tonight.

'We're good to go,' says Baz. 'All secure in the back?'

We are. The cabin lights go out. The cockpit glows in soft red light—this colour won't affect a pilot's night vision. Baz runs through his landing checklist. We line up and descend steadily. Hydraulics whine and flaps extend. The landing gear thunks into place as ground proximity warnings call out in a robotic, North American voice. 'One. Hundred. Feet!' An alarm whoops. Baz silences it. I look back over my left shoulder and out the cockpit window behind me, watching as he lines up the lights, looking relaxed. I'm sure the pilots love the novelty of all this as well.

'Fifty! Feet!' calls the ground warning. There's another alarm. We bounce in the thermals. The runway lights shift as the plane rolls and pitches. The orange flames dance up and down and sideways in the cockpit window, and I wonder how we never clip a wing when we land, or skid sideways in strong winds, and how the pilots always bring the plane down perfectly, and surprisingly gently. 'Don't bloody curse us, Damo!' I can imagine Baz telling me if I'd asked this out loud. It's like walking into an ED and saying 'Fantastic, it's so quiet in here.' You don't do it. The universe hears, and a bus full of unwell people is sure to arrive. Or not—but it's the one superstition that I can't shake.

There's a gentle bump as we land, then loud rumbling as the rubber tyres speed across gravel. The two engines scream their reverse thrust into the dark. We slow fast and turn sharply at the end of the runway to face back the way we came, ready for take-off, and Baz powers down.

'Bloody hell,' says a man as we lower the back door and step out. 'Glad that worked! We were a bit worried they'd flame out before you landed.'

'Nah, you did it perfectly,' says Baz.

A dozen people are here and waiting. They're the quintessential cattle station crew, dressed in jeans, boots and shirts. I'd always assumed that these places were full of rough, outback-type blokes, but they're often run by families, with people of all ages and from many backgrounds working on them. Sometimes there are a few European backpackers as well—young people who'd come for a quick look but stayed on for years. It's hard not to see the appeal of living under these skies, of mustering on horseback, or on a bike or helicopter, but it's a long way from everything. And these properties are huge: just checking the fence line or all the water pumps for livestock can mean camping out in a swag for days. Years ago, we'd landed on a cattle station to fetch an injured man and were then offered a lift in their mustering helicopter or on a quad bike to reach him—even after a long flight, we still had to get across their property.

Tonight, our patient is right here. She's on the back tray of a ute, propped on pillows and blankets, her leg in a homemade splint for a lower leg fracture. I climb up to examine her. Lou, the flight nurse, leans over to insert an IV and give pain relief. The patient was thrown from her horse earlier this evening, and Claire's her name. We check for other injuries and fit a soft neck collar, then put her onto our spine board. Doing all this on the back of a ute is fiddly, but the station crew here have done all this before.

'You happy with their splint?' asks Lou.

'Very. You guys made it perfectly.' Their bandage and timber version is well fitted. The patient's leg has good pulses and sensation, and this is a short flight. It's better to just get going. Other jobs are waiting.

We gently load and secure Claire. Baz shuts the door. The plane powers up. Only a few lamps line the runway this time, but there's a ute at the end to aim for—no need for more flaming dunny rolls for take-off.

'We good?' he asks, hand on the throttle.

We're good.

For almost two years I couldn't work here in Cairns. Borders opened and closed unpredictably. I tried once when I was living in Darwin, but new Covid cases were announced shortly after I landed, so I had to flee before midnight. That was an expensive little round trip. Things have been back to normal for a while, though, or at least relatively normal.

Staffing levels have taken a hit everywhere. Health workers seem bruised and battle-weary after recent years, and working part-time is more common, particularly for front-line services. Many colleagues take extended leave to find that spark again, to shake the mental Etch a Sketch and reset—myself included.

My time off didn't include Maya this time. We broke up—amicably, but sadly. We kept talking for a long time afterwards, trying to reconcile, but it didn't work. The border issues during Covid had been a huge hurdle, but our worlds grew increasingly far apart, especially as family obligations increased. The decision seemed inevitable, as sad as it was.

'Online dating?' Colin asked, when I told him about downloading an app and getting out there. Maya had told me that she was doing this to try to move on—which was far harder to hear than I'd expected—so I thought I should. It'd be a distraction, if nothing else. 'You think you're ready?' asked Colin.

Not at all, I'd said. But judging from the profiles I'd seen, neither are a lot of people on these apps. What possibly couldn't work? 'Here shopping for other humans,' one woman joked on her profile, but it was one of those joking/not joking comments.

And I *had to* remember to switch off the app when I flew out bush.

'I never knew you were that old,' Carol said to me recently. We'd caught up for a pie and Coke—full sugar. She coincidentally mentioned that her granddaughter was back in juvenile detention. A daughter-in-law had died in ICU since we last spoke, and one of her sons had been stabbed walking past a brawl in Cairns. She didn't lead with these stories, either. They came out over the course of an afternoon, as asides. For my family, any single one of these events would be the worst thing that had ever happened in years, a defining story.

'What do you mean about my age?' I laughed. 'I never kept it from you, surely? Maybe it never came up. And anyway, how do you now know how old I am?' I asked. 'Facebook?'

'Nah, my niece in Cairns saw you. On some app,' she said.

Uh-oh. Small world.

Maya has now met someone on the apps, she told me recently, and she thought it could be serious. She sounded happy. I couldn't hope for anything more than that, short of being back together, although it did trigger a phase of melancholic playlists and finally removing the photos of us from my fridge and screensaver.

I also met someone on the apps, an engineer who had spent some time working overseas. We hit it off quickly. 'I have to confess something,' she said, a couple of weeks after we met, and I braced myself. By this stage I'd heard a few colourful backstories with online dating. There was a husband in the mix? She didn't believe in vaccines and hoped that I didn't, either? 'No,' she laughed. 'But I'm actually based in New York,' she said, 'and I've got a few years left on my contract there. I'm only back in Australia for a family thing. I'm sorry, I should've said so at the beginning. But I really feel a connection, and I think the distance thing won't be a problem if we don't want it to be. We could try to make it work, yeah? I think it could be kinda exciting.

We could FaceTime most days? Maybe we could even meet in Bali soon?'

My revised relationship goal: to be based on the same continent.

As for Central, I've stepped away. It was time. Covid made it difficult to get there. There were some other considerations, too. It was sad to leave after so many years, but they're well staffed, far ahead of when I first arrived in town. There's an Aboriginal doctor leading the hospital now, who's great, and knows the region well, so it's a fantastic step forward for the hospital. A very safe pair of hands.

Speaking of Central, Billy died. One of the trainees mentioned it as an aside when she'd emailed me for a reference check recently.

'When?' I messaged her back.

Quite a few months back, she said.

'Peacefully?'

Yes, as far as she knew. I was disappointed that none of the other staff had let me know at the time, but why would they? Everyone interacted with Billy, and often, and for years. My relationship with him was probably no more significant than others'. And sadly, this is the most remarkable thing about Billy's medical story: up in Central, it's *unremarkable*. Death at a young age is not rare. A 30-something-year-old person with severe disease isn't noteworthy. Such is the disparity.

There's another uncomfortable aspect to Billy's story, or in my telling of any of it: it puts me at the centre. This is my version of his story, after all. There's no way I can honestly recount it other than how it relates to me, with all my biases and blind spots. But I'm not at the centre of this. His family and friends are. And many of my colleagues were just as involved as me, if not more so. My interactions aren't unique; nor are my frustrations. Many people work hard there, and for years.

There's another unfortunate fictionalising, too, in my telling of any of this: the cast of characters is far larger in real life. In even a small hospital, or in that Flying Doctors hangar, the cast is rich and deep, and it's impossible to write about everyone. The stories would drown in detail. For Billy, I suspect that I was one of a dozen doctors and nurses he saw often—not the central, single lead. Hopefully we were all kind and competent.

Gloria the artist also died. I found this out incidentally. 'You've got the same surname as Gloria,' I'd commented to a patient, Jacquie, in the clinic. 'You related?'

'She's my mum,' she said.

I'd been trying to get hold of Gloria for a while and I'd missed her calls. 'She left a voice message,' I said, 'but then I never got through. She change her number?'

'Nah, she died.'

'Really?'

'Yeah.'

'I'm so sorry. When?'

'A while back. You didn't come to the funeral?'

I didn't. I can't imagine I'd have been invited. I visit this community occasionally, and I didn't know her that well, not compared to some of the others here. And many staff have worked at this clinic in recent years.

'Lots of clinic people come,' said her daughter. 'You shoulda been there.'

We shelved the medical consult and spoke about Gloria instead. Jacquie had some of her mum's unfinished artwork, she said, and photos of her life. I asked about them. I should come look sometime, she suggested, but I was flying out the next day, and I had paperwork to do that night, and results to check, and—

It was time to stop putting these things off.

Hours later, we sat opposite each other on plastic chairs. We were in an overgrown front yard in the community, under a large tree, chicken wire fence on one side. Jacquie opened scrapbooks and showed me through them. I didn't bring any gifts; the memory of shopping bags for Carol still made me wince, even years later. 'You better move your car,' Jacquie said. But it was a clinic car, clearly marked and parked a few metres up the road, so no one was going to mess with it, surely? She laughed. 'Nah, cheeky kids over there. They maybe gonna muck it up.'

We sat mostly in silence. Litter fluttered past. A bad smell sailed from bins when the wind shifted. A dog nearby scratched itself constantly, then wandered over and licked my arm. I commented on the photos of artworks as she showed me. 'Wow. This one's really beautiful. These colours.' My queries about their pasts got short answers and sometimes silence. *I shouldn't have come*, I thought. But she showed me more photos of them. Together when they were younger. On her boat. Gloria baking ochre in her backyard. Gloria getting her first major award. I remembered the editor I'd spoken with about a possible book draft, and one of her lines: 'Be careful, because it could sound to a reader like you're trying to *collect* Aboriginal people as friends,' she'd said.

'Like you're trying to form these connections, or set up these meetings, to be able to say, Look at me, I spend time with them, I get them, and I get all the issues. Or worse, that you're just doing this for book material.'

Seriously? I'd thought. The comment bothered me hugely. There was no malice in it, I'm confident, just caution. And I've trawled enough of Twitter to know that if something can be misconstrued, it will be. Better then to never engage, though? And who's the arbiter of the 'right way' to engage with another person, anyway?

We sat in silence for a while. Jacquie turned pages. I asked questions. The answers were brief. I wondered if they were dismissive. *I shouldn't have come*, I thought again, and we both seemed uncomfortable, and I left not feeling good about it all. But the next afternoon, as I was packing up for the flight out, one of the nurses came past.

'I heard you had a lovely meeting yesterday,' she smiled. 'Jacquie was working at the arts centre this morning, saying how grateful she was that you'd remembered her mum, and how touched that you took the time to come out to her and chat.'

Really? I was floored. This is how little it takes? To connect with someone? Just a chat and a few minutes?

Maybe so, when the starting point is nothing. When the baseline is zero.

We land in Cairns. There's no wind. It's a deliciously cool night. A little curlew races out from behind the open hangar doors, squealing like an old stove-top kettle about to boil, all legs, like in the road-runner cartoons. An ambulance crew is waiting, and we hand over our patient with the broken leg and wish her the best.

'Good night so far?' I ask the paramedics, as Baz calls the refueller.

'Double shift,' says one.

'Ouch. Sixteen hours?'

'Twenty-four,' she says. 'We're super short.'

'Been okay?' I ask.

'A cardiac case at the start,' she says. 'Then a febrile kid. Then some guy sprinted down the Cook Highway with his clothes off, hitting cars. Probably meth. Ended up being a roadside sedation, cops, all that. This one's a lovely break for us, so thank you! We're ready for bed.'

We commiserate, then repack, grab food, and head to the next cases in a Cape York community. It's a quiet flight. Only a couple of phone calls, so plenty of time for catch-ups. As we descend, I hope that the brolgas and other birds are deep asleep, not startled by us. We'd hit a flock of galahs recently, the poor things, and the landing gear looked like a pink and grey feather duster afterwards. An engineer had to fly up and examine the aircraft before it could take off again.

We touch down. It's pitch dark outside, and at the small airport's gates, I can see the light of the waiting clinic ambulance. There's another car beside it, too. Bats squawk in nearby trees.

'Put your stuff in the back of me ute,' says a barefoot whitefella, the driver of the other car. 'I'll drive you up there. Those blokes are me mates. They're pretty banged up.'

Three trauma patients are in the clinic and we've got a lot of equipment, so we take him up on his offer. Lou goes in the ambulance, and I get in the ute.

'I gotta be honest, mate,' says the driver, as we pull out of the airport car park, 'I'm pretty tanked.'

'Tanked?'

'Yeah. We'd been fishin' all arvo until this happened. Had a fair few drinks.'

'Oh, nah, pull over,' I say. 'I'll drive.'

'Nah, she's sweet as,' he says. 'No one cares up here, mate. We're good.'

He's probably mid-twenties, wearing board shorts and a singlet, and his cap's back to front. They've been travelling through Cape York on a camping trip, he'd said.

'Pull over,' I say again. He debates it a bit. But then he stops, and I drive the remaining minutes to the clinic. I wonder how this would've played out in an occupational health and safety meeting, if I had to explain why our equipment ended up under a rolled-over ute and the doctor was more injured than the patients. 'I mean, he didn't strike me as *completely* wasted,' I imagine saying, trying to defend this. 'Just kinda tipsy, you know? But only in a standard North Queensland bloke way. Standard fishing trip levels. Wobbly, not trashed. Nothing too bad.'

Inside the clinic, the nurse manager and other staff are still busy, long after their home time. I know them well from clinic visits. 'We've got a fourth patient for you,' says the manager. 'Is there a full moon out there or something?'

A middle-aged woman has just arrived. She looks to have had a large stroke earlier today, her right side is completely paralysed.

Her mother is here, too, and I recognise her—Rose, the owner of the jealousin' dress.

'Oh, hello, Rose! No, no good huh. Sorry,' I say. 'I know. We'll take good care of her. We'll get her down quickly, do all the tests.' Her daughter's missed the potential window for a clot-busting drug, but she'll hopefully still improve in coming weeks. It'll be a long road, though, and life-altering. Wheelchairs are difficult to use up here.

Lou and I quickly assess the trauma patients. There's no X-ray operator here tonight. This is going to be another round of Aircraft Tetris, I can see—we can't get them all out at once.

One guy definitely needs to come. His hip is either dislocated or badly fractured, among a few other injuries. He was thrown from a ute tray, and he'll need a stretcher and full spine precautions.

Rose's daughter should come down, too, and on a stretcher. This leaves one seat free, and no more stretchers.

The second trauma patient has a large cut over his ankle with the fractured bone on view, no other obvious injuries. We rinse and dress the ankle, then splint it and give antibiotics, but it takes time. He'll need surgery tonight, so he'll have to sit on the plane with his leg elevated, which is not ideal. I'm confident his neck and spine are okay—or as confident as I can be, based on his story and examining him, and with not having X-rays or CT. That's not a high enough bar by large hospital standards; but out here, tonight, it seems the less risky decision. Leaving him for the next flight is unacceptable. Asking the stroke patient to sit up is impossible. We could justify leaving him now and racing straight back, but the pilots have strictly limited hours overnight, so we probably won't make it. And who knows what else is still brewing out there . . .

Perfect is the enemy of good, I often think.

This will have to do.

But I wonder if it would hold up in court? Someone in the ED will scan all these patients later, from head to toe, and there will almost certainly be something about our management to critique. Hindsight's twenty-twenty, as the saying goes. Everything's easy with a retrospect-o-scope.

Lou and I divide and conquer. The third trauma patient has a forearm fracture and some cuts, nothing else that we can see. He can safely come down in the morning. We 'package' the patients safely for transfer with the help of the clinic nurses.

The car shuffles begin. We use the ute as well. I politely decline the shoeless, boozy bloke's offer to drive us out; even if we don't run off the road, I wonder how Baz will take it if this guy reverses slowly into a wing.

There's a saying I've heard in medicine, that you're 'seeing zebra dung in a horse paddock'. It's usually used when a keen student suggests an obscure, highly improbable diagnosis. 'What are the likely causes of bleeding in a motor-vehicle trauma?' they'd be asked, then nervously blurt out, 'Haemophilia. No? Um, okay, Hermansky-Pudlak syndrome with abnormal clotting? No? No good?'

Nope. No good. It was probably their visible fractures or lacerations. One of our professors, a well-liked specialist, had knelt down quietly onto the floor, in his fine woollen suit, when one of us gave a similar answer, and he'd written it onto the skirting board in tiny print. 'Sure,' he said, standing back up. 'Theoretically. But I'd put it there in terms of likelihood. Any other suggestions?'

Common things are common. We forget this.

In medicine, we make probability-based decisions all the time; frequency gambles. We have to. We overlay experience, studies, the family's concerns, test results and colleagues' wisdom, among much else. To subject every feverish child that we see to painful and unnecessary tests would be unjustifiable—and clog up the health system in a day. Conversely, to miss just one severe cause would be catastrophic. Somewhere in that wide, varied spectrum, we make a judgement. But the tolerance for any error, no matter how improbable, is increasingly disappearing. That's a complex area and a whole other discussion.

But I do wonder whether we're looking for zebra dung in the horse paddock of bigger issues up here. If we're seeking rare, clever solutions to problems for which there are obvious and effective ways of helping now. Many high-impact interventions are known about, and wanted—such as more and better housing; healthy food that's easily available and affordable; employment programs; and alcohol policies that don't shift at every election, and that aren't decided on by people who've never set foot up here, and who never will. We need functioning health services that aren't dismantled and rebranded in an expensive exercise, handed over to another provider, only to struggle with the complexity suddenly foisted on them, and sometimes fail and lose staff—something I've seen a few times—which means that there are no front-line health providers for the most vulnerable people. We need to talk with the people this affects, and treat it all like the public health crisis it is—and it *is* a crisis—rather than the political football it's become.

Our discomfort with uncomfortable topics—the difficult things such as violence, trauma and substance abuse, among many—has to take a back seat to people's actual needs. How 'we' on the outside feel about discussing things is a far lesser consideration. Our discomfort belongs at the skirting-board level of priorities. Everyone here has a right to live their best life. We wouldn't tolerate this in Melbourne. Look at these kids: *all this potential! All this energy!*

Ignoring this is morally fraught.

We can't cherrypick what we'd like to talk about.

There are some wins here, and they're worth noting. Kids are significantly more likely to finish school now. And the gap in life expectancy is narrowing—although not nearly as much in remote areas. I've worked with many First Nations health workers in these places, increasingly so in recent years. And the young doctors and nurses out here, along with those in many other roles, are keen and open-minded. This bodes well. Everywhere I work, I see this: deeply committed people—far more than we suspect in our cynical 'everything's getting worse' moments. Some aren't, for sure, but they drift off. There are far more like Patricia, working on a ward in Chad, and Faith, and Sue, running the night shifts in Central Australia, bandaging heads, chatting with families, creating connections. I've come across community members running programs such as youth centres that open late into the night, to give kids a feed and something to do; and cattle stations that take in troubled youths and train them; and the Night Patrol service that picks up troubled souls and gets them home safely, away from a brawl. In a growing number of remote communities, the general stores now stock healthier foods and subsidise them, as a result of the advocacy of many. And all over the world, right now, millions of dedicated health workers are on shift. Delivering babies, laughing over a coffee, arriving at an accident scene, breaking the worst-ever news, getting up to do an urgent caesarean, commencing HIV/AIDS treatment, and sometimes just debriefing someone or occasionally being yelled at. And showing up again, anyway. Whatever the hour. It's a good tribe.

We load the patients. The major trauma guy is first. It's sweaty work, even on a cool night. 'Gentle with his neck,' we remind everyone.

Rose's daughter goes in last. Her smile's still lopsided and her speech slurred. Her extended family have all come to wave her off, standing at the fence nearby, dozens of them. 'Doctor!' shouts Rose, waving me over.

'Yeah?' I walk towards the gate.

'Give her this one,' she says. 'Toothbrush, phone charger, all that stuff.' She hands me the little bag. 'Tell 'em to look after her.'

'Of course. I promise.'

'We're good to go!' shouts Baz from the door.

I walk back to the plane. The moon's dropped and the stars are out, salting that endless, glorious black vault of a dome. I pause at the bottom of the stairs, crane my neck back. I breathe deeply. This is the same glorious sky I've seen in South Sudan, South Africa, Chad and Central Australia. We all sleep under this same expanse. We all want the same: the best for our loved ones. To be healthy. To enjoy ourselves and have a sense of purpose. We have far more in common than what divides us. We forget.

I climb up the stairs and shuffle past the patients.

I strap into my seat.

This is the best job in the world sometimes. It's a privilege to do this work. I just have to limit my exposure to it at times, and remember the small wins. I struggle with cynicism, I flirt with burnout and I wonder in my flatter moments whether I should've chosen another, less confronting path. But I do love this—mostly. And there's nothing I can reliably see to do but show up, stay well, be competent, find the balance, enjoy the journey. And advocate for what counts. Direct the frustration to be useful.

Lou locks the rear door.

'All secure in the back?' Baz asks, turning around.

'All secure.'

'Bloody beautiful night,' he says. 'Check out those stars, people!'

We all do.

He powers us up.

The phone pings through another job. They're stable, so the morning crew can manage it.

The family at the fence all wave. I tell Rose's daughter, because she can't lift her head to see them, and she smiles. Behind the family, I see the shoeless, tipsy fella wandering towards his ute. *Surely not . . .?* I think. *No way. Is he actually fumbling for his car keys?*

The engine roars.

I lean back.

The horizon falls away.

Acknowledgements

Sincerest thanks to Selena Hanet-Hutchins, who helped me to find the story. Selwa Anthony, my agent, championed the book from the moment she read it, and Elizabeth Weiss at Allen & Unwin provided much guidance and wisdom as she oversaw the entire publication process. Angela Handley and Brooke Lyons both cast their warm, sharply honed editorial eyes over this, saving me from grammatical pitfalls and narrative oversights. Dannielle Viera, Nadine Davidoff and Rod Morrison gave very helpful feedback at various stages.

Several friends encouraged me during this journey and asked important questions. Chris Lack, Ben Goodfellow, Dane Horsfall, Richard Kane, Mel Thompson, Charlene Diamond, Adam Pritchard, Reece Reed and Rhys Harding all went above and beyond, providing helpful feedback. A huge thankyou. And Ali Jarman and Jamie Roberts helped me through those doubt-filled early stages to get started.

For the medical work, I'm indebted to countless medical and nursing colleagues and mentors over the years for the guidance, teachings and chats. Ditto the many pilots for the laughs and safe landings, and the many allied health, administrative and support staff, who're so often the backbone of these services.

For welcoming me into their communities, I'm forever grateful to the many residents and Traditional Owners of all these amazing lands. It's a privilege for me to visit.

And finally, to my parents, Graham and Denise, and my sister, Nicolle, who got me through this process—a million thanks. They endured dozens of doubt-filled phone calls and read hundreds of pages. Still, they encouraged me. They've been unfailingly supportive. And to June, my new niece, thank you for the light relief: the giggling, splashing, and face-painting with spaghetti sauce during our evening FaceTimes. They've been a delightful diversion.

Selected Sources and Reading

BOOKS

Ashenden, Dean, 2022, *Telling Tennant's Story: The strange career of the great Australian silence*, Black Inc.: Collingwood, Vic.

McMillan, Andrew, 2001, *An Intruder's Guide to East Arnhem Land*, Duffy & Snellgrove: Sydney, NSW

Pearson, Noel, 2011, *Up from the Mission: Selected writings*, Black Inc.: Collingwood, Vic.

Pigni, Alessandra, 2016, *The Idealist's Survival Kit: 75 simple ways to avoid burnout*, Parallax Press: Berkeley, CA

Rosling, Hans, Ola Rosling and Anna Rosling Rönnlund, 2019, *Factfulness: Ten reasons we're wrong about the world—and why things are better than you think*, Sceptre: London

Trudgen, Richard Ian, 2000, *Why Warriors Lie Down and Die: Towards an understanding of why the Aboriginal people of Arnhem Land face the greatest crisis in health and education since European contact—Djambatj mala*, Aboriginal Resource & Development Services Inc.: Darwin, NT

Wright, Alexis, 1997, *Grog War*, Magabala Books: Broome, WA

ARTICLES

Fitzpatrick, J.P., Latimer, J., Carter, M. et al., 2015, 'Prevalence of fetal alcohol syndrome in a population-based sample of children living in remote Australia: The Lililwan Project', *Journal of Paediatric Child Health*, 51(4): pp. 450–7

Mahood, K., 2012, 'Kartiya are like Toyotas: White workers on Australia's cultural frontier', *Griffith Review*, vol. 36

Mahood, K., 2015, 'White Stigma: Review of Emma Kowal's Trapped in the Gap', *The Monthly*, August

Wilson, R.M., Michel, P., Olsen, S. et al., 2012, 'Patient safety in developing countries: Retrospective estimation of scale and nature of harm to patients in hospital', *British Medical Journal*, 344

WEBSITES

Australian Government, 2025, *Commonwealth Closing the Gap 2024 Annual Report*, https://www.niaa.gov.au/resource-centre/commonwealth-closing-gap-2024-annual-report-and-2025-implementation-plan

Australian Institute of Health and Welfare, 2024, *Health and Wellbeing of First Nations People*, https://www.aihw.gov.au/reports/australias-health/indigenous-health-and-wellbeing

Australian Institute of Health and Welfare, 2025, *Family, Domestic and Sexual Violence: Aboriginal and Torres Strait Islander People*, https://www.aihw.gov.au/family-domestic-and-sexual-violence/population-groups/aboriginal-and-torres-strait-islander-people?

Dattani, S., Spooner, F., Ritchie, H. and Roser, M., 2023, 'Child and Infant Mortality', OurWorldinData.org, https://ourworldindata.org/child-mortality

Roser, M. and Ritchie, H., 2024, 'Maternal Mortality', OurWorldinData.org, https://ourworldindata.org/maternal-mortality

Also by Damien Brown

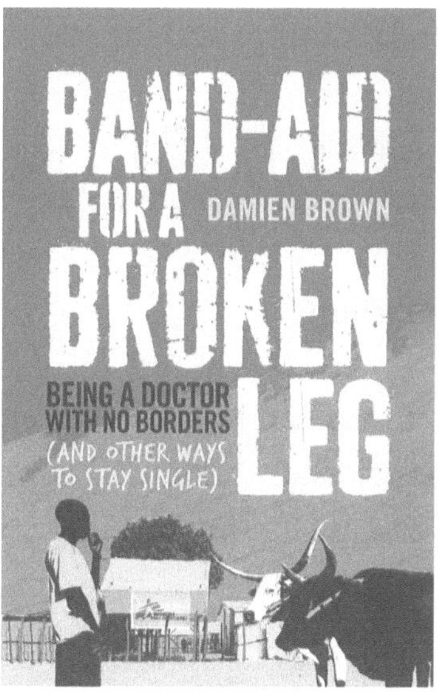

ISBN 978 1 74331 556 9

Praise for *Band-Aid for a Broken Leg*

'. . . as a writer/observer, he is skilful at capturing the moments of sublime joy that living and working in such extremities can provide.' ***Sunday Herald Sun***

'To have such great stories entwined with robust insight into humanitarian aid makes this, for me, the travel book of the year.' ***The Irish Times***

'He writes with wit and humour, at the same time demonstrating his true compassion for his work. A fascinating read.' ***Liverpool Post***

'A young man's boldness is accompanied by a lack of sentimentality and a genuinely questing spirit, and these keep you turning the pages, wondering, as in all the best books, what is going to happen next.' ***Daily Mail***

'. . . a touching memoir of the rewards and the toll of humanitarian work, the power of relationships and the many sides of humanity.' ***The NZ Herald***

'Written with a sense of humility, humour and empathy . . . a book which will stay with me for a long time. Moving and inspiring.' **The Edinburgh Bookshop**

'There is such genuine affection and admiration for Africa and its people it counterbalances the horrifying reality it describes, making it a pleasure to read.' ***Sunday Telegraph***

'Now here is a doctor who can write. His bright debut is a pleasure from cover to cover . . .' ***Cape Times***

'. . . a celebration of the ascension of human spirit in adversity.' ***ArtsHub***

'Heartwarming and heartbreaking in equal parts.' ***Medical Journal of Australia***

'This book reads like a medical TV drama, balancing heart-wrenching moments with hilarious misunderstandings and encounters that you know could only happen in real life.' **Britnae Purdy, *The Quiet Kind***

'A funny, moving account, the book captures the intense highs and deep lows of working in a hospital that has no oxygen, machines or electric equipment.' ***Thomson Reuters***

'It's a fiercely honest account of life that is such a far cry from Australia it might as well be on the moon.' ***Australian Doctor***

www.ingramcontent.com/pod-product-compliance
Lightning Source LLC
LaVergne TN
LVHW091022080826
845145LV00002B/328

* 9 7 8 1 7 6 1 4 7 3 6 3 0 *